# Flesh and Money
# Trafficking in Human Beings

Petrus C. van Duyne
Jon Spencer

**Flesh and Money:** *Trafficking in Human Beings*
*P.C. van Duyne, J. Spencer*

ISBN: 978-90-5850-655-9



Published by:

Wolf Legal Publishers (WLP)
P.O. Box 31051
6503 CB Nijmegen
The Netherlands
Tel: +31 24 355 19 04
Fax: +31 84 837 67 00
E-Mail: info@wolfpublishers.nl
www.wolfpublishers.com

## Table of contents

# The traded human body: The ultimate commercial option?

*Petrus C. van Duyne and Jon Spencer*

## Some historical roots

The concept of trading in human beings is not an economic aberration. Historically the abolition of slavery is not so far behind that it allows us to speak of 'grey history', or that with which we have nothing to do. In 1863 slavery was abolished in the US and the Dutch colony of Surinam, the last slave exploiting states. Prior to 1863 slavery, which had a long and enduring history, was the reality of socio-economic relationships that allowed for the ownership of one person's physical being by another. This meant that the 'body' had an economic value, but the owner of the body was allowed no autonomy over his or her own existence.

Such socio-economic relationships resulted in the 'body' being commodified and therefore available to be traded or used as collateral. For example, when one's luck ran out or when one's resources had been depleted, all that was left of value was one's physical existence. Hence, debtors could become the legitimate slave of a creditor: they became a physical property either set to work for the new owner or traded off for money or another commodity. This custom became obsolete during the Middle Ages. Instead, bad debtors could be imprisoned and kept hostage, which ultimately implied that one exchanged one's physical freedom, a body, against the sum money owed. However, this is not physical *ownership* but a measure to exert pressure on the debtor, which has been strictly regulated in the Civil Code.

In ancient times wars were also a source of slavery. This changed in the medieval warfare: warriors were captured to be traded trade against a ransom. The expectations about the potential ransom were decisive for life and death of the defeated: a noble 'captured body' had potential value; the humble footman was slain without much ado as he had no economic value, other than as a slave.

War and debts were not the only causes of a body becoming a tradable commodity. There is evidence that capturing humans as a 'commodity' was not uncommon. Not only were the population of sub-Saharan Africa victimised by (indigenous) hunters but they were sold by their captors into the flourishing human slave trade to the Americas. In the 17th Century, entrepreneurial seamen of the Barbary coasts were pirates capturing ships and their (Christian) crew but additionally they also raided coastal villages in the Northern Mediterranean. They sailed even as far as Ireland to hunt for human booty. The Algerian historian Ahmed bin Mohammed Al-Maqqari speaks of a 'sea jihad' (Tinniswood, 2011). The trafficking in human beings found many justifications; it was religiously justified by Muslims and Christians alike on the grounds that those trafficked were non-believers.

By the 19th Century the idea of 'hard-core' slavery in the sense of legally *owning* a human person had become offensive to European sensibilities and so disappeared during the 19th Century with economic conditions and the tireless abolitionist zeal of Wilberforce (Simpson and Hill, 2008) hastening slavery's demise, first in the UK (1833: but with the exception "of the Territories in the Possession of the East India Company," the "Island of Ceylon," and "the Island of Saint Helena", to protect commercial interests). As remarked above, the Netherlands and the US were the last civilised modern countries to abolish slavery and its abolition was not economically unproblematic. For the plantation economies the freed slaves fled from the hated plantations leaving them unattended. Facing a serious labour shortage, the authorities of the colony needed to recruit contract-labourers from India and Java. Though these were legally free, they worked under conditions which did not much differ from the conditions of slavery. However, the one significant difference was that the plantation owners did not *own* the contract labourers, but they had direct jurisdiction over all they did. The plantation owners exercised what they viewed to be their implied right to punish the workers without resorting to the courts, for example, for breaking the very loosely interpreted labour contract. This exploitative, near-slavery, system, remained in force until abolition in 1947 (Gobardhan-Rambocus and Hassankhan, 1993).

However, the contract labour system was not limited solely to the Dutch colonies. Many modern developing countries used a system of luring the destitute and desperate with all kinds of promises. Once arrived at the destination the promises were not kept: labour conditions and payment proved to be poor, legal protection against abuse absent and the terms of contracts unfulfilled. Indeed measured against our present standards this way of handling labour would, without a doubt, be considered as human trafficking. It is not difficult to find other historical examples of the movement of humans for their labour: the slave trading of Africans (Pope-Hennessy, 1967), the indentured labour to the US, or Russian farmers on the noble estates (Hoetzsch, 1973). So, what has changed? We think that there has been considerable change but within a context of continuity, so we witness the recurrence of similar patterns but within a contemporary context.

## New Patterns

In the waters east of Somalia the main intention of the pirates is to capture humans for ransom, comparable to the Barbary piracy. However, the Barbary corsairs operated from fortified towns with a proper administration, but the Somalian pirates now operate from a destitute country without a functioning administration and in waters that used to provide a proper livelihood before being emptied by western factory fishing boats. The international response is different too as in the 17th Century admirals from the seafaring nations were occasionally sent with a fleet of gunboats to the North African coast to sink private boats or bombard strongholds without any other 'rule of engagement' than that to liberate captured Europeans and hang the pirates (zu Monfield, 1971). Now there is little to bombard in Somalia while the jurisdiction over the captured pirates is uncertain and delicate, and an unpopular matter because of jurisprudence uncertainties.

As far as coveted – cheap – labour is concerned we meet old patterns in new contexts. Contract labour organised by nation states has disappeared and cross-border mobility has been curbed in a way which is incomparable to the 19th Century when passports, as an interstate instrument, were gradually being introduced. In Western Europe after the Second World War, the recruitment of foreign labour became a critical element in the post-war reconstruction. In particular between 1950 and 1970 tens of thousands of migrant workers from the Caribbean and Asia were encouraged to move to the UK and 'gastarbeiter' (guest workers) were recruited from the Maghreb countries and

Turkey for other European countries. This was a regulated inflow based on permits and licences and wages were supposed to fall under the normal labour conditions. However, with the 1980 recession, less foreign labour was required in the European labour markets. However, the supply from the low-wage countries, such as those in the Southern Mediterranean countries, remained high. This encouraged illegal mobility where new migrants found work in the poorly regulated economic sectors which still could employ (cheap and unrecorded) labour. Depending of the strictness of each country's border controls, on occasions some clever organisational skills were required to get people into the country of destination. Whether this movement of people illegally is be defined as 'organised crime' or human trafficking is elaborated in the chapters of this volume.

There is, of course, a gendered element to this labour mobility and this has been an enduring feature of migratory flows. For example, in the last decades of the 19$^{th}$ Century, and during the hyperinflation of the 1920s, and during the Great Depression (1929-1933), many unmarried German women migrated to neighbouring countries to find domestic work in households. The traditional good commercial relationships between Germany and the Netherlands meant that the Netherlands was popular destination country for such young women. Work was easy to find because of a shortage of young Dutch women prepared to undertake such work, for their preference was to work in factories instead of the low paid jobs under a bullying "lady of the house". However, for some young German women the experience proved to be not as anticipated and so some German female luck seekers engaged in prostitution in one of the big Dutch cities, particularly Rotterdam, as it was the main transit port to Germany (Henkes, 1995).[1] In our contemporary context this would be counted as human trafficking for sexual exploitation.

## New contexts of human trafficking

This leads us to ask if the context of 'human trafficking' has significantly changed over the years. One of the themes of this collection is that while there may be similarities in the patterns the context has changed substantially because of the increased scale. This approach is elaborated in the section of

1 www.vijfeeuenmigratie.nl/dienstboden. Accessed: 23-3-2011

this volume. Both the chapter of *B. de Ruyver, K. van Impe,* and *J. Meese* of the Ghent University and that of K. *Aromaa* and *M. Lehti* of HEUNI (Helsinki), argue that the supply side of women, whether or not voluntarily willing to provide sexual services in another country, has significantly increased. Historically, they argue, there has been a continual inflow of women from Africa (south of the Sahara), the Caribbean region and Southeast Asia. One of the outcomes of the change to the socio-political structure of Central-Eastern Europe after 1989 was increased migration, male and female, from the previous socialist countries of Eastern Europe. However, all writers note the importance of the social conditions in the home country as a push factor in migration. When reading the list of the origin countries it is like reading a rank order of low income countries, particularly concerning Eastern Europe. At the time these chapters were written (2001 and 2007) the low-income country list was headed by Moldavia (as it still is) where living standards and economic prospects provided the push for economic migration.

Aromaa and Lehti argue that many of the undocumented migrant workers are engaged in 'normal' labour. The economics of such labour is explored noting that cheap tomatoes in supermarkets may be picked by underpaid and badly housed undocumented migrants recruited by illegal labour intermediaries: the ubiquitous *koppelbaas* (Van Duyne and Houtzager 2005). This 'modern *lumpenproletariat*' may experience more consistent and extreme exploitation than those undocumented migrants engaged in the sex industry. So, not all of the organised smuggling of humans and not all of the luck seekers can be fitted into the definition of trafficking as defined in the Palermo protocol. The economics of migration no doubt result for many in misery but, not all of it stems from criminal activities or coerced sex-workers.

The cross border flow of migrants has not only its local roots in unemployment and lack of economic prospects but also in social upheaval caused by war or (violent) change of regime. An elaboration of this mixture of push factors is presented in the chapter of *Vesna Nikolić-Ristanović* who describes the situation of the Balkan region in the last decade of the 20th Century. There were many good reasons to leave the devastated and war torn 'economic pastures' of this region. On the other hand, there is also an inflow of women (and children) for sexual exploitation into the region itself (Nikolić *et al.*, 2004). However, the author also notes the pull factors, especially that in many destination countries the hidden economy had increased in size

(Schneider, 2003) thus providing a kind of economic 'welcome' or lure. For example, these economies placed an increased demand for workers both in the construction industry and the agricultural sector in Germany and Austria. The perennial market for sexual services continued unabated and as always there was a demand for 'new faces and new flesh'. Statistics seem to lend support this assumption (Kangaspunta, 2004), despite the large range of uncertainty of official data (Di Nicola and Cauduro, 2007). Indeed, the mounting foreign supply of sex workers appeared to expand in the Balkan region as well as in Western Europe.

The attitude to the sex market remains a constant issue because at the least it is ambiguous if not incoherent. On the one hand, there is the official policy to decriminalise prostitution as a normal 'craft' or service. On the other hand, a negative attitude still prevails from which a strong official association is formed between 'organised crime' and 'foreigners', as observed in the first chapter by *Jon Spencer*. The author observes that the media play an important role in presenting an image of the sex market with sinister 'organised crime' figures when the more probable structure is of a criminal network of *ad hoc* cooperating entrepreneurs. The cross-border element naturally brings in the migrant as the ethnic 'other', particularly if they are constructed as the perpetrators of 'trafficking'. From there it is a small step to the more threatening phenomenon: 'transnational organised crime'. Though this imagery is to a large extent inappropriate, the authorities do not distance themselves from it. Instead, they endorse it as a means of emphasising sex work oriented migration as the usual pattern. This is reflected in the official language within which the underlying reality is described. This creates a distorted reality which is used to replace the daily and mundane on-going dealings of entrepreneurs with the deceived, exploited as well as fully self-conscious luck seekers.

## Organised crime?

Is the whole representation of human trafficking in general and women trafficking in particular a matter of a conceptual reconstruction of the facts to fit a popular organised crime imagery? The closing of the first section seems to hint at that. However, the next two chapters written respectively by *Miroslav Scheinost* and *Almir Maljević* seem to falsify this hypothesis. Scheinost describes the illegal migration and human trafficking against the background of tumultuous changes at all societal levels which took place after the 'implosion' of the socialist regime. Informal and formal controls changed or partly disappeared, while the law enforcement agencies had to be reformed.

Let us first look at Scheinost's study of the Czech Republic. As a small country, the Czech authorities and population faced a substantial increase of cross-border mobility, of which a considerable part proved to be illegal. Most of this mobility was transitional with the richer EU Member States as destination countries. However, there was also a migratory flow into the Czech Republic thus leaving enough migrants, as far as the commercial sex service industry was concerned, to replace the indigenous sex workers who had taken the opportunity to migrate to other European countries. However, with increased border controls and the supervision of illegal/sex labour, the situation of individuals randomly roaming around seeking their luck could not continue. What the author suggests is a growth in organisations for recruiting, transporting and 'handling' young women, deceived about either the nature of their work or the conditions in which they have to work, to maintain the supply of new faces to the market.

Predictably, regions which are in a state of violent social and political upheaval are fertile breeding grounds for underground economic activities, whether consisting of prohibited commodities, services or migration of various kinds. While the situation in the Czech Republic was peaceful, the crumbling Yugoslavian state during the 1990s was a scene of war and crime (Glenny, 1999). The protracted war in Bosnia-Herzegovina can be considered as one of the culminating points of violent political disintegration of this region. After the Dayton Agreement (1994) the new federal state law enforcement agencies presented anything but a bulwark against crime while such agencies and other state institutions were plagued by widespread corruption. *Almir Maljević* depicts this disharmonious background against which to project female smuggling and trafficking arguing that: "Lack of unified political leadership, of harmonised criminal legislation, of state-wide law-enforcement agencies and of judicial and police cooperation" all contributed to the opportunities available for the illegal movement of people across borders (See Spencer *et al.*, 2010).

No surprise that crime-entrepreneurs took advantage of this situation, particularly in the illegal movement of people sector with 90% of the identified victims coming from Moldavia, Russia or the Ukraine. About two third were recruited by friends or acquaintances. Of course, poverty and unemployment were important push factors, but these got only a decisive weight if combined with fractured families or other personal difficulties. The author argues that only a small minority were aware of being recruited for sex work with approximately one third of the women being subjected to physical violence. However, more than a quarter declared to receive friendly treatment and a decrease in personal violence and better treatment correlated with less complaints to the police which may or may not, falsely, indicate less trafficking. The popular myth that foreign peace keeping forces create a market for sexual services appears refuted when near to 80% of the sex workers' clients were local.

A lively description of local as well as of Europe wide sex service organisations is given in the chapter on prostitution in Bulgaria by *Philip Gounev, Tihomir Bezlov* and *Georgi Petrunov*. The findings of their research reflect the cross-border complexities of the recently emerged Bulgarian sex industry. It developed from a virtually non-existent, or a denied, sex market to an internationally extensively varied sexual services industry. The push factors of unemployment, destitution, fractured families recur here. But that is not the whole story as a climate of more liberal attitudes to sex means that voluntary entry into the sex market is no longer an exception. This implies that not all engagements in the sexual service industry are to be considered as tantamount to victimisation, unless one equates commercial sex *per se* with victimhood.

The study of the Bulgarian sex market indicates that elaborate organisations succeed in maintaining control over the market. What have to be controlled are the various layers of the market, from sex-workers with their pimps at the lowest level to club managers employing 'elite' sex workers. The sex business in Bulgaria has to proceed smoothly and efficiently. For example, it has to follow the rhythm of the tourist seasons: from ski resort in winter to the seaside resorts in summer and back again. According to the authors, this market management ranges from the one-man entrepreneur/pimp supervising his whole business, to hierarchical organised enterprises, supervising various levels of the chain of the business at a distance. Such enterprises are usually considered 'real' organised crime which exist alongside a multitude of enterprises which hardly merit this qualification.

## Informal Economy

In describing human trafficking as embedded in an informal economy, Vesna Nikolić-Ristanović takes us to Serbia after the last Balkan wars at the beginning of this Century. It is a country, socially and economically still licking its wounds, while many try to eke out a meagre living in the informal or even 'underground', criminal economy. In such an economy switching from informal (but not prohibited) to underground criminal enterprises is not a big step. Some may not even perceive it as such or find sufficient rationalisations to salve their conscience. Of course, the war has contributed to what the author calls 'structural victimisation' which induces people to criminalise themselves. While engaging in the criminal migration business, whether human trafficking or just smuggling people over the borders, a division of labour and leadership developed: guiding migrants over the frontier, organising hiding places, taking care of transport and on top of this overseeing the whole procedure. In short, a form of 'organisation of crime', which provides the needed income to impoverished households. Whether the schoolboy who guides migrants over the border for € 25 should be considered as a victim, as the author suggests, is a matter of evaluation. We would not blame the kid for thinking differently and for looking forward to a regular flow of 'victims' who need to be guided over the mountains or through the woods. Indeed, who is victim?

While the previous chapters provide a human trafficking picture of three Balkan countries, the following chapter by *Anna Markovska* and *Colleen Moore* elaborates two widely removed countries: The UK and the Ukraine. We may oversee the connection if we neglect the fact that one country delivers the 'victims' or luck-seekers while the other is for many the coveted destination, even if Ukrainian women may also choose perhaps the less rewarding Sarajevo brothel as we have seen in the chapter on trafficking in Bosnia. Apart from that, the situation is different because the Ukrainian victims have to cope with a criminal law system they have reason not to trust. In the UK it is argued the situation is different because there can be trust in the legal system as the Courts are functioning without the reputation of corruption. Nevertheless, conviction rates in the UK are equally low, which may indicate that victims who are required to function as witnesses do not invest much trust in the UK authorities either, particularly law enforcement officers. This reluctance to trust is due to law enforcement professionals lacking the skills in dealing with such victims and lacking experience as well as prejudice against the victims.

The previously noted incoherent mixture of conflicting notions recur again: the 'foreignness' of the victims, the incomprehensible 'voluntary' status of some of them, because sex workers are assumed to be forced into their victimhood, the view of the perpetrator as the 'folk devil' or the rational calculating criminal actor, the 'incarnation of evil', when for many their role was confined to that of travel agent. Add to this the usually inflated statistics plus the organised crime imagery and we have the ingredients for a moral panic which is focussed on 'big crime' while neglecting the undercurrent of the informal/underground economy of this sector.

Moral panic subverts open-minded observations and creates a distance between 'the righteous' citizen and the to-be-rescued victims. Often victims of so-called sexual trafficking have a different opinion about how to further their own interests, being quite aware that this is matter of *their* 'flesh and money' from which they do not want to be rescued. Given that their choices are the less attractive economic options, they do not perceive themselves as 'fallen women' but exploit the commercial opportunities with which they are presented, sometimes with daring perseverance and spirit. This is described by *Dina Siegel* who recounts the 'adventurous' ways in which Russian women try to enter the Israeli sex market. Clearly these enterprising women challenge the prevalent victim image in skilfully circumventing the visa barriers against their entry in Israel: they do not enter Israel directly but take their way through Egypt and then through the Sinai desert to be smuggled into Israel. Why this detour?

The answer lies again in the difference of perception: for the Israeli Customs officer at the airport an unaccompanied Russian women is a suspicious prostitute, while in Egypt she is a tourist bringing in money. And in Egypt she can be tourist as well as sex worker (earning back the travel expenses) or (subsequently) find contacts for a smuggling route with Bedouins through the desert. This is facilitated through contacts of acquaintances that preceded her. The Bedouins who have at least one side-business consisting of smuggling commodities into Israel are amenable to extra income with human smuggling. They can spend their small windfall on increasing their prestige by buying/marrying more women, which is their way of laundering money (as there is no Egyptian FIU which will monitor 'suspicious' marriages to check for laundering). This side-business does not exclude 'hardcore' trafficking but demonstrates the variety of structures. There is also most certainly for some women hardship or a social or economic tragedy behind their rational choices.

So the market of 'flesh and money' is not only filled with 'tears and tragedy'. While recognising the misery and debasement of human dignity, the last chapter by *Jon Spencer* makes clear that the imagery is to a large extent determined by those stakeholders or 'problem owners' who define the problems – often to their own moral satisfaction or to further their bureaucratic status. Often times these definers are the ones who provide victims with access to support or who enforce the law, and this is not always the same. He argues that the process of defining is not a one-dimensional process, because other interests and agendas tend to interfere and one of these agenda issues is 'organised crime'.

Though the chapters in this volume have provided sufficient examples of the organisation of voluntary as well as forced 'sex service mobility', one-man enterprises next to hierarchical structures, drawing in the 'organised crime' theme encourages the use of a whole range myths surrounding such an activity. The problem with the focus on organised crime is that it fails to bring clarity to what is a complex and multilayered issue. What the focus on organised crime does achieve is to move the illegal movement of people across borders and commercial sex enterprises to a higher political priority. In addition, it pretends a semblance of 'understanding' that something more serious is going on than just the basic predicate offences. The latter can range from 'travel services' (forged papers, addresses for the migrant) to providing brothels as intended places to work. Sometimes, and more seriously, this is clearly against the will of the imported sex-workers or the work must be done under dire and humiliating conditions they would never have accepted when they were recruited. However, compounding these various services with the qualification of 'organised crime' leads to an illogical composition of different dimension.

There is evidence in this collection that we should view 'human trafficking' differently and ask searching questions. If we understand it as organising the movement of people illegally and legally across borders we can conceptualise it as a form of management. We may also have to accept that, as indicated again in this collection, that such an activity does not necessarily lead to more harm and it can even result in less harm. The people movers want to ensure that the person is moved efficiently over the border without delay or accidents because this minimises their risk of apprehension. Brothel keepers want to run an efficiently managed brothel as it is more profitable and is likely to be appreciated by the women and the men who look for such a service. And what of violent coercion, particularly exerted against the weaker female victims? There is no doubt that some women are subjected to horrendous levels of personal violence by some of the 'traffickers' but this is not necessarily the norm. Running a crime-enterprise with violence is rarely a sign of good management: it often leads to the undoing of the entrepreneur and in his chapter Almir Maljević observes that many sex workers were treated decently by their 'owners', resulting in less complaints and criminal cases and so increased profits, satisfied customers and satisfied workers. Such an approach does not suggest a lack of organisations but rather that those involved realised what their trade is all about and that essentially organising illegal commercial sex services is about 'flesh and money'

## References

Di Nicola, A. and A. Cauduro, Review of the official statistics on trafficking in human beings for sexual exploitation and their validity in the 25 Member States from official statistics to estimates of the phenomenon. In: E.U. Savona and S. Stefanizzi (eds.), *Measuring human trafficking. Complexities and pitfalls*. New York, Springer, 2007

Duyne, P.C. van amd M. Houtzager, Criminal subcontracting in the Netherlands: the Dutch 'koppelbaas' as crime-entrepreneur. In: P.C. van Duyne, K. von Lampe, M. van Dijck and J.L. Newell (eds.), *The organised crime economy. Managing crime markets in Europe*. Nijmegen, Wolf Legal Publishers, 2005

Glenny, M., *The Balkans 1804-1999*. London, Granta Books, 1999

Gobardhan-Rambocus, L. and M.S. Hassankhan (eds.), *Immigratie en Ontwikkeling, emancipatie van contractanten*, Anton de Kom Universiteit, Paramaribo, 1993

Henkes, B., *Heimat in Holland. Duitse dienstmeisjes 1920-1950*. Amsterdam, Babylon-De Geus, 1995

Hoetzsch, O., *The evolution of Russia.* London, Thames and Hudson, 1973

Kangaspunta, K., Mapping the inhuman trade: preliminary findings of the database in human beings. *Forum on Cime and Society*, 2003, vol. 3, *no. 1 & 2*, 81-103

Nicolić-Ristanović, V., S. Ćopić, S. Milivojević, B. Simeunovic-Palić and B. Mihić, *Trafficking in people in Serbia.* Beograd, VDS/OSCE, 2004

Pope-Hennessy, J., *Sins if the fathers. A study of Atlantic slave traders 1441-1807.* London, Cassel Publishers, 1967

Schneider, F., The size and development of the shadow economies and the shadow economy labour force of 22 transition and 21 OECD countries: what do we really know? In: B. Belev (ed.), *The informal economy in the EU accession countries.* Sofia, Center for the Study of Democracy, 2003

Simpson, Peter and Hill, Clifford (2008) Leadership, spirituality and complexity. Wilberforce and the abolition of the slave trade. In: Turnbull-James, K. and J. Collins (eds.), *Leadership perspectives: Knowledge into action.* Palgrave MacMillan

Spencer, J., R. Broad, K. Aromaa, M. Junninen, A. Markina, J. Saar and T. Viljanen, *Organised crime, corruption and the movement of people across borders in the new enlarged EU: A case study, Estonia, Finland and the UK.* Brussels, European Union, 2010

Tinniswood, A. *Pirates of Barbary. Corsairs, conquests and captivity in the 17th-century Mediterranean.* Jonathan Cape, 2011

Zu Monfeld, W., *Drie duizend jaar zeeroverij.* Spectrum Paperback 68, 1971

# The need for a multidisciplinary and proactive approach to human trafficking. Reflections from two pilots

*B. de Ruyver, K. van Impe, and J. Meese*[1]

## Introduction

During the last decades the phenomenon of trafficking in human beings has taken a universal dimension. This is due to political and socio-economic developments. For example, there are the drastic (r)evolutions in Eastern European countries, there is the persistent political commotion in Africa, South Asia and a number of countries in Central and Latin America and some Central- and South American States, as well as the escalation of economic problems in Southeast Asia. Individuals as well as criminal organisations use the weak spots in legislation to realise their ambitions. These weak spots are to be situated in the field of diverging regulations between different states, but also in the context of national legislation in the countries of origin and destination.

World-wide, the desire to migrate is continuously increasing, but the legal means to do so are, certainly in the United States and Europe, smaller than ever. Consequently, black markets and criminal organisations meet this demand by offering an illegal supply of migration possibilities. Consequently, the migration issue in general is often associated with illegality and criminality, while criminal organisations find a new area of business. As the phenomenon of trafficking in human beings manifested itself during the last decade, policy makers were put under pressure to come up with proper responses. Public concern about the problematic character and the dangerous

---

1 Professor in criminology and researchers at the University of Gent, Belgium. This chapter was first published in: P.C. van Duyne, V. Ruggiero, M. Scheinost and W. Valkenburg (eds.), *Cross-border crime in a changing Europe*. Huntington, Nova Science Publishers, 2001

consequences of human trade led to various initiatives, on both the national and international level.

Three of the four on research projects on human trafficking received funding under the STOP-programme. The first project studied the phenomenon of trafficking in human beings from Poland and Hungary to Belgium and other EU Member States. The second project examined the feasibility and the opportunity of the international gathering and administration of data concerning missing and sexually exploited minors. The third STOP-project aimed at evaluating the phenomenon of transmigration via Poland with a view to controlling human trafficking.

A fourth project was funded by the Belgian State Secretariat for Development Co-operation. It was a two-year bilateral project, promoting a multidisciplinary approach to deal with human trafficking between Belgium and the Philippines.

A common conclusion emerging from these studies is that restrictive measures alone cannot stop human trafficking, as there are powerful push factors in countries of origin as well as pull factors in receiving countries. In order to be effective, a strategy to combat human trafficking needs to be sufficiently comprehensive to address both sets of factors. The research findings have clearly shown that there is no easy or uni-dimensional solution to human trafficking, as the phenomenon originates from a complex set of factors, often in combination with one another.

An effective strategy must address various aspects and must combine and balance punitive and preventive measures, law enforcement and protection of basic human rights, stricter border control and the remotion of the causes of illegal migration. Measures taken by the countries of origin, transit and destination must be part of an integrated approach. There is a real danger that, in order to curb human trafficking as quickly as possible, the receiving countries would attach a disproportionate importance to a set of narrow and ad hoc measures, focussing on short-term cures through border controls and punitive action. It would be unfortunate if preventive action to remove the causes is neglected or receives only scant attention (Ghosh, 1998).

Hereafter, before discussing the need for a multidisciplinary and pro-active approach towards human trafficking, the phenomenon will be analysed and some research findings discussed.

## The analysis of the phenomenon

If we consider the case of Poland the causes of trafficking in human beings can be tentatively identified as follows.

First, the social-economic situation should be examined. The economic revolution that followed the radical political and social changes in several Central European countries since 1989 had a tremendous impact. Although Poland managed to control inflation, the country faced a huge level of unemployment. Mainly young people, aged between 15 and 25, and especially large sections of the female population shared this fate. Besides, the very weak social safety net with extremely low social security benefits, the high burden of tax, the lack of social retraining and reintegration and the need for proper education funds encouraged more and more (young) people to emigrate to the West (Hummel, 1993; Franssen, 1994). Apart from these economic motives, however, it is essential to recognise that for most migrants the desire to improve the quality of their life or enhance their personal status have provided the incentive for migration (Kupryashinka, 1996).

Second, human trade became possible because of the increased freedom of movement (Bruinsma and Meershoek, 1999). Therefore, the existence of a fourth wave[2] of female victims of trafficking in human beings to Europe can be noticed, coming from Central and Eastern Europe (Hungary, Poland, Czech Republic, Russia and Romania) since 1994. The first wave was made up of Asian women (mainly from Thailand and the Philippines, since 1992), the second came from South America (Dominican Republic and Columbia, and to a lesser extent also Venezuela, Brazil and Ecuador since 1993) and the third wave came from Africa (Ghana and Nigeria, since 1993).

The existence of criminal organisations in the countries of origin also facilitates human trade. The fact that smuggling and trafficking in human beings is associated with huge profits and that the burden of proof in cases of smuggling and trafficking makes the work of the judicial authorities very difficult without the victim's co-operation, make this business attractive to criminal networks. In other words, the overall risk of trafficking in human beings is very low compared to other forms of trafficking, like trafficking in drugs. In addition, the profits are large.

---

2 See the IOM report *Trafficking and Prostitution: the growing exploitation of migrant women from Central and Eastern Europe*, May 1995, p. 8 and ff.

The business of trafficking in human beings is increasingly controlled by Eastern European criminal organisations, operating both in the country where recruiting takes place as well as in the destination country. The organisations are characterised by a high degree of specialisation, extreme violence and involvement in other lucrative criminal activities such as vehicle theft and trafficking in arms and drugs.[3] The reason why the smuggling of migrants takes place from or via, Poland, is that certain criminals and their organisations in this country have established more effective networks, consisting of recruiters, traffickers and exploiters.[4]

Another important factor encouraging Polish women to migrate is their search for independence and emancipation. After the Communist regime was overthrown, the new establishment propagated the conservative family model. This evolution together with violence and alcohol abuse in many families, reinforced the intentions of many young women to look for a better future, and employment in the rich West. Women are therefore not only attracted by the myth of welfare and prosperity, but also by the prospects of (financial) independence and a stable family life based on the 'partnership model' where men and women as equals (Oleszczuk and Buchowska, 1996).

Finally, there is increasing competition in the sex industry. Some studies have estimated that more than 40 % of the women working in Warsaw as prostitutes are originally from the former Soviet Union (Gramenga, 1997). Their number is continuously growing, and the police report that Russian women successfully undermine the position of Polish prostitutes. For these Polish women, who are already working in the sex industry, migration to

---

3 See: Migrant Trafficking. Overview. Migration and Organized Crime, in *Trends in Organized Crime*, Transaction Periodicals Consortium Rutgers University, New Brunswich, New Jersey, with the Regional Strategy Information Center, Winter 1996, Vol. 2, no. 2, p. 58-90

4 Zie: *Mensenhandel vanuit Centraal- en Oost-Europa*, afdeling Advies en Informatie, IRT-NON, Internationaal Politie-instituut Twente, Universiteit Twente, De Admiraal, Enschede, 1997, p. 43. Schiffer (1995) uses a very similar classification into three types (Schiffer, K.; *Migrationsprostitution und Frauenhandel. Strukturwandel der europäischen Sexindustrie*, Mr. A. de Graaf Stichting, January, 1995, 42-44). IOM has also worked out a system of classification, and distinguishes occasional traffickers, small well-organised trafficking rings and organised, international trafficking networks (IOM, *Trafficking of women to Countries of the European Union: Characteristics, Trends and Policy Issues*, Conference on trafficking in Women for Sexual Exploitation, Vienna, June, 1996, 10-11). See also Sieber (1998, p. 97-98); Flormann (1995) and Sieber and Bögel (1993)

Germany, the Netherlands, Belgium or another Western European country, making use of traffickers if necessary, seems a plausible solution.

Therefore there are two groups of women coming to the West to work in the sex industry. On the one hand there are those who leave their country of origin knowing that they will end up in prostitution. In other words, these are prostitutes who are hoping to earn more money from doing the same work abroad. The large numbers of sex clubs, massage parlours and escort agencies mushrooming throughout Central and Eastern Europe are the ideal place from which to recruit Polish, Hungarian, Russian, Czech, Romanian and other women. Women in this category are therefore clearly aware of the job that will be awaiting them in the West. As far as these women are concerned, it is only possible to speak of trafficking in human beings if a conflict situation arises in the destination country: for example if they have to prostitute themselves under coercion, are resident in the country illegally and cannot voluntarily leave the sex industry or have to hand over large parts of their earnings.

There is a second group of people who are lured to the West under false pretences, using deceptive artifices, or who are simply deceived. For example, these people respond to the huge numbers of 'job offers' in Polish newspaper advertisements. They sign fictitious contracts of employment for a job in the West as cleaners, household helper, nurses, teachers etc. Others are persuaded by friends and acquaintances. Recruiters seem to be trustworthy, as they help to sort out the formalities, lend money for the trip and often drive customers to the destination country. In other words, recruiters take advantage of the desire and expectations of customers and victimise them by tying them in a web of dependency and obligation. Victims are employed in prostitution, in the construction sector, in cleaning companies, sewing workshops, where they are held and exploited by means of blackmail and violence.

In the case of the Philippines, human trafficking has to be seen as a component within the continuum of the migration cycle.

The phenomenon of trafficking in Filipino women has to be analysed within the context of the massive migration of Filipino workers since the 1970s. The largest wave of migration started in 1974 with the introduction of the Labour Code and the overseas employment program of the Philippines that came with it.[5] Since then and throughout the 1980s, government policy-makers regarded overseas employment as a strategy to boost the sinking economy and partly solve the problem of unemployment, (Ofreneo and Ofreneo, 1998). Overseas employment became an integral and indispensable feature of the global Philippine economy. By the 1980s, the labour migration flow became increasingly feminised with the demand for nurses, domestic helpers, and other types of carers in East Asian countries, the Middle East, and Europe (Go, 1998). During the 1990s, however, government policy officially shifted from exporting the country's labour surplus to managing the tide of labour migration. In reality, the Philippine government currently promotes western lifestyle[6], propagated by media and the stories told by returning migrants. At the micro social level, Filipino women are accustomed to sacrifice herself to help and support the family. This[7] exposes them to many negative –often exploitative– experiences abroad, such as accepting dehumanising work or a marriage proposal from a stranger in order to earn money for the family back home.[8] Nevertheless, in this process, they acquire

---

5 See *Handbook on Labour Representation, Philippine Overseas Employment Administration* 1995, 48 p, with annexes (Republic Act No. 8042.; *Guidelines on the Training, Testing, Certification and Employment of Performing Artists.* Department Order No. 3, Department of Labour and Employment, 1994; X., *Foreign Service Circular No. 221-86*, Ministry of Foreign Affairs; Laurel, S.H., *Rules and Regulations Governing Overseas Employment*, as amended 1991, Department of Labour and Employment; *Administrative Rules and Regulations. Omnibus Rules and Regulations Implementing the Migrant and Workers and Overseas Filipinos Act 1995*, Department of Foreign Affairs/Department of Labour and Employment).

6 The economic situation in the countries of origin (not infrequently developing countries) is and remains the main cause of human trafficking. The fight against this phenomenon therefore requires a fundamental change in North-South/East-West relations and, besides fair international trade relations, solutions to the problem of debt repayment. Poverty is thus unarguable a very important push factor. However, it should be noted that the desire to raise the current standard of living is not infrequently the principal motivation. In other words, individual, well-considered motives, related to the desire to optimise the quality of life or to enhance personal status (and no so much the search for essential means of existence), underlie most migratory movements (Vasquez c.s. 1995).

7 The problem of human trafficking has to be correlated to a significant cultural differentiation. Women play a highly subordinate role in the Philippines, Thailand and the other Mekong countries, especially in rural areas. Gender roles and socialisation in Philippines society are based on values formed by patriarchy that explains the dominant role of men.

8 The profession of prostitute is for many families at the border of the poverty line often a respectable and necessary choice. In this way, village girls have from time immemorial played the traditional role of financial mainstay of the family by forwarding their income earned (abroad). Prostitution is accepted in the region

status and power within her family and in the community. The interaction between economic status (low family income), gender-role socialisation, and the family dynamics (problems/tensions) reinforced by pressures from significant others[9] make Filipino women vulnerable to trafficking.

Several factors are responsible for the attractiveness of Belgium, like other EU countries, as a country of destination. These forces include the high demand for cheap labour for carrying out the so-called three D-jobs (dirty, demanding and dangerous). However, the migration flow between Belgium and the Philippines is also informed by the convergence of a specific demand and supply, particularly in the area of domestic work. The chances for a low-skilled Filipino woman finding a job in Belgium are enhanced by the presence of a large diplomatic community (embassies, EC, NATO) which can afford to hire domestic servants. The Filipinos, on the other hand, are known for their efficiency, for speaking English and for being obedient workers. Aside from domestic work, a number of Filipino women also end up as prostitutes in Belgium or neighbouring countries.[10] The fact that there

---

(Thailand, Myanmar, Cambodia, the Philippines) even when children are involved. Although, this mentality seems to have changed substantially over the last few years which is reflected by recent changes of law. X., *Trafficking in Children B International Labor Office/IPEC Responses in South EastAsia*, 1998, 8 p; X. *Questionnaire on Projects/Activities on Trafficking in Women and Children in ESCAP Region*, 1998, 8 p.; X., *Child Labor: Trends and Challenges in Asia*, 1997, 25 p.; DERKS, A., *Trafficking of Cambodian Women and Children to Thailand*, IOM, Geneva, 1997, 54 p.; X., *IOM=s Regional Strategy and Plan of Action to Combat Trafficking in Women and Children*, IOM, February 1997, 14 p.; X., Combating Trafficking in Children for Labor Exploitation in the Mekong Sub-Region. A Proposed framework or ILO/IPEC Action and Proceedings of a Mekong Sub Regional Consultation, ILO/IPEC, South-East Asia, October 1998, Bangkok, 87 p.;http://intlrel.soc.hawaii.edu/ps321/chapter5.htlm.

9 A considerable number of women is still recruited by agents/ agencies or impresarios but those recruited by friends and family are rapidly increasing. This is a definite shift from formal recruitment practices in the 1970s and 1980s and might mean that cross-border migration is becoming more difficult to monitor and control. Getting information from personal sources seems to be more powerful in influencing the women to migrate, rather than being 'informed' by advertisements and agencies.

10 As a result of booming sex tourism, certain Philippine provinces witnessed a considerable development of the sex industry. Initially, the prostitutes were recruited locally, but from the 1990s onwards the traffickers' focus of attention shifted to the surrounding countries: women from Laos, Cambodja, but mainly from Myanmar entered the Philippine prostitution market. Besides, sex tourism was often led to trafficking in women to countries outside the Mekong region. Germany, Taiwan, but mainly Japan, are currently the most attractive countries, especially for Thai and Philippines women. This trade usually takes place in stages, characterised by exploitation in each intermediate country.

is demand in the West, linked to the reality that foreign victims are easier to manipulate or exploit – because they usually do not speak the language, are unfamiliar with the customs and the laws in the West, cannot fall back on friends or acquaintances and are often mistrustful of the police system - turns human trafficking into a highly lucrative business.

## Tackling the problem

*A multidisciplinary approach*

As mentioned in the introduction, action towards a phenomenon like human trafficking cannot be limited to the expansion of a mere repressive legislative arsenal. A mainly criminal restraint of the phenomenon may cause undesired effect: there is a real danger that a repressive approach will promote rather than halt traffic in human beings. It is believed that by punishing the criminals the problem will be solved, but in reality this one-sided approach often causes several side-effects such as an increased dependence of the victims on the criminal environment, double victimisation and a shift of prostitution towards more hidden forms of sex exploitation. Moreover, the success of a criminal trial is highly dependent on the testimony of victims, who may suffer severe consequences from their decision to provide evidence against those exploiting them.

These elements strengthen the conviction that the best way to tackle the problem is to include a variety of measures and leave repressive measures as a last resort.

- Firstly, measures should be devised in the field of administrative law.
- Secondly, more attention should be paid to the problems that arise in the field of social policy. Only in as far as preventive action fails to tackle human trafficking, criminal legislation should be brought to the task.

It is essential to elaborate this approach on the international, and in particular the European level. To prevent traffickers taking advantage of loopholes and differences in different national legislations, consistent European administrative, social and criminal measures are needed.

## Administrative law

The channels of migration, by which (potential) victims are being traded, are often legal, though they are used in an illegal fashion.[11] Abuse is found in the ways in which work permits are obtained, but also in the way in which visas are requested. For example, visa applicants may claim family reunion and the phenomenon of marriage purposes of (usually with mail-order brides). They may seek authorisation for temporary residence of au-pair girls. Abuse is also rife among applicants to special identity cards for technical staff or staff of embassies and international organisations. The use of false documents is also widespread while abuse of refugee-status, adoption, of student-status, of the regulations for minors and employment-status are frequent.

The migration pressure will not be eliminated by closing all doors and windows, but the replacement of the (de facto) quasi migration freeze with open borders is equally indefensible. That is why we proposed in the context of the Belgo-Philippine research project that the European Union Member States should consider the introduction of quotas for migrants. By giving a fixed number of migrants access to their territory every year, and by giving them access to the labour market, trafficking in human beings and the marginal situation of 'illegal aliens' could be controlled.

In exchange, the countries of origin should commit themselves to an effective fight against illegal human trafficking networks. In order to manage the migration problem, the governments of the countries of origin should therefore primarily focus on channelling the migration flows within a legal framework. This presupposes that the number of - mala fide - recruitment channels (travel agencies, employment offices, marriage agencies) should be curtailed, or generally that a more transparent migration policy should be pursued.

Within the European Union, the diplomatic and consular missions have also a crucial role to play. First of all, they should be better equipped to obtain an overall view of the phenomenon. This requires further computerisation of their services, development of –additional– consultation structures and a more efficient use of visa registers and diplomatic annual

---

11 See Report on the conference on Trafficking in Women, Vienna, 10-11 June 1996, Workshop on Migration Policy, European Commission, Doc. CAB./183/96-EN, p. 47-49; See in this respect: Lap-Chew and Wijers (1996)

reports. In addition a de facto uniform and detailed policy should be pursued with regard to the treatment of visa applications in the diplomatic missions of the different Schengen Member States, in order to prevent 'embassy shopping'.

## Social policy

Most countries still have gaps and difficulties in their social legislation making it almost impossible for the victims to claim their rights and compensations.

For instance, female forced to work illegally in clothing workshops, are regarded as moonlighters. As a rule, the employer does not pay social contributions, while wages are lower than stipulated by law. An employer who is caught has to pay such contributions. In addition, the employee can submit a claim to demand payment of arrears wages in. However, employees taking such a step are faced with a heavy burden of proof. The starting date of employment, the number of hours worked (generally higher than statutorily established) are often hard to prove.

An additional problem arises if the victim is working in the sex industry. Although prostitution is tolerated, Belgian labour law acts as if prostitutes did not exist. For a victim of trafficking in human beings, who ends up in the sex industry, it will be impossible to claim what she/he can normally receive on the basis of an employment contract since an agreement that infringes public order and morality has no legal value. A slight amendment to the (Belgian) Law on Labour Agreements would avoid this, making it possible for any employer to come forward.

## The criminal law

Trafficking in human beings by definition is a crime that, is of an international nature. The fight against this crime necessitates not only co-ordinated action on a national level but also on an international level. The international nature of trafficking, however, is the reason why the various countries involved in fighting it are faced with different practices, different approaches and different legislations. In other words, states increasingly feel the need for an efficient set of rules which can be applied internationally.

However, aiming for international legal measures is not completely satisfactory. More than four international Conventions were drawn in the period 1900 to 1950 dealing with trafficking in persons and prostitution. These Conventions were replaced by the Convention for the Suppression of the Traffic in Persons and the Exploitation of Prostitution on 21 March 1950.

Through these Conventions the signatories of the Agreement of 1950 have introduced stricter rules, ranging from fighting only forced trafficking in human beings to curbing trafficking in human beings and sexual exploitation, in both cases even with the consent of 'the victim' (Hamerlynck, 1992; Kootstra c.s., 1996). The Convention of 1950 in doing so confuses the offence 'trafficking in human beings' with the incrimination of 'smuggling in people'.

When people, undoubtedly most often to make a profit, 'help' others to gain unlawful entry to or a residence in a certain State, this is usually a matter of smuggling people. Trafficking in human beings, on the other hand, should be associated with an aspect of coercion.

The UN Treaty of 1950, moreover, only mentions recruiting, taking away and forcing people into prostitution. In this way, the other aspects of trafficking in human beings, aimed at economic exploitation, are overlooked.

Furthermore, the current developments show that several States are discussing or implementing regulation, if not decriminalization of prostitution. Should not the abolitionist tone of the Treaty of 1950 make way for a more regulatory approach? Should one not consider decriminalization of certain types of exploitation such as prostitution when this take place does not under coercion or, deception?

It is obvious that there is a need to adapt the UN Convention to the current times, by making the Treaty more up-to-date. In this context it's worth mentioning that on 18 May 1999 the Ad Hoc Committee on the Elaboration of a Convention against Transnational Organised Crime adopted the Revised draft Protocol to Prevent, Suppress and Punish Trafficking in Persons, especially Women and Children, Supplementing the United Nations Convention against Transnational Organised Crime. The purpose of this (draft) Protocol is to promote and facilitate co-operation among member states to prevent, investigate and punish international trafficking in persons for the purpose of forced labour or sexual exploitation. To that end, member states shall adopt effective measures to prevent trafficking in human beings, ensure that victims of receive appropriate assistance and protection, promote the co-operation between States, provide in appropriate cases for the safe and voluntary return of victims to their countries of origin, and inform and educate the public.

It is certain that in the absence of a approximation of the legal definition of the crime of trafficking in human beings throughout the EU, it is extremely difficult to carry out a valid analysis of the phenomenon or to develop a uniform prevention and repression policy. This confirms the need for a minimum legal standard on a European level. As far as this is concerned it should be pointed out that article 31, under c) and article 34, under 2,b) of the consolidated version of the Treaty on European Union give the Council the opportunity to ensure by common action the compatibility of the applicable rules and to adopt framework decisions for the purpose of the approximation of the laws and regulations of the Member States.

Before the entry into force of the Amsterdam Treaty, the Treaty on European Union[12] gave the Council, in Article K3, paragraph 2b), the authority to decide on a joint action[13] at the initiative of a Member State. This form of intergovernmental co-operation was situated within the third pillar of the European Union, the areas of justice and internal affairs.

The Joint Action of 24 February 1997 intended to approximate the legislation of the Member States in relation to trafficking in human beings and the sexual exploitation of children more effectively. Next to measures to be taken on a national level, the Joint Action of 24 February 1997 contains a number of provisions concerning international co-operation between Member States, thereby promoting the police and judicial co-operation in this field.

---

12 Treaty on European Union, signed in Maastricht on 7 February 1992, *Official Journal EC*, No. C/191, of 29 July 1992.

13 See in the context of human trafficking: the Joint Action which provides a promotion and exchange program (the so-called 'STOP-program', which tries to facilitate the fight of these crimes by creating a framework for training and instruction activities, studies and exchanges, for the benefit of persons who are responsible for taking action against all possible forms of human trafficking and sexual exploitation of children), *Official Journal* No. L/322/7 of 12 December 1996; the Joint Action adding the fight against trafficking in human beings to the operational scope of the European Drugs Unit (EDU), *Official Journal EC*, No. L/342/4 of 31 December 1996; the Joint Action in relation to the measures to be taken to harmonise the fight against trafficking in human beings and the sexual abuse of children, *Official Journal EC.*, No. L/63/2 of 4 March 1997.

The hope is real that the Joint Action of 24 February 1997 constitutes more than the mere overall result of an ad-hoc policy, and that it may be regarded as a first concrete realisation of the fifteen EU member countries' willingness to pave the way for joint legislation. Within the European Union a fundamental mutual consultation of the Member States is required when dealing with East-European and South-East Asian countries. Isolated projects of EU member countries, set up within the third pillar usually give the impression of being ineffective.

## A pro-active approach

Since human trafficking is one of the ways in which migration takes place, the authorities dealing with immigration issues should pre-empt it by taking measures based on co-operation with sending countries and transit countries. Further co-operation in the field of migration between the EU Member States and, for instance, Russia, have to be encouraged. Another positive element that should be elaborated concerns the regular meetings between CIREFI[14] experts of Central and Eastern European Countries, and their participation to the data-exchange related to illegal migration problems. Also the participation of candidate countries in an early warning system for the transmission of information on illegal immigration and facilitator networks, as proposed earlier this year in the CIREFI group, should be encouraged. Finally, the initiative to establish an European Centre of Monitoring Illegal Migration and Trafficking in Human Beings has to be supported.

## Protection and reintegration

*Protection*

The Joint Action of 24 February 1997 encourages the EU Member States to provide appropriate protection for witnesses. In this respect the hearing of witnesses using (audio)visual equipment (with the possibility to distort the

14 CIREFI: Centre d'information, de réflexion, et d'échange sur les frontières extérieures et l'immigration.

sound and the images in order to avoid recognition and thus intimidation) offers a solution not only for witnesses who wish to remain anonymous, but also for known witnesses and especially for victims of human trafficking and crimes of a sexual nature.

The initiatives relating to the protection of witnesses, informers, etc. which have been developed within the EU Council of Europe[15] are of particular relevance in the fight against organised crime, and should be expanded. This suggestion also emerged during the preparatory stage of the Tampere Summit.[16] It is obvious that, certainly in cases of trafficking in people or sexual exploitation (of children)[17], providing protection to witness is of great importance.

*Reintegration*

Fear of repatriation often prevents victims of human trafficking from co-operating with law enforcement agencies. To encourage victims to co-operate the Belgian authorities developed a system which give the victims of human trafficking a temporary residence permit. Usually, this permit is not extended if the presence of the victim is no longer deemed necessary for the inquiry, or after the trial has been completed.

If after having co-operated with the inquiry, the victim expresses the wish, to return to his/her country of origin, support should be given. In this context, reference can be made to the Resolution of 16 December 1998 on the Communication from the Commission on the Council and the European Parliament concerning trafficking in women for sexual exploitation[18] (in particular to its recommendation No 22). The payment of a reintegration

15 E.g. The Resolution of 23 November 1995 on the protection of witnesses with regard to the fight against international organised crime, *Official Journal*, nr. 97/C 327/04, 7 December 1995; the resolution of the European Council of 20 December 1996 relating to persons who co-operate with the police in combating international organised crime, Official Journal, nr. 97/C 10/01, 11 January 1997: the draft Recommendation of the Council of Europe on the practical application of the European Legal Assistance Treaty, the Recommendation of the Council of Ministers of the Council of Europe on the Intimidation of Witnesses and the Rights of Defence.

16 Council of Europe, 9611/99 CRIMORG 83 JAI 65 CATS 13, 12 July 1999, 3.

17 Recommendation nr. R(97) 13 of the Comittee of Ministers of the Council of Europe.

18 Resolution about the Communication from the Commission to the Council and the European Parliament concerning trafficking in women for sexual exploitation of 16 December 1998, *Official Journal EC,* nr. C 14/39, 19 January 1998

bonus in the country of origin can undoubtedly play an essential role in this respect. Since the victims of human trafficking are mostly not entitled to unemployment benefit, as they often work illegally, a reintegration-premium system could be introduced. In order not to send them home with empty hands (knowing that victims of human trafficking are often treated by their family as failures when they go back as poor as they left) the premium would encourage victims to return to their home country and re-integrate into their family.

The return of the victim to the family environment has important advantages. On the one hand, it can have a preventing effect, as it can dispel the myth the of "making easily lots of money abroad." On the other hand, it is necessary for the self-esteem of the victim.

The best place to work on their self-confidence is the family environment where the person is more than just another victim of human trafficking. However, integration is very difficult if the victim does not meet the expectations of the family. Therefore, giving some kind of re-integration premium would make the way to integration a lot easier for the victim.

To prevent abuse and to reduce the 'attraction effect' as much as possible, the development of a formal payment structure is a crucial requirement. Therefore, contacts between various NGOs in countries of origin and target countries should be stimulated. It would also be appropriate to organise meeting, with NGOs and local assistance centres, so that each returning victim can be accompanied home by an NGO.

## Conclusion

Human trafficking is –by definition– connected with forms of international organised crime and take place in the larger context of illegal migration flows. Human trafficking must be analysed against the backdrop of world-wide economic and political changes. It is a structural problem caused by a complex set of economic and social reasons, commonly called 'the gap between the rich and the poor'. It implies that criminals exploit the desire of victims to find a better life in a new country. The central question is how this phenomenon can been tackled without worsening the conditions of the victims.

The findings of the above mentioned research projects point out that control measures alone cannot stop the flow of trafficking in persons. Moreover, a legal approach relying only on one area of legislation (criminal, social, administrative law etc.) would be too narrow. Only a harmonised approach, both in countries of origin and destination, which integrates all relevant parts of legislation and balance punitive measures and human rights can offer multi-faceted responses to the problem.

## References

Brants, C. and A. Klip, Uitsluiting, criminalisering en migratie. *Recht en Kritiek*, 1997, *no. 4*, 301-314

Bruinsma, G.J.N. and G. Meershoek, Organized crime and trafficking in women from Eastern Europe in the Netherlands, *Transnational Crime*

Buchowska, O., J. Oleszczuk, J. Garnier, I. Dawid, B. Butterweck and S. Kupryashkina, (eds.), *One year La Strada. Results of the first Central and East European program on prevention of traffic in women*, Stichting tegen Vrouwenhandel, September, 1996, p. 27 and

Caquette, T.M., *Needs assessment on cross-border trafficking in women and children in the Mekong Sub-region*, Draft prepared for the UN Working Group on Trafficking in the Mekong Sub-region, Bangkok, Thailand, 1998

Derks, A., *Trafficking of Cambodian women and children to Thailand*, IOM, October 1997

De Ruyver, B.; W. van Eeckhoutte, J. Meese, K.van Impe and S. Vanheste, S., *Multidisciplinary research on the phenomenon of trafficking in human beings from an international and national perspective: a pilot study with Poland and Hungary*, Research Group Drug Policy, Criminal Policy and International Crime, Ghent, 1998

De Ruyver, B., G. Vermeulen, T. Vander Beken, N. Siron, and P. van Baeveghem, *Multidisciplinary research into the phenomenon of transit migration in Poland with a view to the control of human trafficking: a case-study with Poland,* Research Group Drug Policy, Criminal Policy and International crime, Ghent, 1999.

De Ruyver, B., W. van Eeckhoutte, K. van Impe, P. de Somere and M. Delcour, *Research on a multidisciplinary approach to the phenomenon of trafficking in women: a pilot- and case study of the Philippine situation*, Ghent, 1998

Flormann, W., Rotlichtmilieu - Menschenhandel als Teilbereich der Organisierter Kriminalität, *der Kriminalist*, 1995, *no. 4*, 178-179

Franssen, M., *Zicht op vrouwenhandel. Een methodiek van geïntegreerde begeleiding van slachtoffers van vrouwenhandel*, Stichting Tegen Vrouwenhandel (STV), Utrecht, Uitgeverij SWP, 1994, p. 15-16

*Frauenhandel und Prostitutionstourismus. Eine Bestandsaufnahme zu Prostitutions-Tourismus, Heiratsvermittlung und Menschenhandel mit ausländischen Mädchen und Frauen, Anhang: Rechtsexpertise zur Situation in de BRD*, Aktionsgemeinschaft Gegen Internationale und Rassistische Ausbeutung (AGISRA), Trickster, p. 44-48

Gaberle, A., Gruppenkriminalität in Polen als kriminologische und strafrechtliche Erscheinung. In: *Internationale Perspektiven in Kriminologie und Strafrecht für Günther Kaiser zum 70. Geburtstag*, Berlin, Duncker & Humblot, 1998

Galdwell, C., S. Galster and N. Steinzor, *Crime and servitude: an exposé of the traffic in women for prostitution from the Newly Independent States*, Moscow, Global Survival Network, 1997, 16-20

Ghosh, B., *Huddled masses and uncertain shores. Insights into irregular migration*, IOM, Martinus Nijhoff Publishers, The Hague, 1998

Go, S., The Philippines: A look into the migration scenario in the nineties. In: *Migration and regional economic integration in Asia*, Organisation for Economic Co-operation and Development (OECD), 1998

Gramenga, M.A., International conference on the trafficking of NS women abroad. New migration challenges after the Cold War and international responses, IOM, Moscow, 3-5 November 1997

Hummel, D., Lohnende Geschäfte: Frauenhandel mit Osteuropäerinnen und der EG-Binnenmarkt. In: *Beiträge zur feministischen Theorie und Praxis e.v.*, Farbo Drück und Grafik Team, Köln, 1993, p. 58-68

Knudsen, A., M. Gunnarson and F. Forster, *Ongoing evaluation of two pilot projects: Return and reintegration of trafficked and other vulnerable Cambodian and Vietnamese women and children from Thailand and Return of Trafficked and other Vulnerable Chinese Women and Children from Thailand*, IOM, 1997, 27 p.;

X., *Two reports on the situation of women and children trafficked from Cambodia and Vietnam to Thailand*, GAATW/IOM/CWDA, 1997

Kootstra, T., I thought I would be the lady-companion of one man. In: Kootstra, T., O. Oleszczuk, I. Dawid, B. Butterweck and S. Kupryashkina, *One year La Strada, results of the first Central and East European Program on prevention of traffic of women*, September, 1996

Kupryashkina, S., It is not our problem: Society attitudes to prostitution and traffic in women in The Ukraine. In: *One Year La Strada*, STV/La Strada, 1996, 47

Lap-Chew, L. and M. Wijers, M., *Trafficking in women. Forced labor and slavery-like practices in marriage, domestic labour and prostitution. Summary of the preliminary report,* October 1996, Utrecht, The Netherlands, GAAT-W/STV, 22

Licuanan, P.B., A.S. Sta Maria, S.M. Candelaria, M.J.N., Real, M.C.G. Bautista, E.L. Beja Jr., E. Porio, C.S. Crisol, and E.N. Paul, *Philippine-Belgian project against trafficking in women. Final report,* Ateneo de Manila University, 1998, p. iv-ix

Limanowska, B., Trafficking in women - Report from Poland, in *Sim special,* 17

Oleszczuk, O. and S. Buchowsk, The pretty women syndrome. In: Kootstra, T., O. Oleszczuk, I. Dawid, B. Butterweck and S. Kupryashkina, *One year La Strada, results of the first Central and East European Program on prevention of traffic of women*, September, 1996

Ofreneo, R.E., and R.P. Ofreneo, R.P., Prostitution in the Philippines. In: L.L. Lim, (ed.), *The sex sector. The economic and social bases of prostitution in Southeast Asia*, International Labor office (ILO), Geneva, 1998

Phongpaichit, P., S. Pipriyaransan and N. Treerat, *Guns, girls, gas and Ganja. Thailand's illegal economy and public policy.* Political Economic Center, Faculty of Economics, Chulalongkorn University, 1997

Sanghera, F., *In the belly of the beast: Sex trade, prostitution and globalization.* Discussion paper for the Asia-Pacific regional consultation on prostitution. February 17-18, 1997, Bangkok, GAATW, Canada, 1997

Seshu, M., *Trafficking in women and children in the countries of South Asia.* Regional meeting on trafficking in women, forced labour and slavery-like practices in Asia and the Pacific, February 19-22 1997, Asian Women's Human Rights Council, 1997

Sieber, U., Internationale Organisierte Kriminalität. Eine Bestandsaufnahme. *Kriminalistik*, 1998, *no. 2*, p. 98-102

Sieber, U. and M. Bögel, *Logistik der Organisierter Kriminalität. Wirtschaftswissenschaftlicher Forschungsansatz und Pilotstudie zur Internationalen Kfz-Verschiebung, zur Ausbeutung von Prostitution, zum Menschenhandel und zum illegalen Glücksspiel*, Wiesbaden, 1993

Vasquez, N.D., L.C. Tumbaga, and M. Cruz-Soriano, *Tracer study on Filipino Domestic helpers abroad. The socio-economic conditions of Filipino domestic workers from pre-departure until the end of their first two-year contract in Hong-Kong*, IOM, Geneva, 1995, p.25-27)

Wijers M. and L. Lap-Chew, *Trafficking in women, forced labor and slavery practices in marriage domestic law and prostitution.* Foundation against Trafficking in Women (STV), Utrecht, the Netherlands

# Trafficking in human beings: policy problems and recommendations

*Kauko Aromaa and Martti Lehti*[1]

## The problem

There exists a considerable volume of published texts about trafficking in human beings for the purpose of sexual exploitation or otherwise. However, there is not very much that would be based on strong documentation. Volume estimates are vague and variable and often not possible to trace back to research sources. Also, it is often unclear what counting rules have been applied when volume estimates are given. A major problem when analysing the estimates is not only that neither the definition of trafficking nor the sources of data are usually mentioned, but that it is also rarely said what the figures refer to. Do they refer to persons or border-crossings? Do they comprise only those trafficked across international borders or also the victims trafficked within countries? Do they include only new recruits or also victims of earlier years whose exploitation is still continuing? With regional estimates there are additional problems, because the same persons can appear in the estimates of several coun- tries at the same time. For example, a victim transferred through the Balkan route from Ukraine to Belgium is in theory included in the figures of six to ten countries, and would appear as six to ten victims in a joint European statistics compilation. On the other hand, a victim can also appear in the statistics of one single country several times. A foreigner who is trafficked into a country, exploited there in several different towns, and then again trafficked out of the country, should appear at the same time in

---

1 The authors are respectively director of European Institute for Crime Prevention and Control, affiliated with the United Nations (HEUNI) and National Research Institute of Legal Policy.
This chapter was published in: P.C. van Duyne, A. Maljevic, M. van Dijck, K. von Lampe and J. Harvey (eds.), *Crime business and crime money in Europe. The dirty linen of illicit enterprise.* Nijmegen, Wolf Legal Publishers, 2007.

the statistics of those trafficked into, out of, and within that single country, and thus as at least three different victims. Considering these problems one should use only data concerning native victims trafficked out of and within each country as the basis of international estimates. Such a rule is, however, impossible to apply. For most countries only estimates concerning the aggregate total number of victims are available, the use of which inevitably inflate the regional and global numbers.

Keeping these problems in mind, we have attempted to summarise the main facts of which there seems to be at least a low level of consensus in the available literature.

Trafficking for *prostitution* and other forms of *sexual* exploitation[2] dominates the trafficking debate and policy planning in Western countries. This is partly because of the lack of information and an even greater confusion of concepts in the case of other forms of trafficking in persons, with the phenomena even harder to conceptualize. The sex industry is also more visible than other forms of exploitation (domestic servitude, sweatshop industries etc.) and seems to arouse stronger moral implications. It is also economically less important than the other industries using large numbers of trafficked workforce and has less powerful interest groups to defend its interests in Western societies (IOM, 2004, 12).

All this does not mean that trafficking for sexual exploitation would not be a major problem. According to some estimates, 70 to 90 percent of the traffic in women and children in Europe and Asia serve organised prostitution (Omelaniuk, 2002). As for traffic in adult men, sexual exploitation has, however, played only a marginal role. Or is it only the impression we get out of the "data full of gaps"?

---

2 The term *trafficking* is used in this report as defined in the UN Palermo Protocol on Trafficking in 2000: "Trafficking in persons shall mean the recruitment, transportation, transfer, harbouring or receipt of persons, by means of the threat or use of force or other forms of coercion, of abduction, of fraud, of deception, of the abuse of power or of po- sition of vulnerability or of the giving or receiving of payments or benefits to achieve the consent of a person having control over another person, for the purpose of exploita- tion. Exploitation shall include, at a minimum, the exploitation of the prostitution of others or other forms of sexual exploitation, forced labour or services, slavery or practices similar to slavery, servitude or the removal of organs". The terms *trafficking in women* and *prostitution-related trafficking* are used in this article as synonyms for trafficking for sexual exploitation regardless of the sex and age of the victims; the term *traffic in women* refers to trafficking in female victims and the term *traffic in children* to trafficking in minors.

## Europe and Russia

The highest estimates of prostitution-related trafficking in Europe come from Human Rights Watch, the Swedish NGO 'Kvinna till kvinna', and from Malt- zahn in the Australian Women Conference (2001) (it is probable that they all are based on a common unmentioned source), which give 500.000 women and children as the annual volume of trafficking *to the old EU member countries* (EU-15) (or, alternatively, to "Western Europe").[3] According to the latest IOM estimate, the volume of trafficking *to and within the whole continent* is 500.000 annually (whether this is based on the same source as those above is not clear, but it is significantly more modest, since it also includes the countries outside the pre-2004 EU borders). Trafficking to the European Union (EU-15) from and through the Balkans would be 120.000 women and children a year, and from the whole of Eastern Europe about 200.000 women and children. According to the latest estimate of the U.S. Drug Enforcement Administration (DEA), 200.000 women and children are trafficked through the Balkans each year (a figure fairly similar to that of IOM) (*Organized crime situation report* 2001, p. 41; Hajdinjak 2002, p. 51; Laczko, Klekowski von Koppenfels, and Barthel, 2002, 4; 'Trafficking in Persons Report' 2004, 46; *Trafficking of Nigerian Girls to Italy* 2004.4

The volume of trafficking for prostitution has been increasing in Europe for the last fifteen years. Table 2 presents recent estimates, drawn from sources discussed in this text. The demand for prostitution and other sexual services seems to have been increasing in Western Europe, while the former socialist countries in Central and Eastern Europe with their current economic and so- cial problems offer a source area from which trafficking to Western Europe can be organised far more easily and more economically than from the old source areas (Southeast Asia, West Africa, and Latin America). Estimates of the annual turnover vary from 100 million Euros to several billions of Zuros (*Organized Crime Situation Report* 2001, p. 41; Hajdinjak 2002, p. 51; fpmail.friends- partners.org).

The majority of victims come from Albania, Lithuania, Moldova, Romania, Russia, and Ukraine. Of the victims of coerced prostitution

---

[3] All figures in this volume are in (normal) European annotation: the comma for the decimals and the dots for the thousands.

[4] fpmail.friendspartners.org;www.janes.com;www1.umn.edu/humanrts/usdocs.

assisted by the IOM in the last few years, about half have been Moldavians, a quarter Romanians, and a tenth Ukrainian. Trafficking in women to Europe from other continents has significance mainly in the Mediterranean countries and in Western Europe. The main source areas are Southeast Asia (Thailand), Latin America (Colombia, Brazil, and the Dominican Republic), and North and West Africa (Morocco, Nigeria, and Sierra Leone). According to Europol, the extent of this trade has remained about the same in recent years. The increase in Europe is due to trafficking from Eastern Europe (*Organized Crime Situation Report* 2001, p. 41; fpmail.friends-partners.org/pipermail/stop-traffic).

Concerning trafficking in women, Europe may be divided into two parts: the old member countries of the European Union serve as a destination area, and Central Europe, the Balkans, and the Confederation of Independent States (CIS) countries serve as source and transit areas.5 Irregular immigration as a whole has six main routes to and inside Europe:

- from Russia (mainly Moscow) through Lithuania, Poland, or the Czech Republic to Germany and Austria;
- from Ukraine through Slovakia, Hungary, the Czech Republic or Poland to Austria and Germany;
- from the Middle East and Turkey to Greece and Italy;
- from North Africa to Spain and Italy; from Turkey through the Balkans to
- Italy and Austria; and from South and Central America to Portugal and Spain.

These routes also serve as the main routes of trafficking in persons (NCIS 2002, p. 34).

Tables 1 and 2 show the volume of victims of prostitution-related trafficking and numbers of persons engaged in prostitution in the major geographic regions of Europe based on the latest data and estimates available in different European countries. The main sources are the reports of the IOM and the STOP-project (Hollmen and Jyrkinen 1999; *A Study*; *Trafficking in Women* 2001; Laczko, Klekowski von Koppenfels, and Barthel 2002), and some national summaries (Mon-Eu-Traf 2002; Mon-Eu-Traf II 2004). The data mainly describe the situation in 1999-2001.

---

5 However, see Almir Maljevic (2005).

## Table 1.
## Global volume of prostitution-related trafficking (source: national and regional estimates)

| | Annually identified victims in reported crimes/assisted by NGOs | Estimated annual number of victims trafficked within the region | The estimated annual number of victims trafficked to/ through the region | The estimated annual number of victims trafficked to/ through the region | Estimated number of people engaged in prostitution in the region |
|---|---|---|---|---|---|
| Nordic Countries | 0-50 | 0 | 100-1.000 | 0 | <10.000 |
| Baltic Countries | 50-500 | 1.000-10.000 | 1.000-10.000 | 1.000-10.000 | <25.000 |
| Western Europe | 3.000-5.000 | | 50.000-100.000 | | 260.000-500.000 |
| Central Europe | 500-2.000 | | 100.000* | | 60.000-70.000 |
| The Balkans | 1.500-2.000 | | >70.000 | 200.000* | >200.000 |
| Mediterranean | | | 10.000-50.000 | | 100.000-140.000 |
| Eastern Europe | >300 | | | 5.000-100.000 | >200.000 |
| North America | | | 50.000-120.000 | | >1.000.000 |
| Central America | | 10.000-20.000** | | | >100.000 |
| The Caribbean | | 10.000-20.000** | | | >300.000 |
| South America | | 300.000-2.000.000*** | | >110.000 | <10.000.000 |
| East Asia | | 300.000-1.500.000** | | | >3.000.000 |
| Southeast Asia | | 200.000-3.000.000** | | | >2.500.000 |
| South Asia | | 250.000-500.000** | | | <10.000.000 |
| Central Asia | | | | 1.000-15.000* | >10.000 |
| The Middle East | | | 10.000-50.000** | | >20.000 |
| Oceania | | | <10.000 | | >30.000 |
| North Africa | | | >10.000** | | >500.000 |
| West Africa | | | | 50.000-100.000** | >500.000 |
| Central Africa | | | | 10.000-100.000** | >500.000 |
| East Africa | | | | 10.000-50.000 | >500.000 |
| Southern Africa | | 50.000-100.000** | | | |

* Trafficked through and out;
** Trafficked within, to, through and out;
***Trafficked within, to, and through

**Table 2.**
**Annual volume of prostitution-related trafficking in the industrialized countries**

| Countries | Estimated number of annual victims of trafficking | Estimated number of minors engaged in prostitution |
|---|---|---|
| Western Europe* | 60.000-150.000 | >25.000 |
| Central Europe | <50.000** | <5.000 |
| Israel | <5.000 | |
| Canada | 8.000-16.000 | >1.000 |
| USA | 14.500-50.000 | >100.000 |
| Japan | 50.000-250.000 | <100.000 |
| Australia; New Zealand | <10.000 | 5.000 |
| Total | 200.000-550.000 | >235.000 |

* Western Europe, the Mediterranean, and the Nordic Countries;
** An estimate of victims trafficked to the region and from the region elsewhere than western Europe.

# Northern Europe:

## Denmark, Estonia, Finland, Iceland, Latvia, Lithuania, Nor- way, Sweden

Trafficking in northern Europe is regionally to a large extent an internal affair. The main destination area is the Nordic countries: Denmark, Finland, Norway, and Sweden. The source areas are the Baltic countries and north-western Russia. A secondary destination area consists of the Baltic countries, to which women are trafficked from Russia, Ukraine, and other CIS countries. Prostitution from Lithuania and Latvia is mainly directed to Germany, Sweden, and Denmark; and prostitution from Estonia and North-Western Russia to Finland, northern Norway, and Western Europe. A significant number of Baltic and Russian prostitutes are also active outside Europe, in North America, the Middle East, and the Far East (*Kännedom om prostitution* 2000, pp. 27-29; *Trafficking in Women* 2001, pp. 71, 110-11, 123-28, 210-26; *EU Organized Crime Report* 2002, pp. 45, 76; *Norwegian Report on Anti-trafficking Activities*; Lehti and Aromaa, 2002, pp. 50-69; Moustgaard, 2002, pp. 4-9; Leskinen 2003, pp. 9-28).

Prostitution from Russia and the Baltic countries to Scandinavia is mostly mobile: prostitutes come as tourists and work for a few days or a couple of weeks. The level of organisation of this activity usually seems to be fairly loose. The recent entry of the Baltic countries into the European Union (and the consequent relaxing of border controls) has further loosened the grip of panders of Baltic prostitution in Scandinavia (Kontula, 2005, p. 39).

The volume of foreign prostitution in the Nordic countries increased rapidly in the 1990s, but the number of cases of coerced prostitution reported to the police remained almost non-existent. The number of women from Russia and the Baltic countries who work in Nordic prostitution is estimated to be 5.000-10.000. The annual number of victims is probably a couple of hundred at the highest, although much higher figures have occasionally been referred to in public discussion. The low number of reported crimes and the overall loose organisation of prostitution do not, however, support these claims.

Internal prostitution in the Baltic countries and north-western Russia is likely to employ full-time 30.000-50.000 persons. The number involved in part-time prostitution is considerably higher. Most prostitutes working in the Nordic countries also work in prostitution in their home countries. No estimates are available of the number of victims of trafficking in the internal prostitution of the Baltic countries or north-western Russia, but it is probably higher than in the Scandinavian countries (Lehti and Aromaa, 2002, pp. 50-69; Lehti 2003, pp. 9-14; Leskinen, 2003, pp. 13-14).

In all three Baltic countries, most workers in the sex business are natives, especially members of the Russian-speaking minority formed by immigrants of the Soviet era. The core of Baltic prostitutes in Western Europe and Scandinavia consists of local professional prostitutes, whose numbers are estimated at 2.000-3.000 in Estonia, 2.500-9.000 in Latvia, and 3.000-10.000 in Lithuania. The number of foreign prostitutes is largest in Lithuania: 20 to 30 percent of all full-time prostitutes in the country. Most come from the Kaliningrad enclave of Russia, Ukraine, and Belarus. In Estonia and Latvia, the source areas are the same: Russia, Ukraine, and other CIS countries; but the number of foreign prostitutes is estimated to be considerably smaller. Local prostitution, the import of foreign prostitutes, and the export of local prostitutes are partly controlled by 'organised crime' in all three Baltic countries.

The known number of minors in prostitution directed to the Nordic countries seems to indicate that the problem of trafficking in children for prostitution is almost non-existent. In the Baltic countries and the St. Petersburg region the volume of underage prostitution is, however, considerable. The number is estimated to be hundreds in the Baltic countries and thousands in the St. Petersburg region. Their customers include many Scandinavian sex tourists (*Trafficking in Women* 2001, pp. 71, 110-11, 123-28, 210-26).

## Prevention, legislation, and crime control

The factors which create, motivate and direct the global flows of trafficking are the same as those directing the global migration flows as a whole, these are: the deep differences in the standard of living between and inside different geographic regions. It is unlikely that any fundamental positive changes can be achieved unless these differences are removed. The most effective means of preventing trafficking is thus to support, and remove obstacles to a more equal global social and economic development.

Concerning crime control and preventive policies, all measures ought to be global to be effective. It follows, therefore, that measures taken in Europe or North America alone will only have a minor impact on the global situation, as most trafficking takes place outside these areas. The crucial questions for crime control at the moment are:

1. creating extensive and reliable data collecting systems;
2. criminalizing the trafficking in women globally with relatively uniform criteria;
3. developing and increasing the cooperation in crime prevention both inter- nationally and inter-regionally (for example, using as a model the experiences of the European countries);
4. the improvement of the victims´ status and rights in the legislation all over the world;
5. creating efficient witness protection legislation and programmes applicable to the victims of trafficking; and
6. creating effective social and economic shelter programmes for the victims globally.

There is no reliable, comparative information available anywhere on the extent of any type of trafficking. In order to improve the situation, international efforts (for example, by the UN) should be made to create and harmonize national statistics concerning reported trafficking crimes, using relatively uniform criteria and composed by relatively comparative standards. The mere statistics are, however, able to produce only indicative information. In order to obtain better knowledge of the situation and to create a basis for more efficient data collection systems, it is important to increase basic research concerning trafficking and organised prostitution.

The legislation concerning trafficking in women is heterogeneous. The target of the international community should be a harmonisation of the national legislation and an improvement of the legal status of the victims of trafficking:

1. trafficking should be made a special offence;
2. courts of law should have the right to seize assets belonging to convicted traffickers, and
3. victims of trafficking should receive help and protection when necessary: Governments should set up agreements to facilitate the victims' return to their native countries (if they so wish), and victims should be granted, if necessary, temporary residence status on humanitarian grounds.

The ratification of the Palermo Protocol as extensively as possible and an adoption of its obligations in national legislation should be a primary goal.

Some European countries have introduced special witness protection legislation applicable to the victims of trafficking. All of the laws are relatively re- cent, and there is not yet much experience of how they will work in practice. All include the possibility of issuing temporary residence permits. In Belgium and the Netherlands the consent of the victim to co-operate in the investigation and prosecution is required. In Italy all victims have similar rights whether they co-operate or not. In Spain the stipulations of the general witness protection law are applicable. Only Italy and Spain offer the victims police protection, which continues also after the court proceedings have been closed; but even in these countries the right for this kind of protection is largely theoretical. It is also questionable how effectively the victims' willingness to co-operate with the authorities, crucial for the combating against trafficking, can be improved by granting only temporary residence permits (Pearson 2001, 10-13).

The routes of trafficking are so numerous and variable and the organisation of the crime is so flexible that it is not possible to close all the routes and eliminate all the trafficking networks. It makes more sense to focus the crime prevention efforts on the main source countries and on the most important junctions of the trafficking routes. It is also crucial for the effective prevention of all types of trafficking to continue and invigorate the combat against corruption in police forces and on all levels of government, which is rampant not only in many source countries but also in many of the main destination countries (NCIS UK 2002, 34-36; EU Organized crime report 2002).

## Conclusions

The current global extent of trafficking for prostitution is based upon rough estimates only, and in most cases it is unclear how these estimates have been reached. In spite of the wide political and media publicity, trafficking for prostitution is not among the high priorities of everyday crime prevention work in any single country. As a result, exact data about the crime is scarce, and information and studies on the phenomenon are to a large extent based on the same few original sources, and usually repeat tautologically the same story. The topic and data collection is also ideologically biased, which does not always help the interpretation of the data or of the research results. The need to collect and exchange comparative information on trafficking throughout the world, and to allocate sufficient funds to monitor trafficking, to create databases and to carry out further research on this issue should be underlined.

It is usually assumed that prostitution-related trafficking makes up the bulk of up to 70 to 80 % of all global trafficking in persons when measured by the numbers of victims. It is also assumed that the volume of this kind of trafficking and forced prostitution is much larger than shown by available sources.

If we use the Palermo criteria as the definition, it is probable that the first assumption is false. Although available data are sporadic and full of gaps, it is likely that other forms of trafficking, especially traffic of men, women and children for economic exploitation as domestic servants and as workers in agriculture, construction, and sweat-shop industries are globally at least equally common as trafficking for sexual exploitation. In some regions, for example in Africa and North America, this form of trafficking is prevalent.

In spite of this, it is probable that the current estimates of the total volume of prostitution-related trafficking underestimate rather than overestimate the volume. Although the police authorities and the NGOs tend rather to exaggerate than underrate the role of trafficking in international prostitution of adults (the new paradigm of organised crime can easily lead to this kind of exaggeration and many NGOs have an ideological tendency to see all prostitution as trafficking-related), most of the existing estimates underestimate the volume of domestic prostitution of minors, or at least do not include it in the numbers of victims of trafficking. In order to obtain a better knowledge of the situation, and to create a basis for more efficient data collection systems, it is important to harmonize the definitions of trafficking in persons used within national legislations and statistics. The creation of an international database (an idea presented for the first time in the 1913 Madrid Conference) would considerably improve the present situation.

Most of the global trafficking for sexual exploitation is short-distance. According to the available estimates, 60 to 80 % of the crime takes place within countries. The percentage of cross-border trafficking is 25 to 30 of the global volume, and also the bulk of it is regional, taking place between neighbouring countries. The major flows run from rural areas to cities and from economically disadvantaged regions to affluent ones. The proportion of traffic to the major industrialized countries is only 10 to 20 % of the entire global volume; most of the prostitution-related trafficking takes place within and between the third world and the eastern European countries. However, industrial countries have an important indirect role in the crime outside their borders, as Western and Japanese sex tourists forms a substantial part of the clientele of the local prostitution in several Third World countries and in Russia.

Although current statistics and studies very likely overestimate the proportional importance of prostitution-related trafficking for all global trafficking in persons, there are good reasons for keeping the focus of preventive and legislative measures against this particular type of crime. Studies carried out in different countries show that aggravated abuses of human rights are substantially more common in trafficking for sexual exploitation than in other types of trafficking. The victims are submitted to violence and grave intimidation more often than the victims of economic exploitation; their living and working conditions are worse, and their economic exploitation is more outrageous than for the victims of other types of trafficking. The victims are also usually younger than those of trafficking for other economic exploitation, and are less capable of defending themselves or of escaping the abuse without outside help.

The question whether prostitution as such should be allowed or abolished, is a moral and ideological one, and does not belong to the scope of this article. However, there is indisputable evidence that both the criminalisation of the activity of individual prostitutes, as well as the current policies in many countries which criminalise the exploitation of prostitution by third parties but leave the status of prostitutes unclear, creates favourable circumstances for all forms of abuse, including trafficking, of individual prostitutes. It is, therefore, important for the prevention of prostitution-related trafficking, that the rights and the status of prostitution and prostitutes are defined clearly in national legislation and that the prostitutes will be given the same economic, civil and social rights that other citizens and foreigners enjoy.

It is also important to harmonise the legislation concerning trafficking in persons in national legislation globally, as regards the criteria of crime, sanctions, and the status and the rights of the victims. The victims of trafficking should be given legal rights for help and protection when necessary and governments should set up agreements to facilitate the victims' return to their native countries if they so wish. The ratification of the Palermo Protocol as extensively as possible and the rapid adoption of its obligations in national legislations would hasten the harmonisation process and should be a primary goal for the international community. However, even the most effective legislation is not enough if the will and resources for implementation are lacking.

In the long run the best and only way to prevent prostitution-related trafficking as well as prostitution as a whole is to support and facilitate the general social and economic development in the countries on the losing side of the current globalisation process and to make an effort for a more equal and balanced global economic and social development.

## References

*A Study: Trafficking in Women and Children from the Republic of Armenia.* 2001. IOM.

www.iom.int/documents/publication/en/Armenia_traff_report.pdf

*Country report of the Republic of Slovenia. Trafficking in Human Beings.* Permanent Mission of the Republic of Slovenia to the OSCE. OSCE/ODIHR Country Reports

www.osce.org/odihr/attf/pdf/nap_slovenia.pdf

Dutch National Rapporteur on Trafficking in Human Beings, The Netherlands. In: *A study for monitoring the trafficking of human beings for the purpose of sexual exploitation in the EU member states.* Unpublished final draft. Helsinki: Heuni, 2004 *EU Organized Crime Report 2002.* Den Haag, Europol, 2002

GPAT, 2005, *Regional Patterns of Trafficking in Human Beings.* Global Programme Against Trafficking in Human Beings. www.unodc.org

Hajdinjak, M., *Smuggling in Southeast Europe.* CSD Reports 10. Sofia, Center for the Study of Democracy, 2002

Hollmen, L. and M. Jyrkinen (eds.), *Building up a network for monitoring, analysing and combating trafficking in women and children.* Helsinki, Ministry of the Interior, 1999

IOM, *Analysis of Data and Statistical Resources Available in the EU Members States on Trafficking in Humans, Particularly in Women and Children for Purposes of Sexual Exploitation. A Project of the International Organization for Migration (IOM) for the European Commission's STOP Programme. Final Report.* Geneva, IOM, 1998

IOM, 2000, *Migrant Trafficking in Europe: A Review of the Evidence with Case Studies from Hungary, Poland and Ukraine.* Geneva, IOM, 2000

IOM, *Victims of Trafficking in the Balkans. A Study of Trafficking in Women and Children for Sexual Exploitation to, trough and from the Balkan Region.* Geneva, IOM, 2001a

IOM, *Deceived Migrants from Tajikistan. A Study in Trafficking in Women and Children.* Geneva, IOM, 2001b

IOM, *Irregular Migration and the Trafficking in Women: The Case of Turkey.* Geneva,

IOM, 2003a

IOM, *The Trafficking of Women and Children in the Southern African Region.*

*Presentation of Research Findings*. Geneva, IOM, 2003b

IOM, *Trafficking in Persons. An Analysis of Afghanistan*. Geneva, IOM, 2003c

IOM, *First Annual Report on Victims of Trafficking in South Eastern Europe*. Geneva, IOM, 2003d

IOM, *Who is the Next Victim? Vulnerability of Young Romanian Women to Trafficking in Human Beings*. Geneva, IOM, 2003e

IOM, 2004, *Revisiting the Human Trafficking Paradigm: The Bangladesh Experience. Part I: Trafficking of Adults*. Geneva, IOM, 2004

Kontula, A., *Prostituutio Suomessa*. Helsinki, Sexpo, 2005

*Kännedom on prostitution 1998-1999*. SoS-rapport 2000: 5. Linköping, Socialstyrel- sen, 2000

*Labour migration*. 2005. www.iom.int/en/who/main_service_areas_labour.shtml

Laczko, F., A. Klekowski von Koppenfels and J. Barthel, Trafficking in women from Central and Eastern Europe: A review of statistical Data. Paper presented at European Conference on Preventing and Combating Trafficking in Human Beings, Brussels, September 18-20, 2002

Lehti, M. and K. Aromaa, *Trafficking in Human Beings, Illegal Immigration and Finland*. Helsinki, Heuni, 2002

Lehti, M., *Trafficking in Women and Children in Europe*. Heuni Papers 18. Helsinki, Heuni, 2003

Leskinen, J., Organisoitu paritus ja prostituutio Suomessa. In: *Rikostutkimus 2002*. Helsinki, Keskusrikospoliisi, 2003

Maljevic, A., Trafficking in Women in Bosnia and Herzegovina. In: P.C. van Duyne, K. von Lampe, M. van Dijk, and J.L. Newell (eds.), *The organised crime economy. Managing crime markets in Europe*, Nijmegen, Wolf Legal Publishers, 2005

Mon-Eu-Traf, *A pilot study on three European Union key immigration points for monitoring the trafficking of human beings for the purpose of sexual exploitation across the European Union*. Final Report. Brussels, European Commission, 2002

Mon-Eu-Traf II. *A study for monitoring the trafficking of human beings for the purpose of sexual exploitation in the EU member states*. Unpublished final draft. Helsinki, Heuni, 2004

Moustgaard, U., Bodies across borders. *NIKK magasin* 1/2002

Muhonen, P., Interview in „Ajankohtainen kakkonen", YLE TV2, 26.7.2005

NCIS UK Threat Assessment 2002. 2002. www.ncis.co.uk/ukta

Niemi-Kiesiläinen, J., Naiskauppa, paritus ja seksin osto. *Lakimies* 3/2004.
*Norwegian report on anti-trafficking activities.* Royal Ministry of Foreign Affairs.

OSCE/ODIRH Country Reports.
www.osce.org/odihr/attf/pdf/nap_norway.pdf

Omelaniuk, I., Trafficking in persons: Nature and logistics. Paper presented at the conference on Trafficking: Networks and Logistics of Transnational Crime and International Terrorism, Courmayer, December 6-8, 2002

*Organized crime situation report 2001.* Strasbourg, Council of Europe, 2003

Pearson, E., The need for effective witness protection in the prosecution of traffickers: a human rights framework for witness protection. Paper presented at the First Pan-African Regional Conference on Trafficking in Persons, Abuja, February 19-23, 2001

Trafficking in Persons Report Office to Monitor and Combat Trafficking in Per-sons, June 14, 2004. *Trends in Organized Crime*, Vol. 8, No. 1/ 2004, 38-45

*Trafficking in Women and Prostitution in the Baltic States: Social and Legal Aspects.* Helsinki, IOM, 2001

*Trafficking of Nigerian Girls to Italy.* Torino, Unicri, 2004

# Trafficking in migrants a European perspective

*Andrea Di Nicola*[1]

## Introduction

This chapter seeks to answer questions related the trafficking in migrants in Europe: are there organised criminal groups who are involved in human trafficking, and if so which groups? How do they organise their business? Which routes are most widely used? While answering these questions, I will try to identify, though tentatively, the role played by Western, Central and Eastern European states, sometimes as sending, sometimes as transit or destination countries. The analysis will also try to identify the most common illicit acts performed by organised criminals while trafficking in migrants.

There are reasons to believe that this illegal business, when conducted by organised criminal organisations, is very dangerous because it links international and local criminal aspects. The more the traffic is organised, the more it is related to the exploitation of victims in the local criminal markets of destination countries. Trafficked people, once in the host countries, are of then pushed into deviant or criminal markets, such as those of illicit drugs, prostitution, begging or theft. These activities may cover the cost of being smuggled.[2]

The second part of this essay sets some guidelines in order to build up a feasible and comprehensive strategy, at the European regional level, to fight

---

1 The author is researcher at Transcrime, Research Group on Transnational Crime, University of Trento.
This chapter is from: P.C. van Duyne, V. Ruggiero, M. Scheinost and W. Valkenburg (eds.), *Cross-border crime in a changing Europe*. Huntington, Nova Science Publishers, 2001

2 Part of the crimes committed by immigrants in host countries can be referred to as the state of dependence and exploitation in which trafficked people are kept by traffickers who help them, at high costs, to enter the desired destination countries. In order to receive payment, traffickers may force clandestine people to engage in criminal activities. See, on this issue, TRANSCRIME, 1996; Savona, Da Col, Di Nicola, 1997: 154-229; Savona, Di Nicola, 1998.

the international migrant trafficking. In particular, it suggests that interventions should be devised country by country. This should not only focus on criminal law but start from the consideration that some Central and Eastern European countries are the main sending countries, while Western European countries, are mainly receivers of illegal migration.

## Organised crime and the trafficking in migrants in Europe

Perceived differences between nations concerning the welfare of citizens is a main factor contributing to migration. Overpopulation, high unemployment rates, ecological disasters, deprivation of civil rights, political persecution and low standards of living, all lead some to seek a better life elsewhere. All of these also create new opportunities for criminal organisations, which are better equipped to offer alternative migration services. Facing these disadvantages and others, thousands from developing countries wish to flee their birthplaces for better lives in industrialised nations. Of course, the industrialised countries are responding to these emigration pressures to suit their own needs, tightening migration policies in times of high unemployment and making them more liberal when a supply of cheap labour is desired. For example, with high unemployment rates across the continent, Western European countries have enacted legislative restrictions on immigration, and this legislation has stemmed the flow of legal migrants and asylum seekers. Unfortunately, since the desire to emigrate has not been affected by these laws, a strong market for illegal migration has developed, and criminals (particularly organised ones) have begun to service it. If opportunities have increased for criminals with respect to illegal immigration, it must also be noted that the risks associated with these opportunities have remained uniformly low. In many countries, trafficking in aliens is not even considered a crime and in others it is only lightly penalised.[3] This is the case in some Central and Eastern European nations and even in the Western European nations, where sanctions against human smuggling often do not

3 For further treatments of this subject, see Belgium, Austria and ICMPD, 1995; Secretariat of the Inter-Governmental Consultations on Asylum, Refugee and Migration Policies in Europe, North America and Australia, 1995a; Siemens, 1996; IOM, 1998: 20.

exceed a two year term of imprisonment and sometimes simply amount to fines. Finally, law enforcement standards are low in many countries and – along with high levels of corruption– help to explain the spread of illegal smuggling (Savona, Lasco, Di Nicola, Zoffi, 1997: 8-9).

As a consequence of all this, illegal immigration represent a huge source of profit for traffickers in Europe as elsewhere. The *International Centre for Migration Policy Development* (ICMPD), considering the fact that in 1993 from 100 to 220 thousand of the illegal immigrants seemed to have used traffickers' services, estimates that the overall gain of the trafficking syndicates operating in Western Europe accounts to between 100 million and 1,1 billion dollars. The global profit margin in this criminal sector for one year is alleged to be around 5 to 7 billion dollars (Widgren, 1994: 5-6). For the year of 1996, estimates of the world business turnover for traffickers was 8 billion dollars (Paiva (IOM), 1996: 382). These huge profits are due to the high prices migrants pay for the services they require. The average cost to reach a European country, for instance, is from 2 to 5 thousand dollars (with a maximum 35-40 thousand for Chinese people).

The growing skills and organisation of illegal traffickers[4] are probably the most important development in illegal migration world-wide. This is not to say that 'amateur' smugglers or less organised criminals do not operate in this sector. However, large criminal organisations prevail in the business. Let us see why. Taking advantage of the fact that trafficked aliens who make their way to a new country are often quite vulnerable (because of their limited access to legal income and assistance), some criminal organisations exploit these recent illegal immigrants by introducing them into the drug market, prostitution, begging or theft. This exploitation is likely to leave the recent illegal immigrant enmeshed in the world of crime, although this involvement may be best described as induced rather than freely chosen. Thus, the high rate of illegal aliens involved in criminal activities in host countries can be understood within the context of the following circuit: trafficking leads to exploitation which leads to induced criminality (Transcrime, 1996: 53-72; Savona, Da Col, Di Nicola, 1997: 191-207; Savona, Di Nicola, 1998).

Because organisation in the traffic in migrants is of essential importance, the analysis that follows provide overview of major European-based organised criminal groups involved in this illegal activity. In the European continent

---

4 As far as organisation of traffickers is concerned see Salt, Stein, 1997.

organised groups trafficking in migrants very rarely devote themselves to this activity exclusively. It is more likely that they start this illegal business as a result of the experience built up while performing other kinds of traffics. This applies to the criminal groups that can be defined as opportunistic, i.e. able to shift from one illicit activity to another spreading their operative sectors only on the basis of mere opportunistic criteria. Like legal enterprises, these illicit organisations seek to maximise profits (and the traffic of migrants can bring huge ones) minimising losses (and the traffic of migrants implies very few losses). To minimise losses means to minimise the risk of being caught and convicted and having one's goods seized and confiscated. It means, in the case of conviction, to be reasonably sure of receiving a very low penalty. Organised criminals, being good international entrepreneurs, constantly monitor different opportunities and the risks connected with different crimes in the countries in which they act. They exploit the legislative loopholes and the low qualitative standard of the law enforcement system in some countries. As the trafficking in migrants is increasingly characterised by organisation, we can note an increased flexibility available to traffickers when choosing their logistic bases and the countries to be used as transit points to reach their destinations. In performing this choice, they draw their attention to those countries where criminal legislation is weak, where police control activity is low and possibility of connivance with governments is high. The analysis that follows may possibly clarify these remarks.

Some routes are preferred by traffickers to take their human cargoes to the economic core of Europe. Every route seems to be linked to specific countries and to some Mafia groups.

The first route was defined for some time as the Balkan route. It is still alive though its traffickers had to modify it as a consequence of the events which took and are taking place in the former Yugoslavia and of the increase in border controls along some European areas. The Balkan route crosses Turkey and the Balkan States, usually terminating in Germany. It has various possible patterns. From Bulgaria it is possible to go through Romania and Hungary terminating in Germany or to enter Macedonia or Albania and there make your way to Italy, where you can stay or continue the journey towards the Federal Republic of Germany or other Western European States. Different kinds of criminal groups act in this way; some of them individually and some in a sort of joint criminal venture. It is an area of interest for the

Albanian Mafia, the Italian Sacra Corona Unita and, more recently, for the new and dangerous Greek-Turkish-Pakistani Mafia.

Today there is great concern about the Albanian Mafia, because it combines the traffic in human beings with that of drugs and for its ability to keep immigrants in severe conditions of exploitation, once they reach their destination. In Italy Albanians have established contacts with the Sacra Corona Unita, which controls both the distribution and the exploitation of trafficked immigrants all over Italy and the connected drug traffics. Around 250 illegal immigrants (especially Curds, Pakistani, Iraqi and Chinese, though Albanians are sometimes also involved) are thought to be trafficked to Italy every day. In the summer of 1997 estimates were around 5.000 per week.[5] The average cost to be transported from the Albanian to the Italian shores is about 800 US dollars for a foreigner and 400-500 for an Albanian. A further extension of the illegal business of these organisations is represented by the exploitation of Albanian girls in the Italian markets of prostitution[6] and of children in begging.

Once again, along the Balkan route a new criminal joint-venture formed by an illegal strategic alliance among Greek, Turkish and Pakistani criminal groups appears to operate in the field of human smuggling. In Italy there have been new testimonies in recent criminal proceedings that allow us to infer the existence of this connection. This may also be supported by media reports on sea disasters in connection to human traffic and by passengers' stories. The link among the three criminal organisations can also be inferred from the increase in illegal immigration between Turkey and Greece.[7] Istanbul is said to be a gathering point for illegal migrants, most of all of Asiatic origin. From the Turkish capital some migrants are transported to coastal towns (such as

---

5 See Italy: New Law, Albania. In: *Migration News. Europe*, vol. 5, *n. 3*, March 1998.

6 See, for instance, Eastern European Newsletter, vol. 10, *n. 20*, 26 September-12 October 1996, as cited in IOM, *Trafficking in Immigrants. Quarterly Bulletin, n. 13*, Geneva, December 1996; IOM - Migration Information Programme, 1996a; Tantalo, Merzagora Betsos, 1997.

7 In the last few years diplomatic contrasts between Turkish and Greek authorities have arisen right because of this question. For example, in April 1996, a Greek police patrol boat fired at Turkish fishing boat that was believed to clandestinely transport Iranian refugees towards the Greek territory. Turkey lamented that the Greek action had not taken place in Greek territorial waters, while the government of Athens accused the Greek one of "protecting slaves' dealers", turning a blind eye on traffickers (P.J. Smith, Smuggling People into Rich Country Is a Growth Industry. In: *International Herald Tribune*, 28 June 1996). See also Incidents - Turkey-Greece. In: IOM, *Trafficking in Immigrants. Quarterly Bulletin, n. 16*, Geneva, September 1997.

Izmir, Kas, Kousadasi), where they are shipped in boats leading towards the Aegean islands, easily reachable from the Turkish coasts. Other immigrants are packed into trucks or other means of transportation and cross the land borders between Turkey and Greece. The joint-venture among Greek, Turkish and Pakistani criminals focuses its attention on particular ethnic groups (mainly Asian, Kurd and Middle Eastern people) and it is very powerful, thanks to its ability to infiltrate the legal systems of their counties and to its significant relevant contacts in different European areas. The Greek-Turkish-Pakistani Mafia prefers sea shipments, very often using 'old crocks' bought for the purpose[8]: traffickers get migrants to flow from many smaller boats into a bigger one, which transports them over long stretches of water. They are then regrouped into lighter boats to facilitate their landing on destination shores. The preferred landing points are usually in Italy, mainly in Sicily or Calabria.[9] Malta is also used as a sorting point.

The second preferred route is the Baltic route. It spreads from Asiatic countries, through Russia and the Baltic states, to Scandinavian countries and, from there, often trough Poland, to the core of the European Union. It has been increasingly exploited since the collapse of the Soviet Empire.[10] The poverty of controls, the inadequate criminal response, and the high corruptibility of officers make countries such as Russia, Lithuania, Latvia, Estonia and Bello Russian strategic crossroads to gain access to richer European countries (Ulrich, 1995). For example, according to the German government (The Government of the Federal Republic of Germany, 1994: 3), the traffic in migrants in Russia[11] has been facilitated by rules on visas and on entry permits not properly in line with Western European countries' standards and by corruption among police officers. The Russian Mafia, which is a clear example of opportunistic organised crime for its ability to adapt to new criminal needs and perform new activities, is taking advantage of the

8 A boat of medium dimension costs, at the used boat market, around 50 thousands US dollars and every journey it brings in about one million of dollars (just calculating 250 passengers at an average cost of 4 thousand dollars each). Only one journey is widely sufficient to refund the price of the ship and to be safe from the risks coming from the freezing and confiscation of the good.

9 See D. Frisullo, Buon Natale Clandestino. In: *Narcomafie*, anno V, *n. 9*, September 1997, pp. 3-5; D. Frisullo, La holding degli schiavisti. In: *Narcomafie*, anno V, *n. 9*, September 1997, pp. 6-9.

10 See, among others, IOM - Migration Information Programme, 1997.

11 On the traffic in migrants which involves Russia see Center for the Study of Transnational Crime & Corruption at American University, 1999.

situation. Moscow has emerged as a transit conduit for those illegal migrants wishing to find their way towards the West. An estimated 300 thousand immigrants, coming from developing countries, are believed to be illegally present in the Russian capital waiting to be smuggled into Western Europe (Ulrich, 1995: 10-11). Several investigations have revealed that Russian criminal groups are also involved in the traffic in women towards Western Europe.[12] Traffickers seem to be often protected by the police, by members of KGB and the FSB (the National Investigative Agency) and they can easily falsify visas and other documents.[13] There is also evidence that criminals succeed in obtaining authentic passports of many countries of the former Soviet Union (The Government of the Federal Republic of Germany, 1994: 3).

Traffickers wishing to reach Western Europe also use some Central European countries (such as Bulgaria, Czech Republic, Poland, Romania, Hungary) as transit or gathering points waiting for a further movement. This might happen because of the loopholes or lack of criminal law provisions in these countries[14] and/or because of their lax visa regulations and/or for the inadequacy of border control activities. By controlling the trafficking operations from these nations, traffickers guarantee themselves a substantial impunity. Cities such as Prague and Warsaw (see Salt, Stein, 1997: 475) have become gathering points for many migrants waiting to move towards the West and centres where documents used for trafficking purposes are counterfeited (IOM, 1994: 11). If, for instance, we look in greater detail at the situation in Poland, we see that this is both a sending and transit country, especially as far as women are concerned. 'Trafficking in Poland has acquired the character of organised crime proceeding according to the same principles and methods used in the traffic of weapons, nuclear material, cars and drugs, even if on a smaller scale. Criminal rings of four to five traffickers with German-Polish cross-border links sometimes also operate on larger trafficking

12 The traffic in Central and Eastern European women towards Western European countries is a phenomenon that, in the last years, has become more and more alarming, assuming bigger and bigger proportions. See, on this topic, IOM - Migration Information Programme, 1995; 1996; 1996a.

13 See Caldwell, Galster (of the Global Survival Network) in collaboration with the International League for Human Rights, 1997: 3-4.

14 See Belgium, Austria and ICMPD, 1995; M.A. Siemens, 1996; Belgium, Poland and IGC, 1996. See also IOM, *Trafficking in Immigrants. Quarterly Bulletin*, Geneva, *n. 12*, September 1996.

rings. It is precisely the increasingly organised character of the crime that makes traffickers powerful and a threat for female victims'. (Commission on Human Rights, 1996: n. 59).

The Strait of Gibraltar is another gateway towards Europe. It is exploited by African criminal groups that are certainly far less stable than the Russian Mafia or their Turkish/Greek/Pakistani counterpart. Anyway, they represent a real threat because, they simultaneously engage in drug smuggling[15] and encourage trafficked people to work in the drugs markets of the destination countries.

At the end of this brief overview it is worth underlining the variety of illicit acts that can accompany the trafficking in migrants. These acts go far beyond the simple activity of transporting migrants and violating immigration laws. They include the counterfeiting of documents, the corruption of public officers, the use of accomplices offering food and lodging to illegal immigrants, the exploitation of trafficked people once they have reached their destination (in the black labour market, in prostitution rings, in the drug market, in theft, and in begging). These illicit acts are linked among themselves by what could be defined as 'vertical interdependence'. Vertical interdependence arises when organised criminals or other criminal subjects, with the aim of committing a final offence, go through a series of intermediate or instrumental crimes: in order to finalise a crime of particular importance (in terms of effects or gains), a chain of offences is committed. It is a typical *modus operandi* of organised criminals: it can be recognised in illicit activities other than the trafficking in migrants and shows that a process of specialisation is occurring in criminal organisations (Adamoli, Di Nicola, Savona, Zoffi, 1998: 16-18).[16]

---

15 From 1993 Spanish officers estimate that about 1.000 people are drawn in the attempt of crossing the Strait of Gibraltar (Illegal Immigration: Spain/Marocco. In: *Migration News. Europe*, vol. 5, *n. 3*, March 1998). In relation to the traffic from the African continent see D.A. Kornbluth, 1998: 174-175.

16 Legislator, in the field of the traffic in migrants, such as in other organised crime activities, when using criminal law, should become aware of these interdependencies in the a view of an effective and efficient criminalisation (see next paragraph).

## Building a Global Strategy at the European Level

The analysis carried out so far highlights how some Central and Eastern European countries act as major starting, transit and/or gathering points for illegal migrants. In other words some European states can be considered weak spots of a protective net built around Europe.

It might be useful to explain why traffickers prefer some countries to others in which to conduct their operations. In this respect, the following aspects should be considered. There are legislative loopholes in the criminal law, legislation is often ignored, the police lack resources, corruption is rife, and socio-economic conditions are poor. In other words, countries lacking legislation on trafficking in migrants or failing to implement such legislation, and countries where corruption is widespread are highly exposed to criminal entrepreneurs engaged in illegal migration.[17] On the other hand, rich European countries, are rapidly closing their borders, and by introducing more restrictive policies they are encouraging the use of traffickers. Western European countries also lack serious structured polices concerning the planning of legal migration flows.

As a consequence of all this, almost every European state seems to have its own responsibilities. This is the reason why, at the European level, it should be understood that the only way to try and tackle this problem is to design a global response, agreed upon by several countries collaborating together to reach a common result. Consequently, in Europe like elsewhere, the most correct strategy against the traffic in migrants would seem to be a mixture of prevention and control policies harmonised at the regional level. That is to say rich and poor European countries should perform different but important roles, accepting their different responsibilities and their respective areas of intervention. In other words, it would be appropriate that some European countries intervene in the field of the criminal law or in that of law enforcement, while others focus on admission policies or, more generally, on the reduction of criminal opportunities.

Let us try to analyse a possible European strategy.

---

[17] From the analysis on the phenomenon of the traffic in migrants above carried out, Baltic States and many Central and Eastern European countries have emerged as points of origin, of gathering or of transit of migrants. From these states traffickers control the trafficking operations for they are reasonably sure to have a substantial impunity. The same could go for countries such as Albania or Turkey.

With regard to the criminal law, efforts should be made to harmonise the legislation and law enforcement strategies among European states. Traffickers should find their roads blocked by a regional wall constructed by standardised criminal law. This means that a similar level of sanctions all should be applied, with penalties reflecting the gravity of this illegal behaviour. The types of legal definition should also be similar, with a view to improving the co-operation in the field of judicial and police matters. This development should be relatively smooth in Western European countries, where adequate rules are already in place. However, difficulties may be encountered in Central and Eastern European countries, where legislative loopholes exist. Therefore, differentiated efforts should be made by European countries, though harmonisation should be the common task. Furthermore national legislators should try to design criminal legislation which consider the 'criminal interdependencies' which take place in such traffics.[18] The trafficking in entails corruption of officials, the forgery of documents and, exploitation of women and children. Consequently, these should be regarded as that these further aggravating circumstances of the main offences, i.e. the crime of trafficking in migrants. Particular attention should also be devoted to the establishment of efficient confiscation systems. In order to pursue this goal, especially in the New Independent States, financial transparency should be seen as a powerful preventive tool (Global Survivor Network, 1997).

Criminal law in the book, anyway, is useless if it is not implemented. Too often we witness laws which are only symbolically implemented. They represent mere declarations, sometimes enacted only to please the international or the national community. The problem is serious, most of all because of the likelihood that a few of the poorest European countries have little resources to be used in police activity. The only instrument to get rid of this difficulty is represented by police co-operation, first and foremost intended in a sense of material co-operation. Rich European countries should provide poorer ones with the necessary instruments (in terms of resources, technical instruments, skills) to develop serious law enforcement policies.

In any case, the traffic cannot be stopped by resorting solely to the criminal law. Preventive measures should support the criminal law in the fight against big criminal organisations with a view to reducing criminal

18 See paragraph 2 in the end.

opportunities. In the field of these prevention policies, rich European countries should play a prominent role. Here below are a few examples.

Governments of rich European states should enact policies that make would-be migrants aware of the serious risks they face when they trust in traffickers and in alternative, illicit ways of migrating.

All countries touched by trafficking routes should act, at the national and regional level, to reduce the infiltration of organised crime in the legal arena and do their best to limit opportunities for corruption, possibly through a system of incentives for public officers, a constant monitoring of their activities and an increase in their professional standards.

All countries, particularly the wealthier ones, should 'promote' the morality of employers, through tight controls over their activities and incentives encouraging them to comply with labour legislation. This would reduce the number of entrepreneurs who resort to traffickers as a means of finding low-cost 'black' labour.

All receiving countries should avoid producing those 'factors of social construction' which associate migrants with deviance and criminality (Pastore, 1995). States, through institutional measures and immigration policies, may influence the dynamics of traffic and exploitation of immigrants. For example, sudden and unconditional closure of borders can increase the number of persons requiring traffickers' services.

In countries which do not provide irregular residents with a minimum standard of social welfare trafficked immigrants may resort to criminal groups to obtain such welfare. These groups, in turn, will strengthen their control over illegal immigrants.

To conclude, every country should consider modifying criminal law, police control strategies and policies and aim at reducing opportunities for criminals. Simultaneously, countries should combine prevention and control, and harmonize meansures at the regional level. This should involve all European states in an attempt to design policies which are specific nationally and effective internationally. Shared responsibility and joint actions are, therefore, the keywords in the fight against the traffic in human beings.

## References

Adamoli, S., A. Di Nicola, E.U. Savona, P. Zoffi, *Organised crime around the world*. Publication Series No. 31, European Institute for Crime Prevention and Control, affiliated with the United Nations (HEUNI), Helsinki, 1998

Belgium, Austria and ICMPD, Harmonization of Legislation to Com-bat Trafficking in Aliens, report prepared for the *Third meeting of the expert group of the Budapest Group*. Budapest, 15-16 June, 1995

Belgium, Poland and IGC, *Anti-Trafficking Model Legislation. Report of the Working Group of the Budapest Group*, Oslo, 3-4 October, 1996

Caldwell, G., S. Galster, (of the Global Survival Network) in collaboration with the International League for Human Rights, Crime & Servitude: An exposé of the traffic in Russian women for prostitution. Paper prepared for the Conference on *Criminal Justice Issues in the International Exploitation of Women and Children*, U.S. Department of State, U.S Department of Justice and the Federal Judicial Center, Washington, 7 April, 1997

Center for the Study of Transnational Crime & Corruption at American University, *Organized Crime Watch - Russia*, vol. 1, *no. 2*, February 1999

Commission on Human Rights (U.N. Economic and Social Council), *Report of the Special Rapporteur to Poland on the Issue of Trafficking and Forced Prostitution of Women*, Washington, 10 December, 1996

Global Survivor Network, *The Trafficking of NIS women abroad; an international conference in Moscow*. Moscow, 3-5 November, 1997

IOM (International Organisation for Migration), Trafficking in Immigrants: Characteristics and Trends in Different Regions of the World, paper presented at the *Eleventh IOM Seminar on International Response to Trafficking in Immigrants and the Safeguarding of Migrant Rights*. Geneva, 26-28 October, 1994

IOM (International Organisation for Migration), *Analysis of Data and statistical resources available in the EU Member States on trafficking in humans, particularly in women and children for purposes of sexual exploitation*. Geneva, 1998

IOM - Migration Information Programme. *Trafficking and prostitution: the growing exploitation of migrant women from Central and Eastern Europe*. Budapest, May 1995

IOM - Migration Information Programme, *Trafficking in women to Austria for Sexual Exploitation*. Budapest, June 1996

IOM - Migration Information Programme. *Trafficking in women to Italy for sexual exploitation.* Budapest, June 1996a

IOM - Migration Information Programme, *The Baltic Route: The trafficking of immigrants through Lithuania.* Budapest, January 1997

Kornbluth, D.A., Illegal migration from North Africa: The role of traffickers. In: ISPAC, *Migration and crime. Proceedings of the International Conference on 'Migration and crime. Global and regional problems and responses'.* Courmayeur, *5-8 October, 1996*, Milan, 1998

Paiva, R.G. (IOM), Multilateral efforts to combat trafficking in immigrants: An international agency perspective. In: ISPAC, *International Conference on 'Migration and crime. Global and regional problems and responses'.* Courmayeur, 5-8 October 1996, Milan, 1998

Pastore, M., *Produzione normativa e costruzione sociale della devianza e criminalità tra gli immigrati,* Quaderni I.S.MU. 9/1995, Fondazione Cariplo - I.S.MU., Milan, 1995

Salt, J., Stein, J., Migration as a business: the case of trafficking. *International Migration*, 1997, vol. 35, *n. 4*

Savona, E.U., in co-operation with G. Da Col, A. Di Nicola, Migrazioni e criminalità in Europa. In: L. Tomasi (ed.), *Razzismo e società plurietnica. Conflitti etnici e razzismi giovanili in Europa*, Franco Angeli, Milan

Savona, E.U., A. Di Nicola, Migrazioni e criminalità. Trent'anni dopo. *Rassegna Italiana di Criminologia,* vol. IX, *no. 1*, 1998

Savona, E.U., in co-operation with F. Lasco, A. Di Nicola, P. Zoffi, Globalisation of crime. The organisational variable. Paper prepared for *The 15th International Symposium on Economic Crime.* Jesus College. Cambridge (UK), 14-20 September, 1997

Secretariat of the Inter-Governmental Consultations on Asylum, Refugee and Migration Policies in Europe, North America and Australia, *Summary description of the legislation on alien trafficking in states in Europe, North America and Australia.* Geneva, December 1995

Siemens, M.A., European responses to the phenomenon of illegal migration: National and international initiatives. Paper presented at the International Conference on *Migration and crime. Global and regional problems and responses.* Courmayeur, 5-8 October, 1996

Tantalo, M., I. Merzagora Betsos, Immigrazione femminile e vittimizzazione possibile. Riflessioni per un'analisi fenomenologica, paper presented at the XI National Congress of the Italian Society of Criminology on *Nuove sfide per la criminologia: migrazioni, violenza giovanile, didattica*, Gargnano del Garda (Brescia, Italy). 21-24 May, 1997

The Government of the Federal Republic of Germany, International cooperation in fighting illegal immigration networks. Paper presented at the *Eleventh IOM seminar on international response to trafficking in immigrants and the safeguarding of migrant rights*. Geneva, 26-28 October, 1994

TRANSCRIME, *Migrazione e criminalità - La dimensione internazionale del problema*, CNPDS, Milan, 1996

Ulrich, C.J., *Alien smuggling and uncontrolled migration in Northern Europe and the Baltic Region*. HEUNI Paper N° 7, Helsinki, 1995

Widgren, J., Multilateral Co-operation to combat trafficking in immigrants and the role of international organizations. Paper presented at the *Eleventh IOM Seminar on international response to trafficking in immigrants and the safeguarding of migrant rights*. Geneva, 26-28 October, 1994

# Illegal markets, human trade and transnational organised crime

*Vesna Nikolić-Ristanović*[1]

## Introduction

Transnational organised crime in general, and human trade in particular, have recently became the subject of many criminological studies. At the same time, the study of crime in the social context of globalisation rather than within the boundaries of individual nation states has started to attract the attention of criminologists (McDonald, 1995; Findlay, 1999). Moreover, the approach from the market perspective (van Duyne, 1996; Williams, 1999; Ruggiero, 2000), apart from studies looking at it from human rights, organised crime, migration and labour perspectives, have tremendously improved our understanding of the trends and dynamics of the human trade in the contemporary world.

However, not so many authors tried to combine a global and a local approach. As well observed by Hobbs and Dunnighan (1998: 289), 'a serious shortcoming of global-transnational-international studies of organised crime is that they ignore or substantially underestimate the importance of the local context as an environment within which criminal networks function'. Consequently, for better understanding of transnational organised crime it is necessary to study the dynamics of the local context of 'trading networks and transformative systems of criminal and legitimate commercial activity' as well as the dialectic between the local and the global. The use of a 'glocal' approach (Hobbs and Dunnighan, 1998: 291) seems inevitable.

---

1 the author is professor of criminology at Belgrade University (Serbia).This paper is the result of the research project No 1642 Serious forms of crime in conditions of transitions, partly funded by Serbian Ministry of Science.
This chapter is from: P. C. van Duyne, M. Jager, K. von Lampe en J.L. Newell (eds.), *Threats and phantoms of organised crime, corruption and terrorism*. Nijmegen, Wolf Legal Publishers, 2004

It is of special importance when human trade and transnational organised crime in, through and from Balkan countries are analysed. Having in mind both its geographical position as a bridge between East and West and the high level of interdependence between Western demand of illegal labour and the supply of people from Eastern Europe, the Balkan is playing a very important role in connecting local and international markets. Thus, market and 'glocal' structural approaches are inevitable if we want to understand causes and build adequate prevention and repression strategies.

The main aim of this paper is to explore, focusing largely on the example of the Balkans, the connection between the expansion of neoliberal market economy and war, and related to it the growth of illegal markets and the shadow economy, on the one hand, and the victimisation by human trafficking, on the other. By locating human trade within expanding local and global illegal markets, I am arguing that, without taking into consideration wider social contexts, which create structural incentives for illegal markets and transnational organised crime, we can hardly understand the causes, let alone build effective strategies to combat and prevent it. Consequently, on the basis of the analyses of human trade as a form of both transnational organised crime and illegal markets, I am suggesting some strategies (short-term and long-term) for the prevention and control of human trafficking on both the micro and macro level.

## Overview of the most important notions and global context

Bearing in mind that there are different definitions and sometimes a confusion of terms in relation to transnational crime, particularly concerning human trade, for a better understanding of the text which follows, it is necessary to start with a clarification of the concepts I am using in this chapter. In addition, since, as already mentioned, an understanding of the local context of trafficking in people from, to or through Balkan countries, is not possible without a consideration of the global context, in this chapter I am also providing an overview of the main global factors which contribute to development of illegal markets in general and human trade, in particular.

The meaning of the notion of transnational crime, which seems to have been developed over the last decade, is described by Mueller (Mueller, 1999, quoted by Williams, 2001: 61) as 'criminal activities extending into and violating the laws of several countries'. Thus, the most common and distinctive feature of transnational crime is that it 'involves the crossing of borders or national jurisdictions' (Williams, 2001: 61). However, as well observed by Williams (2001), the notion of transnational crime is much more complex than it looks like at first glance, since there are several components of border-crossing, which appears to be multi-dimensional. These components include border crossing by perpetrators, products, people who are treated as commodities, profits and digital signals. Transnational crime may take form of organised crime, but it may also be committed by individuals.

Transnational crime involves the existence of illegal market, which Arlacchi (1998: 203, 2001: 5) defines as 'a place or principle within which there is an exchange of goods and services, the production, selling and consumption of which are forbidden or strictly regulated by the majority of states and/or by international law' (drugs, arms, human beings). However, for organised crime in North-western Europe (Van Duyne, 1996: 341) and even more in the Balkan countries, it seems more appropriate to make a distinction between two kinds of criminal markets: illegal trading in goods and services that are themselves forbidden, i.e. whose trade is strictly prohibited (e.g. drugs and people) and illegal trading in otherwise legal goods and services (e.g. goods such as cigarettes, liquor or petrol and other scarce goods during embargo in Serbia). This latter form of crime market is sometimes called informal market or informal (shadow) economy (UNDP, 1998: 4; Ruggiero, 2000: 66) and this is how I am going to call it in this article. Also, similarly to Ruggiero, I will define as the 'hidden economy' the social and productive space where both informal and illegal economies operate.[2] It is the part of the larger context of the shadow economy, which is expanding not only in developing, but in developed countries as well. For example, in most of OECD countries, the shadow economy was far below 10 per cent of GDP in 1970, while in 1990s it increased in some of them, such as Belgium, Denmark, Italy, Norway, Spain and Sweden to almost 20 per cent of GDP

---

[2] However, unlike Ruggiero, I use the term illegal rather than criminal market since, having in mind the social context of Balkan, both informal and illegal markets are criminal.

(Schneider and Ernste, 2000: 41, 44). The understanding of both distinction and connection between these two markets is especially important for understanding the trafficking in people in Balkan countries. In these countries the distinction between legal and illegal is very loose and as such serves as an incentive for organised crime.

Trafficking in people, as a form of transnational crime, is often confused with people smuggling. This is not unusual, having in mind that they often are done in connection and by same criminal groups. However, it is very important that a distinction is made between these two phenomena in general, and in the study of the connection between illegal/informal markets and human trafficking, in particular. But, since both smuggling and trafficking in people are connected to illegal migration and illegal markets, there is a need for studying both their commonalties and distinctions. While smuggling is bringing someone across the border for money, trafficking can be done within the same country. In addition, and more importantly, unlike people smuggling, trafficking always include the wish to exploit someone or bringing someone in conditions of slavery. Thus, a smuggled migrant wishes to be smuggled, while trafficked persons usually do not have a choice (IOM Pristina, Situation report, 2000-2001), since they are deceived or pressurised into economic dependence. Also, while people smuggling may be connected to criminal markets, trafficking in people is the form of criminal market itself, often connected to other criminal markets as well. However, the fact that people smuggling can easily turn into trafficking should not be ignored. In fact, as illegal migrants, smuggled people most often do not have much choice but to turn to illegal markets for job opportunities. This brings them into conditions of exploitation or slavery, often turning them into victims of trafficking. In these situation, the distinction between smuggling and trafficking becomes blurred, so that in reality the major difference is in the amount of money that the person is paid prior to departure from the country of origin. The distinction may be determined only after the individual has arrived in the destination country: a smuggled person pays the whole amount in advance and after coming to the destination country he/she can walk free. However, trafficked person pays either percentage or nothing and is kept in debt bondage, i.e. cannot walk away from the smuggler. This is the point when the smuggled person may become a trafficked victim (Aronowitz, 2001: 167).

This usually happen when a smuggled person cannot afford an independent life as illegal migrant and remains dependent and exploited by smuggler or the person in whose service he or she is brought.

Although transnational (organised) crime has always accompanied economic regulations, its increase in the 1980s and 1990s has been accompanied and influenced by global trends, among which the most important ones are:

1. increasing inequality on the global level, and development of a 'glo-bal market society';
2. significant population movement;
3. more lax exit border controls connected to the dissolution of the Soviet Union and the Warsaw Pact, as well as to the democratisation of a number of African, Asian and Latin American countries;
4. globalisation of trade, technology, transportation, communication, information and financial systems;
5. global 'market culture' and colonisation or commodification of sexuality;
6. expansion of the hidden economy (illicit markets and informal economies) and the incorporation of the informal within the formal economy (Ruggiero, 2000: 94).

Leading to both significant increase in inequality and the process which generates quite destructive concentrations of very pronounced economic deprivation (Taylor, 1999: 53), 'market society' (as defined by Currie, quoted by Taylor, 1999: 52) had furthered crime both nationally and internationally. In addition, the increasing gap between rich and poor countries generated significant population movement, driven by a mixture of push and pull factors.

Push factors are ranging from ethnic conflict and environmental degradation, the desire for material survival or economic improvement, to the escape from increasing gender inequality, family problems, domestic and sexual violence and homelessness (Kelly, 2002: 24; Nikolić-Ristanović, 2002a: 136). The increase in migration and the growth of ethnic networks that transcend a whole range of national borders has proved valuable to the operations of criminal organisations (Williams, 2001: 68). This especially became evident in 1990s with the collapse of communism and ethnic conflicts in Eastern Europe, since the increase in migration was not accompanied with the increase but rather with the erosion of the tolerance of receiving countries.

The development of global 'market culture' contributes as a strong pull factor. According to Taylor (1999: 62), 'market culture' 'trades openly with the idea and the range of possibilities of globalisation', feeding the fantasy that the 'solution' to problems of material poverty 'may live not within individual nation-states but within a global market place'. In addition, in contemporary 'market society' everything is for sale: everything is 'commodity', including human body and sexuality. Moreover, colonisation or commodification of sexuality is now playing an increasing role in the public culture of marketing societies throughout the world (Taylor and Jamieson, 1999: 264). This includes not only developed but developing countries as well, where commodification of everything was imported as a new way of life and offered as a norm of civilization or normal life (as opposite to what was reality of communism). (Kotzeva, 1999: 87). As a consequence, increasingly more jobs for women became available within the sex industry. All that serves as a strong pull factor for trafficking in people from undeveloped countries in general, and for trafficking in women in particular, either through feeding their unrealistic expectations about the West[3] or by luring them into local prostitution and other dubious jobs. And although this trafficking is not a new phenomenon, what is new is its geographical distribution as well as the growing involvement of organised crime in the market and its specialisation in smuggling and trafficking of people (Aronowitz, 2001: 170).

Transnational crime can in part be seen also as a response to interdependence and globalisation, or as 'the dark side' of it (Williams,2001: 66, 67). The importance of interdependence and globalisation in terms of facilitating transnational organised crime is especially evident in the field of trade, technology, transportation, communication, information and financial systems, where globalisation provides new opportunities for criminal enterprises to operate across national borders. It is not unusual that illicit trade develops a parasitic relationship with licit trade. However, the free trade system has made it especially easy to insert illicit products in a number of

---

3 One of the very strong pull factors is the myth of independence and emancipation supposedly awaiting women in the West (Wijers and Lap-Chew, 1997: 44). The other is connected to a better life and easy access to employment. The picture of the West comes from the global media, cinema, advertisements, etc., where everything seems possible and everyone is happy (Konig, 1997:87).

(licit) imports and exports, comprising at present international trade (e.g. illegal aliens transported with legal goods). Thus, as observed by Williams (2001, 66), 'as licit business has become transnational in character, so has much enterprise crime'.

The development of organised crime, and trafficking in people as a significant part of it, is also connected to the expansion of the hidden economy, since it seems that there is a very clear interdependence between illegal and informal markets. The consequence is that the tolerance toward the latter one is feeding the development of the former. This can be observed especially in Balkan, but it exists in Western countries as well. Consequently, 'informal economies and conventional criminal activities end up almost coinciding' (Ruggiero, 2000: 64).

However, an especially important aspect of trafficking in people is the absorption of the informal economy into the formal in 'the sense that hidden practices, parallel procedures, and forms of illicit economic conduct are increasingly required to bear fruit for the official economy' (Ruggiero, 2000: 64). Illegal markets emerge partly 'as the result of the growth of the instruments aimed at protecting society from the destructive effects of market forces themselves' (Polanyi, 1974, quoted by Arlacchi). However, the alleged threats posed by the informal economy tend to be turned into opportunities for the formal as well, having in mind that 'some official industries are able to set up their own illicit services to boost their economic performance (. . .) the official economy adopts illegitimate practices, while illegitimate entrepreneurs strive to gain access to the official economy' (Ruggiero, 2000: 105). One of the best examples for that observation is found within illegal labour market in Britain, which provides cheap labour and increases the profits of main British supermarket chains like Tesco and Sainsbury.[4] Other examples are the horticulture in Spain and the Netherlands to produce cheap vegetables. Not surprisingly, those who seek employment on the illegal labour market are illegal migrants, who often enter the countries through smuggling channels and sometimes end in slavery-like conditions.

---

[4] This is very well described in BBC Panorama program on illegal migration.

## Transition, war and illegal markets

Social changes in Eastern and Central European countries connected to political and economic transition led to the creation of conditions favourable to the development of illegal markets. In addition, in the Balkan countries, influences of the transition are interlaced with negative influences connected with war. The example of the Balkans is very telling in that regard, since it shows how illegal markets are developed in connection to the demand/supply ratio in scarce goods, cigarettes, drugs, weapons, illegal migrants etc., influenced by a combination of war, transition and globalisation related factors (Nikolić-Ristanović, 2002). Among the conditions created by the transition from communism, political and economic liberalization played the most significant role.

The political transition in Eastern Europe led to the opening of borders of East European countries and to an increased mobility of people. However, at the same time, the EU closed its borders. EU restrictive immigration policy mirrored in the Schengen agreement (1985), known also as 'Fortress Europe' or 'Fortress EU' (Goody, 2002: 135) led to an increase of illegal and criminal penetrations – a well known effect of prohibition on the emergence of illegal markets. In addition, it also contributed to the organised crime's penetration of legitimate economy, which, however, seems to remain 'limited to small companies' (Van Duyne, 2003).

As observed by Rees and Webber (2002: 89):

> 'The EU's model of internal security has arisen in response to perceptions of an increased threat to the Union from organised crime. The EU has recognised its vulnerability as a region in which there is free movement of goods, services, money and people within the boundaries of the single market. Organised crime exploits this situation and involves itself in the creation of illicit markets as well as the penetration of legitimate ones.'

Economic liberalization, i.e. the replacement of a state-planned economy with a market economy, enabled the easy flow of goods, including drugs and human commodities. Thus, as Andreas puts it, 'loosening of government controls over the flow of goods, services, information and capital encourages both legal and illegal economic activity' (Andreas, 1995, 1996, quoted by Lewis, 1998).

In conditions of poverty, increasing unemployment and severe tax policy, many people are forced to look for either a primary or additional (second) job within the informal sector which, together with its associated labour markets, is growing in many transition economies. Not so rarely, the informal sector offers better paid jobs than the formal one and a section of the population earns significant additional income from such activities (UNDP, 1998: 4). The growth of the informal labour market entails that more people (both women and men) are relatively unprotected and vulnerable to exploitation in their jobs (inappropriate wages, prolonged working hours, lack of any rights etc.). (UNICEF, 1999: 6; Efremov, 1998: 138; Vaknin, 2000: 1).

The upheaval of transition, on the one hand, and the growth of the sex industry as an informal sector most interested in attracting women, has led to a rapid rise in the number of women who are, willingly or unwillingly, working as prostitutes, with a high risk of becoming exposed to violence and exploitation.

All above-mentioned conditions are further aggravated by armed conflicts, 'when criminalised paramilitary and state-intelligence organisations invest in, sponsor, or directly enter' (Lewis, 1998: 217) criminal markets. Consequently, war zones become centres of organised crimes related to the illicit trade of drugs, fuel, weapons. There were also allegations of trafficking in human organs (Nikolič-Ristanovič, 1998: 466). In the Balkan countries, war related economic sanctions against the FR Yugoslavia and Greek sanctions against Macedonia also contributed to the development of a large scale informal economy in the whole region. The informal economy offered both labour and scarce goods (Nikolić-Ristanović, 1998: 462) and as such compensated for the non-existent or ineffective formal economy.

The economic crises in FR Yugoslavia, for example, which had resulted from both the war and UN sanctions, led to a criminalisation of society as a whole. During the war, almost every citizen in the FRY was involved in some kind of illegal activity. Enormous inflation and the impossibility of earning a significant income legally, encouraged a large number of people to acquire and use foreign instead of national currency, smuggle and sell scarce goods on the black market or resort to other illegal activities in order to survive Nikolić-Ristanović, 1998: 471). The hidden economy included both criminalised businessmen engaged in major import-export deals, and a small-scale or street-corner economy, involving 'thousands of impoverished 'ordinary' individuals who are trying to earn their elementary living' (Bolcic,

1995: 153). As observed by Bolcic (1994: 143), everyday life of people became a painful struggle for survival, leaving not much room for thinking about the legal status of one's actions. Moreover, the scale of illegal activities was so extensive that it was useless to threaten people with sanctions. The law seemed to have become non-existent, while destructive individualism spontaneously established itself as the dominant cultural pattern. In this way, the state of anomie reached an extreme point and in 1990s illegal markets became cornerstones of economies of many Balkan countries (Derens, 2000: 186).

In sum, political destabilisation, war and militarisation of the region proved advantageous for development of illicit businesses, at the same time offering a number of specific incentives for organised crime to go transnational: low risk, high profit, high demand for drugs, arms, women, a large supply in people willing to cross borders illegally etc. (Williams, 2001: 69). For example, militarisation and the large presence of international organisations and businesses, as a strong pull factor, has created a significant demand for the products and services that criminal organisations (can) supply. For example, the establishment of military bases in the Balkans created a demand for a sex industry. At the same time, highly developed sex markets in Western Europe and the revenues that they promise play a significant role as well.

Apart from being destination countries, Balkan countries are also important transit and supply countries for Western countries. On the one hand, this means that criminal organisations operating on the Balkan use the existence of a large 'supply' of desperate refugees and economic migrants from both Balkan and other post-communist countries to meet the huge demand from Western sex industry and other illegal labour markets. On the other hand, the traffickers misuse the myths about the West by giving women and men from Eastern Europe false promises of well paid jobs there, and then traffic them to the Balkan as temporary or final destination.

Similarly, the increasing demand for cigarettes and drugs in the Balkan countries, connected with the lack of perspective of large parts of the population and small supplies available on local markets led to the development of other illegal markets as well. Drug trafficking, weapons and cigarettes smuggling and other illegal businesses are often combined, but criminal organisations also shift to the human trade as a less risky but highly profitable alternative. Black markets of all sorts of commodities, from fuel and food to drugs, weapons and illegal migrants are a reality in Bosnia (for example, the well-known Arisona market[5]), Montenegro (e.g. Tuzi) and in the border areas of Serbia, Romania, Macedonia and Bulgaria.

Differential regulation and laws, as well as differential risks, are especially important factors of development of illegal businesses. Lax and poorly implemented regulations, especially in critical sectors such as financing and banking (e.g. in the post-conflict Balkan countries like Bosnia and Kosovo) are especially attractive for organised crime, as it tends to move from jurisdictions with stricter regulation to more lax ones. Thus, the criminal organisations try to contain or minimise the risks by continuing to operate primarily from a low-risk jurisdiction. Good examples are found in Serbia and Bosnia which, especially during the war, have been transit countries for the smuggling of Chinese, Kurdish and Romanian migrants, women from Eastern Europe, as well as of cigarettes, drugs, etc.

## Human trade and illegal markets

As mentioned above, human trade is one of the most profitable illegal markets. It exists on a global, regional and national level, with a black market for illegal immigration adjusting 'permanently to changes in the legal framework of immigration within Europe' (Albrecht, 2002: 17). The markets in migrants, women and children are similar to any other illegal market, since, from the point of view of criminal organizations, people, mostly women and children, are commodities, like any other (Williams, 1999: 147). However, there are also some distinct features of trafficking, such as slavery, and some specificity of the dynamics of supply and demand. Women and children are treated as 'consumer durables to be used and abused repeatedly

5 The irony is that the Arizona Market, established by peacekeeping forces after the war to foster trade between Serbs, Croats and Muslims, has grown 'into five square miles of sinister black facade, where women from the former Soviet Union and elsewhere in Eastern Europe are sold to the highest bidder'. The Market is situated near the towns of Brcko and Tuzla, which boast 'one of the highest concentrations of the international police force created to establish law and order in Bosnia, one of the largest American army bases and one of the biggest UN -administered aid packages of the post-war years (K. Holt 'Captive Market', *The Sunday Times Magazine*, February 18, 2001).

by clients, and to be passed on from one trafficker or brothel owner to another or as modern form of slaves' (Williams, 1999: 148).

The dynamics of supply and demand are manifested in different combinations of push (economic problems, political instability, conflicts, violence against women) and pull factors (employment opportunities, including sex industry, myths about Western countries, presence of military and international organisations and businesses).[6] The main incentives for the development of both demand and supply are found in the very structural context of the present day world: the demand for illegal labour in general and for commercial sex in particular is increasing, while the opportunities in licit sectors are limited, both in post-communist and in Western countries (especially for illegal migrants, with women being particularly vulnerable). Moreover, the mapping of main channels of trafficking in women shows (Global Survival Network, 1997) that it is always market oriented, going from the countries with large supply to countries with large demand: East-West, East-East or from developing to developed countries, from war affected to developed countries, but also from poor to less poor developing countries and even from poor to war affected countries.

Structural changes in post communist and war-affected societies are the source of criminalisation risks as well. Criminalisation is connected to unemployment, poverty or the desire to become rich over night, to marginalisation and social exclusion etc. As many authors suggest, both victims and perpetrators usually belong to the same ethnic communities (Ruggiero, 2000: 54; Fekete and Webber, 1997: 71). According to Ruggiero, 'it is extremely rare that immigrant criminal entrepreneurs manage to recruit West European sex workers, who are instead more likely to be self-employed or employed in the protected luxury sectors of the sex economy.' (Ruggiero, 2000: 54). Also, according to strain theory, crime is organised along ethnic lines, and, whenever American authors apply this theory to empirical research, it always pertains to immigrants who attain the American way of life (Bovenkerk, 2001: 119). As pointed out by Taylor, 'immigration is one of the contexts in which criminalization and social exclusion are coalescing' (Taylor, quoted by Coutin, 2002: 20).

Although history provides such examples as well, in the present day world immigration waves are followed by criminal organisations on a more global

---

6 For more details about how these factors are functioning in Balkan countries see V. Nikolić-Ristanović (2002a).

scale, and to a large part they include both victims and criminals from Eastern and Central Europe. For example, in Europe, Asia and North America, Albanian, Chinese, Colombian, Nigerian, Russian, Chechnyan, Ukrainian and other ethnic criminal groups can be found working within new immigrant communities (Friman and Andreas, 1999: 12). According to Albrecht (2002:7), 'the price immigrants pay today for a safe place in European countries in many instances consists of a prolonged period of uncertainty, illegality and an enormous risk of criminalisation'. This is not surprising, having in mind that they are totally marginalised. Thus, they are ready to co-operate with organised crime for obtaining services, like mediation on the labour market, getting greater rewards than those available in the licit economy in their home country (Williams, 2001: 68). Entering Europe through clandestine routes makes them also exposed to all sorts of criminal and other victimisation. The connection between victimisation, criminalisation and social exclusion is evident in East European countries as well, where both prostitutes and pimps/traffickers tend to come from the marginalised poor. A good illustration for this is the quotation from an interview I have conducted with Julija, a prostitute from Budapest:

> 'Many pimps would not work in prostitution if the economic situation were better. If they were employed. Many of them are not criminals like in the Western countries. They are unhappy people who are not able to find a job. Sometimes, they live from the prostitution of their wives, girlfriends and daughters. Sometimes, they do not earn anything for several days. Poverty is common for pimps. There are a few who have a network, a good car, etc, but the majority live only from the prostitution of their wives or daughters.' (Nikolić-Ristanović, 2002a:127).

Another connection between unemployment and development of criminal networks is also shown in the example of Russia. According to the findings of the Global Survival Network, many members of the Russian mafia are former employees of the Russian national security agency, the KGB, which was replaced after 1991 by the FSB (the state intelligence bureau). As a consequence of this (transition-connected) change, thousands of people, highly skilled in intelligence work and the use of force, became unemployed. Because security police often have 'political connections, access to weapons, and knowledge of the banking and business worlds, they are well-positioned to participate in international criminal activities' (Global Survival Network, 1997: 33).

It is obvious that socio-economic changes in the everyday lives of both women and men in post-communist countries (e.g. unemployment and/or loss of previous social positions/privileges) play an important role in them becoming involved in prostitution and human trafficking (Feher, 1995: 76). The labour distribution is strongly gender biased, so that among recruiters (who get the least profit[7]) women participate in equal measure as men, while men dominate in higher places in the hierarchy.

There is a connexion between victimisation and criminalisation as well. For instance, drug addicts, refugees, illegal migrants and victims of trafficking often become drug dealers or recruiters. In these cases, crime is used as survival strategy,i.e. the way of coping with drug addiction or slavery-like position.

Human trade, as a manifestation of illegal market, cannot function without the existence of other connected (illegal) markets of both goods and services. The most important connected markets are black market in documents (passports, visas, work and residence permits) and black labour market. Some traffickers limit themselves to the provision of smuggling service, but some provide addresses of prospective employers along with smuggling services. The second type of traffickers act as intermediaries between migrants and small businesses, and can be regarded as hidden employment agents (Ruggiero, 2000: 94).

Criminal organisations, in the form of criminal enterprises, are an integral part of an illegal market, but 'they are certainly not the only players' (Williams, 2001: 79-81). The essential point about these markets is that criminal enterprises are at the core of the supplier networks. These networks are then extended along functional lines to include all other components necessary for a smoothly operating trafficking process: brokers and agents who recruit women, brothel owners, corrupt officials who assist in the provision of passports, corrupt police officers, officials who take payoffs for turning a blind eye to the sex trade in their jurisdiction etc. To veil their intentions, some of them are legally registered firms and individuals to whom victims have confidence (e.g. tourist agencies, friends acting as recruiters, employment agencies that offer both registered and clandestine jobs etc.).

7 For example, criminal gangs buy women from recruiters for small amounts of money such as $ 50-150 and resell them for $ 5.000 and more.

Ruggiero (2000: 95, 96), for example, reported on a variety of agencies specialising in the recruitment of men and women from developing countries who seek employment in developed countries and co-operating both with illegal traffickers and state officials. In some cases, legally registered agencies and illegal traffickers entered into temporary or long-term partnerships with police officers assigned at airports, acting as 'visa dispensers', and with consulate employees, in an effort to obtain visas for their customers (e.g. in France, Italy and Britain). Trafficking in servants often involves officials of foreign embassies and international organisations (e.g. Switzerland and France). Moreover, legally registered agencies may attempt to monopolise the business. For example, in the above mentioned case of immigrants from Eastern Europe found without a legal permit in some workshops and middle-sized factories operating in the food industry in Britain, none of the individuals and agencies involved (e.g. tourist agents, employment mediators, transport entrepreneurs etc.) had any affiliation with crime. This may suggest that 'the functions elsewhere performed by criminal groups were taken over by legitimate business groups' (Ruggiero, 2000: 99).

## Instead of conclusion: building control mechanisms and prevention

Structural causes connected to the development of a liberal (global and local) market economy and to war have played a significant role in the rise of various illegal markets, including the trade in humans. The market and 'glocal' approach that I have used in this paper not only appears to be useful for addressing the problem of human trafficking as the darkest side of globalisation. It also seems to be very useful for assessing the possibilities for building control mechanisms and devising preventive measures on a long term and short term basis.

Long-term goals should include, in the first place, a closer control of global markets and a decrease in the gap between rich and poor countries worldwide. Also, and in close connection with that, is the need for real democratisation, state sovereignty and independent economic development of developing, but also developed countries. These, of course, are goals that need time and a lot of efforts of different (progressive) actors world-wide, committed to regenerate the welfare state in both Western and East European countries.

At the same time, short-term goals should include a number of measures to be undertaken on either European or nation state level.

Since 'Fortress EU' has proved to be a strong incentive for the development of illegal markets, one of the most urgent measures to be undertaken on the European level is obviously removing barriers to free movement of people across EU and non-EU borders, with the tightening of the border control for criminals. The usual fear of high costs of migration deregulation in terms of the uncontrollable influx of economic migrants and refugees is unfound, especially having in mind experiences so far: lifting or loosening of visa regime for some East European countries (e.g. Bulgaria and Romania), did not cause any spectacular increase in migration.[8] Similarly, the deconstruction of myths about migrants and Eastern Europe as dangerous 'others', which only furthers marginalisation, social exclusion, victimisation and criminalisation, is very important as well. In addition, when the Balkan as destination of human trafficking is involved, demilitarisation and de-internationalisation of Bosnia and Kosovo are the condition sine qua non for the elimination of the demand for cheap labour in general, and for cheap sex work in this region in particular.[9]

Among the measures, which are needed on a nation state level, two groups are of special importance:

1. creation of market barriers at all stages: supply, trafficking, and demand (Williams, 1999: 157);
2. development of democratic institutions and rule of law.

The creation of market barriers include a range of measures such as:

- education/prevention programs that alert women and men to the dangers and increase of training and employment opportunities for women, more opportunities for licit jobs in general etc. (supply level);

---

8 Of course, the cost/benefit ratio needs to be researched carefully before the decisions are made. However, my own experience of traveling from the country with strict visa regime shows that visa regime is much more effective in humiliating law abiding citizens than in preventing illegal migration, let alone organised crime.

9 This is not to be understood as the critic of the presence of international forces or organisations themselves, but the critic of their role in development of illegal markets on the Balkans.

- awareness raising among officials, legal and policy changes, prosecution of perpetrators and protection of victims, co-operation between officials in EU and non-EU countries (trafficking level);
- changes in policy regarding prostitution and illegal migration (decriminalisation or/and partial legalisation, delay in deportation etc.) and more opportunities for licit jobs for women in destination countries as well (demand level).

So far many education/prevention programs, awareness raising campaigns and legal/policy changes have been undertaken in a large number of countries, including the Balkan and other post-communist countries. Moreover, these measures, which are largely undertaken by or upon the initiative of non-governmental organisations, seem to be more widespread in developing than in developed countries (Kelly, 2002: 54; Copic, 2002). However, the pressure that the international community is exerting on the governments of post-communist countries to undertake decisive steps toward prosecution of offenders, without having enough resources for that policy, let alone for addressing causes and protecting victims, is one more proof of hypocrisy of this same international community, as it is unrealistic relying on women's NGOs in the struggle against powerful criminal networks (see Kelly, 2002:54). In addition, the threat of transnational organised crime is exaggerated when it comes from Eastern Europe and particularly from the Balkans, while, on the other side, the danger of the 'groups that originate and operate throughout Europe' is underestimated in spite of the reports that suggest that they 'pose the significant greater threat' (Rees and Webber, 2002: 81, 95).

All above-mentioned measures may be effective only if the proper legal and political measures toward a distinction between licit and illicit activities are undertaken on both the global and nation-state levels. This is especiallysignificant in post-communist countries in general, and in war affected Balkan countries in particular. As shown in the above analyses, the overall criminalization and the status of anomie have been among the main incentives for transnational organised crime to operate from the Balkan countries. However, these changes cannot be effective if they are not accompanied by appropriate legal and political measures in developed countries as well. Thus, it appears that development of strong social welfare state, democratic institutions and the rule of law is a *conditio sine qua* non for the prevention and control of transnational organised crime, illegal markets and human trade in contemporary world.

## References


Albrecht. H.J., Fortress Europe? - Controlling illegal immigration. *European Journal of Crime, Criminal Law and Criminal Justice*, 2002, *no.1*, 1-25

Altink, S., *Stolen lives*, London, Scarlet Press, 1995

Arlacchi, P., Some observations on illegal markets. In: V. Ruggiero, N. South and I. Taylor (eds.), *The new European criminology: crime and order in Europe*. London, Routledge, 1998

Arlacchi, P., The dynamics of illegal markets. In: P.Williams and D.Vlassis (eds.), *Combating transnational crime: concepts, activities and responses*. London and Portland: Frank Cass, 2001

Aronowitz, A., Smuggling and trafficking in human beings: the phenomenon, the markets that drive it and the organisations that promote it. *European Journal on Criminal Policy and Research*, 2001, vol. 9, *no. 2*, 163-195

Bolcic, S., O 'svakodnevnici' razorenog drustva Srbije pocetkom devedesetih – iz socioloske perspektive' (About everyday life destroyed society in Serbia at the beginning of 1990s - from sociological prospective). In: Prosic-Dvornic (ed.), *Kulture u tranziciji (Cultures in transition)*. Beograd, Plato, 1994

Bolcic, S. (1995) Izmenjena sfera rada (Changed Sphere of Work). In: S. Bolcic, (ed.) *Drustvene promene i svakodnevni zivot: Srbija pocetkom 1990s*. (Social Changes and Everyday Life: Serbia at the Beginning of 1990s). Belgrade, Insitut za socioloska istrazivanja Filozofskog fakulteta u Beogradu, 1995

Bovenkerk, F., Organised crime and ethnic minorities: is there a link? In: P. Williams and D. Vlassis (eds.), *Combating transnational crime: concepts, activities and responses*. London and Portland: Frank Cass, 2001

Coutin, S., Questionable transactions as grounds for legalisation: Immigration, illegality, and law. *Crime, Law and Social Change*, vol. 37, *no. 1*, 19-36

Copic, S. Trafficking in human beings in the Balkan's post-war societies: legal reforms and practical issues, Paper presented at British Criminology Society Conference 'Crossing border'. Keele, July 17-21, 2002

Derens, J.-A., *Balkans: la crise*. Paris, Gallimard, 2000

Duyne, P.C. van, The phantom and threat of organised crime. *Crime, Law and Social Change*, 1996, vol. 24, 341-377

Duyne, P.C. van, Money-laundering. Fears and facts. In: P.C. van Duyne, K. von Lampe and J.L. Newell (eds.), *Criminal finances and organising crime in Europe*. Nijmegen, Wolf Legal Publishers, 2003

Efremov, B., Nerabotenosta i sivata ekonomija (Unemployment and Shadow Economy). In: B.Nanevski and V.Stojanova (eds.), *Socijalnata sigurnost na naselenieto vo R Makedonija vo uslovi na tranzicija*. Skopje, Friedrich Ebert Foundation, 1998

Fekete, L. and F. Webber, The human trade. *Race and Class*, 1997, vol. 39, *no. 1*, pp.67-73

Feher, L., Forced prostitution and traffic in persons. In: M. Klap, Y. Klerk and J. Smith (eds.), *Combating traffic in persons*. Utrecht, SIM, 1995

Friman, R. and P. Andreas, (eds.), *The illicit global economy and state power*. Lanham, Boulder, New York, Rowman and Littlefield Publishers, 1999

Findlay, M., *The globalisation of crime: understanding transitional relationships in context*. Cambridge, Cambridge University Press, 1999

Goody, J., Whose security? Organised crime, its victims and the EU. In: A. Crawford (ed.), *Crime and insecurity: the governance of safety in Europe*. Devon, Willan Publishing, 2002

Global Survival Network, Crime and servitude - an expose of the traffic in women for prostitution from the newly independent states. Washington D.C: Global Survival Network, 1997

Hobbs, D. and C. Dunnighan, C., Glocal organised crime:context and pretext. In: V. Ruggiero, N. South and I. Taylor (eds.), *The new European criminology: crime and order in Europe*. London, Routledge, 1998

IOM Pristina, Situation report, 2000/2001

Kelly, L., *Journeys of jeopardy: a review of research on trafficking in women and children in Europe*. IOM, 2002

Kotzeva, T. Re-imaging Bulgarian women: the Marxist legacy and women's self-identity. *The Journal of Communist Studies and Transition Politics*, 1999, *no.1*, 83-99

Konig, I., (ed.), *Trafficking in women*. Vienna: Federal Chancellery, 1997

McDonald, W., The globalization of criminology: the New Frontier is the Frontier. *Transnational Organised Crime*, 1995, *no.1*, 1-22

Lewis, R., Drugs, war and crime in the post-Soviet Balkans. In: V. Ruggiero, N. South and I. Taylor (eds.), *The new European criminology: crime and order in Europe*, London and New York, Routledge, 1998

Nikolić-Ristanović, V., War and crime in the former Yugoslavia. In: V. Ruggiero, N. South and I. Taylor, *The new European criminology: crime and order in Europe*. London and New York: Routledge, 1998

Nikolić-Ristanović, V., Sex trafficking: the impact of war, militarism and globalization related factors. Paper presented at British Criminology Society Conference 'Crossing border'. Keele, July 17-21, 2002a

Nikolić-Ristanović, V., *Social change, gender and violence: post-communist and war-affected societies*. Dordrecht, Kluwer, 2002b

Rees, G. and M. Webber, Fighting organised crime: the European Union and internal security. In: A. Crawford (ed.), *Crime and insecurity: the governance of safety in Europe*. Devon, Willan Publishing, 2002

Regional Monitoring Reports, No.6., Florence: UNICEF International, Child Development Center, 1999

Ruggiero, V., *Crime and markets: essays in anti-criminology*. Oxford, Oxford University Press, 2000

Schneider, F. and D. Ernste, *Shadow economies around the world: size, causes, and consequences*. IMF Working Paper, International Monetary Fund, 2000

Taylor, I., *Crime in context: a critical criminology of market societies*. Cambridge, Polity Press, 1999

Taylor, I., and R. Jamieson, Sex trafficking and the mainstream of market culture. *Crime, Law and Social Change*, 1999, vol. 32, *no. 3*, 257-278

Transnational Organised Crime, 1999, Special Issue: *Illegal immigration and commercial sex - the new slave trade*. (ed. P. Williams), vol. 3-4., 145-170

UNDP, Poverty in transition - Republic of Bulgaria. Geneva, UNDP, 1998 UNICEF, Women in transition, The MONEE Project CEE/CIS/Baltics

Vaknin, S., The grow out of unemployment, http:/samvaknin.tripod.com-2000

Wijers, M and L. Lap-Chew, *Trafficking in women: forced labour and slavery-like practices in marriage, domestic labour and prostitution*. Utrecht: STV, 1997

Williams, P., Trafficking in women and children: a market perspective,

Williams, P., Organizing transnational crime: networks, markets and hierarchies. In: P. Williams and D. Vlassis (eds.), *Combating transnational crime: concepts, activities and responses.* London and Portland: Frank Cass, 2001

# Media constructing organised crime concepts in an extended criminal Europe
## Trafficking women for sexual exploitation

*Jon Spencer*[1]

## Engaging with the problem

There is a considerable body of academic literature that discusses trafficking for sexual exploitation (see for example: Schloendart 1999, Chapkis 2003, Weitzer 2007, Goodey 2004 and O'Connell Davidson 2006) and official reports (see for example Home Office UK 2007 and UNODC 2006). There are a number of debates within the literature concerning the definition and nature of prostitution (Weitzer 2007 and O'Connell Davidson 2006), and the relationship between prostitution and 'trafficking' (O'Connell Davidson 2006 and Goodey 2004). There is an exploration of the relationship between trafficking for sexual exploitation, prostitution and political anxieties (see for example O'Donnell 2006 and Weitzer 2007). Some writers are sceptical of the scale of 'sex trafficking' problem and take a non-abolitionist position in relation to prostitution (O'Donnell 2006 and Weitzer 2007). Weitzer (2007) argues that the some of the academic writings are skewed and form the basis of a 'moral crusade' rather than an understanding of the 'issue' that is based on methodologically sound social science research. He argues that:

> "My analysis demonstrates that the crusade's core claims regarding both trafficking and prostitution are generally quite dubious, yet activists have met with remarkable success in getting their views and demands incorporated in government policy, legislation, and law enforcement practices." (Weitzer 2007: 447)

---

1 Director Anglo-Baltic Criminological Research Unit, School of Law, University of Manchester.
This chapter is from: P.C. van Duyne, J. Harvey, A. Maljevic, K. von Lampe and M. Scheinost (eds.), *European crime-markets at cross-roads. Extended and extending criminal Europe*. Nijmegen, Wolf Legal Publishers, 2008

The media have also been an important variable in the social construction of the problem of *trafficking for sexual exploitation*. By investigating how the media report criminal cases it is possible to understand the response of policy makers and practitioners. The media is selective in the cases it promotes for public consumption; such cases being decided by a series of complex and mutually rewarding relationships. Harcup and O'Neill argue that: ". . . the media . . . may also be responsible for the prominence of many apparently manufactured stories that have little relation to actual events." (Harcup and O'Neill 2001:277) and Romer, Jamieson and Aday (2003) conclude that television news programmes do have an influence on where viewers both perceive the locations of crime and who are the likely perpetrators. Dowler (2003) contributes to the discussion by exploring media consumption and its relationship to the fear of crime, although providing a more speculative conclusion than some other writers by noting the differential effects of different types of television programmes.These relationships between journalists, media managers (public relations) and other agencies such as the police interact to develop the 'news stories' so that they have a fit with contemporary news values. These stories also draw together other social anxieties and at times provide either a sense of society in decline or a society under threat.

Recently in the UK there has been a growing concern in the media about immigration, particularly after the enlargement of the EU in 2005 and 2008. An element of this concern focuses on those migrants entering the UK from Central and Eastern European countries such as Poland, Lithuania and Romania. One of the anxieties about migrants is evidenced by a concern with human trafficking (Green and Grewcock 2002), particularly of women into the sex industry. Human trafficking is a complex area, with definitional problems (Kelly 2005) and considerable difficulties in estimating the numbers of people who are trafficked as opposed to smuggled or facilitated2 (see for example Goodey 2003 and Salt 2000). As Hagan and Palloni (1999) have argued the media response to migration establishes a link between migration and crime and this can be easily identified in the UK with media reports in relation to human trafficking. Included in these reports of trafficking crimes are either direct or indirect references to organised

2 For the purposes of this chapter, the definition contained in the UN Protocol to Protect Women and Children is used. Thus, trafficking is defined as being the recruitment, transportation, transfer, harbouring or receipt of persons, by means of the threat, or use of force or other forms of coercion, of abduction, of fraud, of deception, of the abuse of power or of a position of vulnerability or of the giving or receiving of payments or benefits to achieve the consent of a person having control over another person, for the purpose of exploitation

crime, so the circle is squared by bringing together migration, trafficking and organised crime. In the next section we shall explore two recent high profile cases in the UK to underline how the reporting of trafficking is linked to migration and organised crime.

## Identifying the victims and the villains

In attempting to define human trafficking crimes Coster van Voorhout (2007) argues that human trafficking offences are usually defined as being:

> ". . . undertaken by organised crime groups that transfer women and girls illegally from their home to a country in which they are forced into prostitution, the escort branch, sex entertainment, web cam sex, or pornography." (Coster van Voorhout 2007:44)

However, as Coster van Voorhout (2007) argues immigration crime associated with labour exploitation is much more complex than being simply about the activities of organised crime. Different jurisdictions across Europe define and treat the crime differently and the European Council Framework3 definition is also viewed as being highly problematic. The lack of an agreed definition and policy approaches to trafficking result in a failure to achieve harmonisation of policy at the EU member state level, and as Coster van Voorhout (2007) argues, harmonisation is 'crucial':

> ". . . because it (a) avoids that traffickers can make use of gaps in the criminal legislation of other countries or other types of legislation, and (b) enables unique measures for an effective combat." (Coster van Voorhout 2007:46-47).

It needs to be noted that effective combat may not be the outcome of enhanced cooperation. However, as Green and Grewcock (2002) argue there are similarities of responses to the problem of illegal immigration by EU member states that include the use of

> ". . . increasingly restrictive immigration policies that exclude refugees, a policy emphasis on border protection, increased use of armed forces or military methods of border policing, increasing levels of cooperation between

[3] Council Framework Decision of 19 July 2002 on combating trafficking in human beings (2002/629/JHA).

> state agencies, a focus on trafficking and smuggling as an aspect of transnational organised crime, analogous to drugs or terrorism and a desire to externalise border controls." (Green and Grewcock 2002:89)

So, whilst there may be legislative gaps, there appears to be a congruence of policy and practical response to the perceived problem of illegal immigration. Furthermore, the response also includes the concept of organised crime as being a crucial factor in the commission of illegal immigration and this is particularly highlighted in the cases of human trafficking.

The role of the media and the formation of public attitudes have a long history of scholarship and research (see Dowler (2003) for a review of the research; Van Duyne, (2004) concerning organised crime). Therefore, it is important to understand the relationship between the consumption of media reports and the formation of public attitudes:

> "The public's perception of victims, criminals, deviants, and law enforcement officials is largely determined by their portrayal in the mass media. Research indicates that the majority of public knowledge about crime and justice is derived from the media. Therefore, it is imperative to examine the effects that the mass media have on attitudes toward crime and justice." (Dowler 2003:109)

Romer *et al* (2003) also provide considerable evidence that there is a significant relationship between fear of crime and television news coverage at a local and national level. However, it is not simply from news reports, television, internet and print based, that individuals glean their understanding of crime and organised crime. It is also culled from other forms of media constructions, especially popular fiction whether it is film based such as 'The Godfather' series of films or the more socially explicit 'Pulp Fiction' and 'LA Confidential'; literature based, for example the writing of Ian Rankin[4] or television based programmes such as the recent 'Sopranos' series. UK statistics for television viewing indicate that eighty-eight per cent of the population watches television at least once a day with ninety-three percent of those watching news programmes. Drama programmes had a high rate of viewing across all age groups, and especially younger adult viewers (Social Trends ONS on line 2008). So, it would seem that many people

4 Ian Rankin is the author of the Scottish based Rebus novels that have as a central character a locally based organised crime boss Big Ger Rafferty. However, many countries have their own 'home grown' thriller writers using the genre as a means of social comment.

construct their understanding of ideas and concepts, such as organised crime, by bringing together news reports and other elements of popular culture. News reports are reflexive in that they utilise such constructions when reporting the news and so we see a constant flow of re-affirming definitions and ideas between news, popular culture and public attitudes. The conflation of different constructions of organised crime and human trafficking are also utilised in official reports:

> "Human trafficking is often carried out by organised crime groups who exploit loopholes in policy and legislation to enable them to carry out their businesses." (Home Office and Scottish Executive 2007:91)

And:

> "Human trafficking is linked to a broader spectrum of criminality and is often carried out by organised crime groups. It is a high profit crime." (Home Office and Scottish Executive 2007:90)

And:

> "Although violence and force are often encountered in trafficking cases, evidence suggests that in the initial stages the vast majority of victims are recruited by deception . . . Additionally, some victims of organised crime gangs end up in prostitution as a result of "debt-bondage" arising from money paid to the gangs to facilitate their illegal entry in to the UK." (Home Office and Scottish Executive 2007:15)

These quotes demonstrate how organised crime is linked to issues of human trafficking and how organised crime is seen to be engaged in high profile and high profit forms of criminality. However, we should not accept these constructions as being an accurate representation of the structure or activities of organised crime (for example see van Duyne 2003 and 2006a, Hobbs 1998). So, the villains are constructed as being members of organised crime gangs with trans-national affiliations.

There are also a number of constructions applied to the victims of human trafficking: generally the victims are female, young and presented as being innocent. They are seen to be victims of the manipulations of the ruthless and exploitative organised crime members ". . . victims are coerced, deceived or forced into the control of others who crudely and inhumanely seek to profit from their suffering" (Home Office and Scottish Executive 2007:2). Against this background, as Matthews (2005) noted, it is understandable that there has been a change in the construction of the prostitute from offender to victim with the men who use prostitutes being seen as offenders. Goodey (2004) argues that this is a relatively new development:

> "With trafficked women, until very recently bracketed in the same category as illegal immigrant and 'undesirable other', their treatment as victims of crime, rather than complicit offenders, is a new development. Traditionally, trafficked women have been responded to as illegal immigrants, as being associated with a criminal underworld, and as prostitutes, and, therefore, as women who have fallen outside the range of acceptable female behaviour."
> (Goodey 2004:32)

However, O'Connell Davidson (2006) is slightly more sceptical than Goodey, suggesting that prostitution is still viewed in a highly negative manner:

> "...it seems that despite the extensive attention paid to rights violations in the sex industry and a raft of new international protocols and declarations, national laws, and policy initiatives designed to combat such abuses, very little progress has been made in terms of promoting or protecting the human or labour rights of those who prostitute." (O'Connell Davidson 2006: 6)

In relation to migrant women in general there is a contradictory process that constructs the migrant as trespasser, as outsider and so viewed as being a net drain on the UK's resources and as placing local communities and services under severe pressure. *The Daily Mail* claimed in 2007 that Eastern European migrants were '. . . swelling the population of English Towns by 10 pc" (Daily Mail 2007a) and at times migrant women are seen as being scheming enough to take advantage of their status even when they are no longer migrants:

> "Dark-haired Angela, 31, works long hours as an office supervisor but she still relies heavily on child benefit from the state to make ends meet. Every week, she puts Martina and Alan in the back of her blue Renault Clio and drives the five minutes journey to the cash point at her local bank. There, she draws out the £33-a-week put into her family account by the British government. It totals £1.650 each year. Yet this young Polish mother does not live in Britain. Her home is thousands of miles away in Lubin, a town near the picturesque city of Wroclaw in south-west Poland and close to the German border." (Daily Mail 2007b)

Migrant female prostitutes experience a form of double jeopardy. Not only are they an 'outsider' as a migrant but their status as a victim is not automatic, usually having to be negotiated and traded (O'Connell Davidson 2006). Therefore, migrant women who are involved in the sex industry are either constructed as being 'legitimate' victims and to be so defined have to present themselves as trafficked women or they are seen as accomplices and removed to their country of origin if possible. So, *victimhood* is constructed by how the victim negotiates her experience with law enforcement and how she defines her experiences within the sex industry in order to negotiate her status. It is to an investigation of a number of UK based cases that we now turn to further explore the relationship between the media and the utilization of organised crime and victim constructs.

## Infamous Cases?

There are numerous press reports in relation to human trafficking cases but since the introduction of the Sexual Offences Act 2003 there have only been 48 prosecutions for Human Trafficking (Hansard 2008) and those prosecutions have decreased year on year. In 2006 the UK government established the United Kingdom Human Trafficking Centre (UKHTC), the aim of the UKHTC is to combat and reduce human trafficking. The UKHTC was established after 'Operation Pentameter', a police led operation which discovered some 88 'potential victims' of human trafficking. The UKHTC provides a focal point in relation to human trafficking, demonstrates the 'political will' to stop trafficking and a link between government and the media in publicising cases. It is this relationship between state and the media in the area of human trafficking and organised crime that concerns us here. To explore this relationship further and to understand how the criminals and victims are constructed three cases will be discussed.

In 2005 Vullnet Ismailaj, with others, was convicted of offences of trafficking for sexual exploitation. The defendant was not in the UK legally, he had arrived in the UK from Albania and his lack of legal status and his Albanian origins were all utilised as a means of increasing the sense of external threat; that trafficking is a 'foreign activity', one undertaken by non-UK criminals. The circumstances of the offences were that Ismailaj along with two other men had been involved in the recruitment of women, mainly from Lithuania, to work in the UK as prostitutes. Ismailaj had paid the transport costs for the women, however, the women paid him the bulk of their earnings and they were required to work in a manner they did not want – for example with drunken clients and when they were menstruating. Ismailaj was observed by the police driving women to brothels in London and Birmingham to work. On one occasion two of the victims reported that they had been introduced to another man by Ismailaj and were told that this man was to be their new boss. Ismailaj, the police alleged, was paid money by other brothel and massage parlour owners for women, however, on this occasion, as detailed in the official court report, the victims objected to being made to work apart from each other and 'packed their bags' (Westlaw 2008a). The account of the offences committed by Ismailaj suggests that he was involved in recruiting and providing prostitutes to massage parlour and brothel owners which he did for money. However, the victims were all consenting prostitutes and do not fit the definition of having been trafficked as set out in the UN Protocol. At the original hearing Ismailaj was sentenced to eleven years, he appealed and on appeal the prison term was reduced to nine years. The appeal court ruled that

> ". . . the women had come to the United Kingdom for the purposes of prostitution and had not been corrupted in any way. They had been coerced by reason of the conditions in which they were required to work. There had been a high degree of planning and organisation and there was some evidence of threats and restriction of the women's liberties and the confiscation of their passports." (Legislation on Line 2008)

The case was widely reported in the media. The headline in the Times was 'Illegal Migrant jailed for Sex-Slave Ring' (Times on line 2008a). The newspaper report claims that Ismailaj ran an 'organised and sophisticated prostitution empire' (Times on Line 2008) and that he had amassed a fortune of over £300.000 which had been remitted back to Albania. However, it is clear from the appeal judgement that the case was considered to have only a small element of coercion:

> ". . . the victims of these offences were not only adult prostitutes, but they came to this country for the purpose of carrying on a trade as prostitutes. The coercion to which they were subjected was extremely minor . . ." (Legislation on Line 2008)

The newspaper reporting of the Ismailaj cases suggests that there are links to criminal networks in Albania and that Ismailaj was a 'ring leader' and that the operation was a form of transnational organised criminality. However, whilst it is clear that Ismailaj was involved in organising and providing prostitutes there is little in the official accounts of the case that suggest he was in charge of an empire or ran a sex slave ring. Essentially Ismailaj recruited prostitutes and either found 'new bosses' for them and he was paid for his efforts or he drove women to work at various locations.

One of the most notorious and widely reported cases was that of the Demarku brothers who were convicted of human trafficking for sexual exploitation offences in 2005. The circumstances of the offences were that the brothers were organising and running a number of brothels. Many of the women who were working at the brothels were from Central-Eastern Europe. The brothers were charged with trafficking offences and there was evidence that they lured women to the UK and then held them against their will, making them work as prostitutes. The brothers received long jail sentences (Westlaw 2008). Once again the case had a number of news values including the coercion of the victim and the Albanian ethnicity of the brothers. In reporting the case The Times described the brothers in the following terms:

> "Agron, the ringleader, who was described as an "intelligent and resourceful man" and Flamur, the firm's "money man", were both jailed for 18 years Xhevair and Bedari, said to be junior partners." (Times On Line 2008b).

The *Guardian* reported the case in similar terms:

> "Four brothers and a friend who ran a family empire trafficking eastern European women into Britain for prostitution were jailed yesterday. The Albanian gang forced their victims to work round the clock in seven West London vice dens." (The Guardian 2008b)

These two cases outlined above were concerned the trafficking of women into the UK, or once women had arrived to the UK knowing that they were going to be involved in prostitution.

The third and final case to be outlined is the one that concerned the raid on *The Cuddles Massage Parlour* in Birmingham. *Cuddles* was a massage parlour which acted as a front for a brothel. Initially it was claimed that nineteen women had been 'freed' from sex slavery (Daily Telegraph 2008a). The victims were reported to be of Eastern European origin and there are claims that the women were locked into the brothel to work and escorted back to the premises where they were staying. The Times (2008c) quoting a police officer involved in the raid construct the operation as one against human trafficking:

> "We went to the property to execute a warrant in human trafficking, and intelligence suggests the girls were brought into the country under false pretences, sold on and held against their will in the massage parlour. These

girls could be subject to violence, sexual assaults and forced to work as prostitutes." (The Times on Line 2008c)

*Cuddles* was presented as being part of an organised transnational sex crime syndicate that exploited women through trafficking. The police raid took place in October 2005. The keeper of the brothel, the maintenance man and the woman who owned the brothel appeared before the courts in August 2006. The brothel keeper received a prison sentence of two years, the sentence being passed for possessing a fire arm and the woman brothel manager and maintenance man were given community based non-custodial sentences. In early 2007 two other defendants were jailed for 40 months and 28 months respectively: Kinga Andrea Borcsok, and Atilla Makai procured women to work in brothels through the internet and met them and introduced them to brothel owners, they recruited women to work in *Cuddles*. This was a breach of the 2003 Sexual Offences Act and they both served prison terms for offences of human trafficking for sexual exploitation. However, Atilla Makai appealed against his 40 month sentence on the basis that he was essentially only procuring women to work in brothels in the UK and that the women knew when they were recruited, the type of activity they would be engaged in. The appeal against sentence was allowed and the term reduced to 30 months (Westlaw 2008b).

The other outcome of the *Cuddles* raid was that the majority of the women who were 'working' at the premises were removed as they were in the UK illegally. So, the raid on *Cuddles* that initially *rescued* nineteen women was nothing more than a raid on a brothel that resulted in a relatively small scale prosecution and the expulsion of those 'rescued' women who were illegally in the country.

## Making Sense of it all

The press reports of the case studies above have three common themes; the perpetrators are all 'foreign', and in many cases are Central-Eastern European with a particular focus on Albania; the cases are all concerned with the sex industry and finally they are presented using the signifiers of 'organised crime'. Many of the cases outlined could be defined as 'serious criminality' as many are concerned with forms of sexual offending, violence or possession of weapons.

*Managing facilities*

The similarities between the cases cited are the following, First each case concerns the sexual exploitation of women through *managed* prostitution or rather, prostitution facilities. The defendants in all of the cases were involved in the management of brothels and women all were 'entrepreneurial' in as much that they had to manage the brothel as a business to ensure continued viability. In the Ismailaj case the Court of Appeal recognised that the women had all come to the UK for the purposes of prostitution and that they had been openly recruited to work in the brothels that Ismailaj managed. Essentially Ismailaj's criminality can be analysed not only in moral terms but also in terms of business and economics. In order to ensure a lucrative business Ismailaj was required to maintain a supply of women prepared to work in the sex industry. Data from interviews conducted with law enforcement personnel during the AGIS Illegal Movement of People Across Borders Project[5] indicates that the need by brothel managers for women to work in the 'off-street' sex industry (brothels and escort services) can be met from either migrant women or locally resident women. However, the locally resident women will enter legitimate and safer forms of employment if such opportunities exist in their local area. Consequently, in areas of high employment it was evident that there was a greater influx of migrant women to meet the demand for women to work in the 'off-street' sex industry than in areas of more restricted employment opportunities. Therefore, to understand the structure of the 'off-street' sex industry and where it is probable that migrant women will be engaged in greater numbers, we need to analyse and understand the structure of the female labour market. The case of *Cuddles* indicates a similar finding; a significant number of foreign national women who were deported after the raid because of their lack of legal status as migrants.

All of the defendants, except those in the *Cuddles* case had resorted to some form of coercion, in the Ismailaj and others case it was acknowledged but not viewed as being at the 'serious' end of the scale, whereas in the case of the Demarku family there was a high level of physical violence and threat. What is apparent from an analysis of each of the cases is that those convicted utilised the 'weapons' of intimidation and threat common within the realms of serious criminality. All of the defendants can be defined as serious violent offenders. In

---

5 This research was undertaken with financial support from the AGIS Programme European Commission Directorate General Justice, Freedom and Security.

attempting to interpret the activities of these criminals we need to pay attention to what van Duyne has to say: "Naturally, the illegality determines the entrepreneurial risks in terms of law enforcement intervention" (Van Duyne 2006:180)

In general the 'off-street' sex industry is not overly policed. With only one of the UK's forty two police forces having a separate 'Vice Squad', the sex industry is policed through those strategies that are aimed at violent, serious and organised crime. However, the recruiting of women from other EU countries or bordering countries requires time and investment and the maintenance of links with other crime entrepreneurs. This results in potential problems as Van Duyne notes:

> ". . . fellow criminals may become police informants. In general the criminal trader operating in a basically hostile environment has an information risk problem. The criminal trader has a dilemma in finding the right balance between information concealment and information dissemination. Concealing too much information about who he is and what he has to offer limits the scale of his business. Disseminating too much information puts him in danger of the law and jealous fellow criminals." (Van Duyne 2006:181)

One of the intrinsic problems with the 'off-street' sex industry is that, law enforcement will always have a watchful eye on the criminal traders It is a relatively high risk 'business zone' and this may go some way to explaining why it is that the 'off-street' sex industry appears to attract illegal migrants or migrants from significantly poorer regions of the EU member states. It was suggested by the data in the AGIS Illegal Movement of People Across Borders Project that the sex industry is highly visible, and is resource intensive in terms of requirements, for example premises and workers, and has a number of attached risks. That means that once criminals have made money they tend to diversify into other areas of serious criminality but with lower risk. Consequently, the relatively risky 'off-street' sex industry is not one that is highly contested between criminal interests.

It is also an industry where there are high levels of demand. Van Duyne highlighted four risks to the criminal trader. One of them concerns attracting customers' attention. However, there can be no open advertising for their illicit goods. In the sex industry this is different: in the 'off-street' sex industry there is a lot of advertising in local newspapers and across the internet. Recruitment of 'reliable staff' poses additional difficulties, as indicated earlier. In the sex industry this is a problem in terms of recruiting women. In this regard the use of information and communication media are problematic as they leave either a 'paper' trail or a human trail and finally human error, either through behaviour that draws attention to the individual or the jealous ex-colleague who tells all (van Duyne 2006). The victim of human trafficking is a very real risk for the crime entrepreneur as they can provide significant amounts of information and report on a serious offence (Van Duyne 2006). The Daily Telegraph reporting on changes to the nature of the off-street sex industry claimed that:

> "The gangs are moving hundreds of women out of the "overt" sex industry – massage parlours and other brothels – and into the "covert" industry, because it is more lucrative, to increase their control over the victims, and to make it more difficult for police to find them." (Daily Telegraph 2008b)

Using Van Duyne's analysis this management strategy described above would be about risk minimisation and profit maximization in what is an openly hostile environment. So, the activities of policing may have a direct bearing on the means by which those managing brothels re-structure the off-street sex industry to protect investment, reduce risk elements and resource costs. As Matthews (2005) comments the structure of off-street prostitution has significantly changed over the past decade with:

> ". . . enormous growth nationally in the number of massage parlours, saunas, escort agencies, gentlemen's clubs, hostess clubs, lap-dancing venues as well as women working from private flats . . . in many urban centres in England and Wales, we have a form of quasi-legalisation in which a growing number of brothels are allowed to operate virtually undisturbed" (Matthews 2005:891)

So, it may not be as the Daily Telegraph claims that canny criminals are moving their operation to avoid detection and apprehension but rather, a significant shift in the policing approach to off-street prostitution that allows for a more liberalised market.

*The evilness*

The second similarity between the cases outlined above is that each of them is presented as being a large organised crime structure. The media reports use terms such as '*evil empire*', to describe the criminal business activity and by inference making a moral judgement on those who are involved. Again in order to suggest the scope of the activity another report claimed '*Britain's biggest people smuggling and sex-trafficking empires*', and the use of the word empire being a key feature in determining the scale of the operation. Often officials are quoted, especially those from law enforcement who are seen to be able to provide a rational evaluation of the situation. So as one policeman said "*. . . a highly sophisticated gang, one of the most sophisticated I've come across in 29 years in the police force*" underlines the serious nature of the criminality and provides an 'informed' assessment of the organisation of the criminal enterprise. It is this construction of human trafficking as a highly organised crime that makes links to the popular constructions of organised crime.

Many of the reported cases also highlight the 'family' link between the offenders. So there are "*. . . family trafficking empire[s]*", and as one report stated: "*Four brothers and a friend . . . ran a family empire trafficking Eastern-European women into Britain for prostitution . . .*" This press report constructs the idea that the 'empire' is run by four brothers and a close family friend who is trusted and loyal. This has similarities to the mafia style organised crime constructions often utilised in popular fiction. A press report of the Demarku case brings this image of a family firm into sharper definition:

> "Agron, the ringleader, who was described as an "intelligent and resourceful man" and Flamur, the firm's 'money man' . . . Xhevair and Bedari, said to be junior partners." (Times On Line 2008b).

The allocation of roles, Agron as the ringleader, who used his intelligence and resources in a wily and criminal way was supported by Flamur, the 'firm's money man'. In many of the reported cases the issue of money is also critical with allegations of considerable sums of money being remitted back to the country of origin. The men are all constructed as being cunning in the way they have managed to return a large part of their 'profits' to their home country. The many press reports comment on the seizure of documents, bank books and papers that evidence the large sums of money made through prostitution. Once again these topics of reporting make direct links to the idea of organised crime with money laundering processes and larger family ties in other countries thus making the activities trans-national.

*The foreignness*

The third element of commonality between many of the reported cases is the 'foreignness' or 'otherness' of the criminals. So those convicted with Ismailaj were of Albanian origin as were the Demarku family. Both were reported to have Lithuanian links and the two convicted of organising the women to work at *Cuddles* were Hungarian. However, what is not reported or commented upon is that these criminals originate from the areas of Europe which have less buoyant economies and where the opportunities for improvement in living conditions are significantly limited. For Albanian people legitimate access to the UK is not easy due to the perceived problem of immigration which makes the entry for many illegal. Once here illegally there are usually two main choices: find work that will be unpleasant, poorly paid and exploitative, or engage in criminal activities that are similarly unpleasant if apprehended, go to jail and be deported.

'Foreignness' provides an opportunity to recruit women from the country of origin and provide the routes and means of illegal entry into the UK. This is a simple exploitation of contacts and the desire by some women to enter the UK and work in off- street prostitution. This is viewed as a better life than the one experienced in their own country. In understanding why women are prepared to migrate for the purposes of prostitution it is necessary to first acknowledge the link between poverty and prostitution and second that the decision to turn to prostitution may also act as an impetus to the decision to migrate, as – one may speculate – prostitution in their own country is less rewarding as well as less anonymous. Both decisions are in some ways dependent on each other. Edlund and Korn (2002) provide an economic model of prostitution and argue that:

> "The marriage market cost is linked to whether potential spouses know that the woman has prostituted herself . . . One way to reduce the risk is to migrate, and . . . our model predicts that prostitution will be linked to high levels of migration and to the extent that domestic and foreign prostitutes co-exist, foreign prostitutes would be cheaper. . . " (Edlund and Korn 2002:211)

So, a decision to enter the sex industry can be seen as a rational solution of a dilemma. It requires a woman to try and protect her personal reputation in order to enhance her marriage prospects in her country of origin where there are meagre prospects of a decent income. Hence, those factors which encourage women to engage in prostitution are driven by economics. It is interesting to note that the countries of origin of many of the women, and those convicted of human trafficking offences, are in the poorer parts of Europe. However, there is little evidence that the criminal groups referred to in the press reports are trans-national or thoroughly organised across borders. The criminal groups fit more comfortably within what Hobbs (1998) has described as local serious criminality (see also Fijnaut 2000).

> "The connection between sets, the relationships that lie at the core of serious crime groups, can be based on familial, interpersonal, geographic or

commercial sets, and often a combination of some or all of the above." (Hobbs 1998:417)

The cases of media reports concerning trafficking for sexual exploitation are not great in number and tended to be more visible at the time when prosecutions were more prevalent. So, the three outlined in this chapter may not be representative due to the untypical nature of sex trafficking offences and the small number of cases, but they provide a window into how the media construct and report such cases. All of the cases discussed in this chapter meet the conditions as defined by Hobbs (1998) of serious local organised crime. The offenders can all be defined as members of serious crime groups and furthermore that there is a connection between different groups, so that the owner of *Cuddles* had a connection with the Hungarian couple who were recruiting and introducing women. This was simply a commercial relationship; the origin of the women and the ethnicity of the recruiters was immaterial. In the Demarku case there was a strong family relationship, probably because this minimises the risks to the criminal enterprise as defined by Van Duyne (2006). The familial relationships are also good for business inasmuch that they reduce costs. However there was also an element of the interpersonal in the Demarku and Ismailaj cases, they were joined by a long standing friend where presumably loyalty and mutual interests were not in question. Finally there was a geographic link and whilst it is not possible to know from the information to hand whether they worked together because of their geographical links (country of origin) and area of UK residence or whether they worked together because they 'happened' to live in the same area; what is apparent is that the structure of these 'organised crime' groups fit into the model proposed by Hobbs (1998) and the strategies to avoid the threats as defined by Van Duyne (2006) are also evident. Indeed, if we sum up these entrepreneurial conditions, there is little of well thought-out sophistication: it is 'human, all too human'.

## Conclusion

There are number of conclusions that can be drawn from an analysis of press reports that focus on human trafficking and prostitution. First, the organised crime construct is frequently utilised to describe the activities of criminal groups. The construct most frequently employed is that of a familial gang. However, on closer inspection it is apparent that these so called 'gangs' are relationship 'sets' (Hobbs 1998) that function at a number of different levels but primarily they are locally based rather than trans-nationally organised forms of criminality. The transnational element of the criminal activity gains impetus from the relationship between migration and prostitution. The push and pull factors that drive migration and prostitution are never fully addressed in press coverage as this would make the short-hand organised crime construct harder to utilise. Instead of simply projecting the case within a simple and tested imagery, the problem would have to be understood in a much more complex and multi-layered manner. Instead of a fixed mould, the relationships between different elements of the criminal enterprise would have to be understood to change and diversify over time.

Second, the use of ethnicity as a definer of organised crime is prevalent: essentially the management of prostitution is viewed as being a 'foreign' criminal activity. There is no detailed reporting on the economic structure of the 'off-street' sex industry. It may be that this is the one area that is possibly less contested among criminal groups as there are 'rich pickings' for all. Furthermore for a migrant who may not be in the country legally, the off-street sex industry is only lightly policed thus reducing the chances of apprehension and deportation. It is therefore a less risky form of criminal enterprise where there are a number of threats, all of those mentioned by Van Duyne (2006b), and also the potential hazard of deportation and loss of assets if apprehended.

Third, there is a strong link between government constructions of the problem and those of the press. This suggests that either government has very little understanding of the issue or that there is a symbiotic relationship between press, law enforcement and government that constructs the problem in a particular manner – one that is common to all participants. It is a shared imagery with a common language (Van Duyne, 2004). There also appears to be a lack of knowledge or a failure to implement the findings of criminological research that provides a model of how crime is organised. An application of criminological knowledge in this area would suggest that a detailed understanding of the off-street sex industry would provide good forms of intelligence that would indicate areas where there is more probability of a thriving 'off-street' sex industry. The variables concerned are: its economic variations, its geographic differences and for example regions where there are greater concentrations of transient people. It is here that you would expect to find a greater concentration of foreign national women working in that industry. It is here that the understanding of how crime is organised would also prove to be beneficial.

Finally, an application of criminological knowledge in the way outlined above would prevent the construction of human trafficking as a problem focused on the sex industry only. There is a considerable movement of people across borders to facilitate other labour market requirements, especially in the highly casualty prone and less regulated employment sectors. There is no doubt that at a local level there are some very serious levels of criminality, some of which is involved in the sex industry. However, the use of organised crime motifs to understand such criminality does little to ensure an effective engagement with the problem and a protection of victims. What is required is a much more effective analysis of locally based crime structures and how crime is organised at the local level.

## References

BBC (2008)

Chapkis, W., Trafficking, Migration and the Law. Protecting Innocents, Punishing Migrants. *Gender & Society,* 2003, vol. 17, *no. 6*: 923-937

Coster van Voorhout, J. E.B., "Human Trafficking for Labor Exploitation: Interpreting the Crime". Available at SSRN: http://ssrn.com/abstract=1083639

Daily Mail (2007a) *Revealed: Immigrants swell populations of British towns by 10pc* Daily Mail. May 3rd 2007

Daily Mail (2007b) *£1m of child benefit paid out a month - to mothers in Poland* Daily Mail September 21st 2007

Daily Telegraph (2008a) '*Sex slaves' rescued in massage parlour raid* http://www.telegraph.co.uk/news/main.jhtml?xml=/news/2005/09/30/ubrothel.xml&sSheet=/portal/2005/09/30/ixportaltop.html (Accessed 21st |March 2008)

Daily Telegraph (2008b) *Sex trade moves its modern-day slaves into the suburbs.* http://www.telegraph.co.uk/news/main.jhtml?xml=/news/2007/02/18/nsex18.xml (Accessed 26th March 2008)

Dowler, K., Media consumption and public attitudes towards crime and justice: The relationship between fear of crime, punitive attitudes, and perceived police effectiveness. *Journal of Criminal Justice and Popular Culture*, 2003, 10 (2): 109-126

Duyne P.C. van, Greasing the organisation of crime-markets in Europe. In:. P.C. van Duyne, K. von Lampe, and J.L. Newell (eds.), *Criminal Finances and Organising Crime in Europe*. Nijmegen, Wolf Legal Publishers, 2003

Duyne, P.C. van, Fears, naming and knowing: an introductions. In: P. C. van Duyne, M. Jager, K. von Lampe and J.L. Newell (eds.), *Threats and phantoms of organised crime, corruption and terrorism*. Nijmegen, Wolf Legal Publishers, 2004

Duyne, P.C. van, Counting clouds and measuring organised crime. In: P.C. van Duyne, M. Maljevic, M. van Dijck, K. von Lampe and J.L. Newell, (eds.), *The organisation of crime for profit*. Nijmegen, Wolf Legal Publishers, 2006

Duyne P.C. van, The organisation of business crime. In: P.C. van Duyne, M. Maljevic, M. van Dijck, K. von Lampe and J.L. Newell, (eds.), *The organisation of crime for profit*. Nijmegen, Wolf Legal Publishers, 2006

Edlund, L. and K. Evelyn, A theory of prostitution. *Journal of Political Economy*, 2002, vol. 10, *no 1*, pp 181-214

Fijnaut, C., Transnational Crime and the Role of the United Nations in Its Containment through International Cooperation: A Challenge for the 21st Century. *European Journal of Crime, Criminal Law and Criminal* Justice, 2000, vol. 8; 119-128

Goodey, J., Migration, crime and victimhood. *Punishment and Society*, 2003, vol. 5, *no. 4*, p.415-431

Goodey, J., Sex trafficking in women from Central and East European countries: promoting a 'victim-centred' and 'woman-centred' approach to criminal justice intervention. *Feminist Review*, 2004, 76: 26-45

Green, P and M. Grewcock, The war against illegal immigration; State crime and the construction of a European identity. *Current Issues in Criminal Justice*, 2002, vol. 14, *no 1*, 87-101

Guardian, *Immigrants tell of forced prostitution and slavery as trafficking gang is jailed.* 2008a
http://www.guardian.co.uk/uk/2005/nov/02/immigration.ukcrime.
(Accessed march 15th 2008)

Guardian, *Family gang jailed for sex trafficking*. 2008b
http://www.guardian.co.uk/uk/2005/dec/02/ukcrime.rosiecowan Accessed 21st March 2008

Hagan, J. and A. Palloni, Sociological criminology and the mythology of Hispanic immigration and crime. *Social Problems*, 1999, vol. 46, *no. 4*, pages 617-632

Harcup, T. and D. O'Neill, What Is News? Galtung and Ruge revisited. *Journalism Studies*, 2001, vol. 2, *no 2*, 261–280

Hobbs, D., Going down the glocal; the local context of organised crime. *The Howard Journal*, 1998, vol. 37, *no. 4*: 407-422

Home Office and Scottish Executive, *UK Action Plan on Tackling Human Trafficking*. Home Office, London, 2007

Kelly, L. "You Can Find Anything You Want": A critical reflection on research on trafficking in persons within and into Europe. *International Migration*, 2005, vol. 43, 235-241

Legislation on Line (2008) Court of Appeal - case of R. v Lorenc Roci and Vullnet Ismailaj *(2005)* [2005] EWCA Crim 3404. http://www.legislationline.org/legislation.php?tid=178&lid=7467&less=false (accessed March 5th 2008)

Matthews, R., The policing of prostitution: Ten years on. *British Journal of Criminology*, 2005, vol. 45, *no. 2*: 877-895

O'Connell Davidson, Will the real sex slave please stand up? *Feminist Review*, 2006, *no. 83*: 4-22

Office of National Statistics (ONS), Interest in television programme type: by age, 2002: Social Trends 34, 2008 www.statistics.gov.uk/StatBase/ssdataset.asp?vlnk=7181&More=Y (Accessed on 19.02.2008)

Romer, D., K. HallJamieson and S. Aday, Television news and the cultivation of the fear of crime, *Journal of Communication Studies*. March 2003

Salt, J., Trafficking and human smuggling: A European perspective *International Migration* Special Issue 2000/1

Schloendart, A., Organised Crime and the Business of Migrant trafficking; An economic analysis. *Crime, Law & Social Change*, 1999, vol. 32**:** 203–233

The Sun (2008) *Sex trafficking duo jailed.* http://www.thesun.co.uk/sol/homepage/news/article190858.ece. (Accessed March 15th 2008)

Times On Line (2008a) *'Illegal migrant jailed for sex-slave ring'* (2005) http://www.timesonline.co.uk/tol/news/uk/article517854.ece. Accessed March 10th 2008

Times On Line (2008b) *Leaders of sex slave gang jailed for 18 years.* (2005) http://www.timesonline.co.uk/tol/news/uk/article744771.ece. Accessed 21st March 2008

Times On Line (2008c) *19 'sex slaves' rescued in raid on massage parlour* http://www.timesonline.co.uk/tol/news/uk/article573215.ece. Accessed 23rd march 2008

Westlaw (2008a) R-V-Demarku (Agron) [2006] EWCA Crim 2049

Westlaw (2008b) R. v Makai (Atilla) [2007] EWCA Crim 1652

Weitzer, R., The social construction of sex trafficking; ideology and institutionalisation of a moral crusade. *Politics & Society*, 2007, vol. 35, *no. 3*: 447-475

United Nations Office on Drugs and Crime (UNODC), *Trafficking in persons: Global patterns.* United Nations, Vienna, 2006

# Transnational organised crime and cross-border trafficking in human beings in the Czech Republic

*Miroslav Scheinost*[1]

## The roots

Under the conditions of the previous regime, before 1989, the problem of organised crime in the Czech Republic (or in the Czechoslovak Socialist Republic) was not very prominent. The former economic and political power model and the relative isolation from the free world did not further the emergence of any large scale 'classical' forms of organised crime. Usual organised crime activities, like racketeering, drug trafficking, trafficking in human beings and arms, thefts of expensive cars, porno-business, were too risky due to the totalitarian police regime, while the market for trading illegal goods and services was too limited to generate large illegal revenues. Therefore we cannot speak of the 'classical' organised crime and about extensive criminal organisations of a Mafia-type before 1989, either domestic or international.

Despite this police regime, some domestic forms of crime, particularly economic crime (illegal exchange of currency, import of some scarce commodities etc.) were to certain extend tolerated by the regime, although they had some characteristics of organised crime as described in the West. The offences were carried out by usually small crime-groups, characterised by a division of labour, some having corrupt contacts with officials.[2] The means

1 The author is the deputy director of the Institute of Criminology and Social Prevention in Prague.
This chapter is from: P.C. van Duyne, V. Ruggiero, M. Scheinost and W. Valkenburg (eds.), *Cross-border crime in a changing Europe*. Huntington, Nova Science Publishers, 2001

2 For example illegal changers of foreign currency (veksláci), overtly operating mainly on the streets in full sight of the police.

of corruption consisted of providing some scarce goods or services including 'special' ones like prostitution.[3]

It means that though officially denied even in the former CSSR there were some tokens of small scale organised criminal activities, including corrupt contacts with law enforcement officers, state and communist party officials, but they existed relatively isolated without international connections. They were based on a social and economic structure which differed substantially from the open capitalist societies.

Emerged in the so-called shadow economy in the former CSSR, forms of local organised crime reflected its structure and scale. Compared to the shadow economy in the former USSR, it did not match its importance in economic and political terms. Under the conditions of a state managed 'deficit economy', the shadow economy took the form of a system of mutual exchanges of advantages and scarce goods and services, which were available only to some privileged professions ('networks of mutual favours'). These exchange relationships involved usually the abuse of state property for personal purposes. This phenomenon was very common and widespread, but it still concerned mainly minor offences, though some succeeded in amassing a substantial, undeclared wealth.

It should be reminded, that the Czech society was going through deep historical experience, connected to a radical conversion of officially presented value systems and behaviour patterns during the lifetime of the last three generations, which affected the identity and certitude of the people. Under the rule of the communist regime the power of the state was in principle superior to the law. The individual has been reduced to an object, manipulated by the state power. This resulted in an engrained distrust and decreased feeling of belonging to or a responsibility to a community. The informal social control nearly disappeared or it was limited to the trusted circle of the own family. The society became more and more atomised, sceptical and dissimulating. The tendency to take advantage and prejudice the own vicinity and of course the authorities became one of the important outlets of 'purposeful' behaviour. Moreover, the communist regime in the former CSSR nationalised nearly all the property exceeding the personal

3 Prostitution has not been criminalised in the Penal Code, but it was prosecuted as so-called 'parasitism'. Nevertheless, the activities of networks, composed of prostitutes, taxi drivers, receptionists in hotels etc. were tolerated and prostitutes, working in hotels were used by the secret police as informers.

needs of people. Property had no longer concrete owners: it was designated as 'all-people-property' and therefore it became in fact anonymous. Gradually the relationship of people to this anonymous property became divorced from the daily morality. Abusing or even pilfering this property became accepted as something not uncommon or reprehensible (Osmaník, 1996).

## After the Change

After 1989 our society has undergone the deep conversion. This conversion was „conditio sine qua non" to overcome the period of stagnation and isolation and to open up the space to establish the democratic society. Nevertheless, the development brought some risky factors which must be taken into account.

The fundamental economic transformation was connected with an enormous shift of property, with the broad privatisation process of the previous state property and with a rapid establishing of a liberal market under a situation of critical shortage of capital. The economy broadened significantly. The motto of this process was that it is more required to keep up its speed than to slow down it by excessive control and the application of strict legal provisions. It meant that the opportunities for various illegal activities increased, which was not only due to the economic transformation process itself and the unpreparedness of the legislation and supervising authorities, but also due to the insufficient control and the underestimation of an adequate legal framework for this process.

The open economy and a free and open society requires open borders, which implies that the restrictions concerning the movement of people, goods and capital had to be abolished. It is obvious that the CSFR and later the Czech Republic is geographically favourably situated between the states of European Union and the states of former socialist block. Czech territory is well accessible from the countries of former Soviet Union and from the Balkan. Consequently this means broad opportunities for transit, for the mobility of goods, capital and people in the legal but as well as the illegal economy, which implies an abuse of the Czech facilities as a starting point for the 'penetration' from East to the countries of EU and visa versa (for example the sale of stolen cars). At the same time the Czech Republic, as well as the whole European continent, has been affected by a wave of migration, including the illegal one. The Czech Republic is mainly a transit country. However, the number of migrants crossing our territory have reached tens of thousands per year, contributing to an increase of the foreigners who remain behind in this country.

The Czech law enforcement authorities, i.e. police, courts, state attorney offices, customs service went through a fundamental reform, affecting the organisational structure as well as the staff. It resulted not only in an exodus of officials compromised by the collaboration with the communist regime (and sometimes not compromised but simply wanted to be better paid), temporarily weakening the effectiveness of the police and the justice system, which was not redeemed by the recruitment of many new people, sometimes without experience and required qualifications. The justice and police bodies has been understaffed and unprepared to face the growth of crime or to solve the more sophisticated problems resulting from the changes in the economy, from the privatisation process and other social-economic forces. In addition the justice and police are still suffering from the mistrust of people (Scheinost, Cejp, Musil, Brabcová, Budka, 1997).

The Czech legislation went through a similar fundamental rebuilding and the means of effectively combatting new forms of crime have only been recently developed. For example, the provision concerning the so-called criminal conspiracy was introduced into the Penal Code in 1995. In the same year the possibility to obtain information concerning the bank secrecy for the purpose of police investigation and prosecution was enlarged under certain conditions. At the same time the witness protection was modified too. The amendment of the Police Law enabling to use undercover agents has also been enacted in 1995. The anti-money laundering act has come into force only a year later (Karabec, 1998).

From the previous description it may be concluded that after 1989 Czech society had come at risk for being highly attractive for the penetration by cross-border crime and foreign organised groups, along with the potential rise of domestic forms of organised crime on the background of increasing crime rate in general.

## The expansion of crime in general

The increase of the crime rate was huge: the number of registered crimes tripled in 1993 compared with 1989 (1989: 120, 768 registered crimes, 1993: 398, 505), followed by a slight decrease and relative stabilisation. In the last two years the crime rate rose again. Not only the numbers but also the structure of crime has changed. The growth of property crimes has been the most remarkable. Their proportion in the total of all registered crimes increased from 49% in 1989 to 82% in 1993 and 74% in 1998, which was the most significant factor contributing to the growth of the general crime rate. As far as economic crime is concerned, it cannot be compared with the situation before 1989, because of the fundamental change of the economic landscape and legislation. Nevertheless, from the beginning of 1990s till 1995 its proportion did not exceed 5%, but in 1997 it rose to 7,5% and 8,5% in 1998. Much more significant is the amount of damage caused by economic crime. Since 1995 the economic crime accounted for 60% of the total loss caused by criminality (in 1998 it was 62,7%). Expressed in Czech crowns it means 14 billion Czech crowns in 1995 and almost 21 billion in 1998. Compared with 1990 the loss caused by economic crime expressed in Czech crowns have risen fourteen times, corrected for inflation. The relative number of violent crimes decreased, but its absolute numbers increased twice in comparison with 1989 and 1998. A growing brutality could be observed. The most serious offence, i.e. murder, shows a rising tendency: 126 murders and attempted murders have been registered in 1989, contrasting with more than 200 from 1990 till 1997, being surpassed in 1998 with 300 cases. A remarkable increase could be observed also in the number of drug related offences. In 1993, only 261 drug related offences were registered and 251 offenders were prosecuted. In 1998 5.234 such offences were registered and 1.355 offenders were prosecuted with a growing participation of juveniles and women.

The outcomes of victim research provide an illustration for the crime statistics. The international comparative victim research, carried out in the Czech Republic in 1992 and 1996, shows that the personal experience with eleven selected kinds of crime had increased. While in 1991 every fourth citizen became a victim of at least one of the selected crimes, in 1995 it was every third citizen. With this rate of victimisation the Czech society has not been slow in reaching the level of the industrialised western countries and in some aspects (or kinds of crime) even surpassed the European average (Válková, 1999). The impact of crime has become a part of personal experience of a substantial part of population, indeed. It could result in the radicalisation of the public opinion in the sense of a growing fear of crime and a development of more severe punitive attitudes or -on the contrary- the acceptation of crime as a 'normal' part of public life. Both tendencies could be observed in the Czech society.

A remarkable and serious phenomenon is that the proportion of habitual offenders (recidivists) of the total prosecuted offenders has decreased from 41% in 1991, 33% in 1993, to 29% in 1995, after which it stabilised at this level. The number of all prosecuted offenders increased from 1989 till 1998 with 58.000, while the number of recidivists increased with only 8.500. This means that an increasing number of people with no previous criminal record begins to engage in crime. Though these first offenders cover all age groups, there is a predominance of younger people. People with higher professional qualification and organisational ability are represented as well. In connection with other criminogenic factors this may provide the breeding ground for a potential collaboration with (foreign) criminal organisations and for the emergence of sophisticated domestic organised forms of criminal activities.

The resulting crime rate in the CR. is not extraordinary compared with the one in the developed western countries. However, the question remains why this increase took place so rapidly and why so many people started breaking the law.

To answer this question we have to take into account the profound changes in social consciousness. The social structure in the Czech republic has altered, together with the development of new values and social status symbols. The prevalent liberal attitude that has determined the major social climate, created another pattern of desirable social behaviour based on values like the individual liberty, success in business, a high material standard of living, the principle of competition and the criterion of high performance. Some social groups have been characterised by high aspirations and by the effort to accomplish a rapid vertical mobility accompanied by impatience and by a relatively strong orientation to consumerism. However, not all of them have been capable of fulfilling their ambitions while remaining within the law. Some people who have been flung into 'open space' of individual liberty and free market with the new vision of personal success often did so with weakened moral standards due to the situation under the previous regime. Other social groups have been marginalised in the turmoil of the social changes and subsequently felt frustrated because of the inability to reach the coveted standard of living and a higher social status.

The social consciousness after 1989 was characterised by a high level of positive expectation. Based on the research carried out in 1991 45% of people expected the rapid improvement of the social and economic situation in the near future. It was found in 1994 that 33% of population expected the improvement of their level of live within one year, 64% of people within five years (Mladá fronta Dnes, 1994). If this high level of positive expectations came in conflict with the reality (and it came) it may cause an increased risk of deviant or even pathological forms of solution. Taking into account the previously mentioned criminogenic factors the trends in the development of crime may be interpreted along three possible lines:

1. Crime as the product of the process of social disintegration resulting from the transformation of the Czech society. This disintegration manifests itself in a form of disorganisation of social institutions and social relations as well as in a form of disorientation, leading to a change and relativisation of social values and patterns, which could be the explanation of some part of the criminality of youngsters and first-time offenders.
2. Crime as a rational choice of an adaptation strategy. This means the intentional and wilful law breaking. This conduct derives from a rational evaluation of potential gains and risks with regard to the opportunities offered by the social situation (see the Merton's concept of deviant behaviour as an innovative reaction of adaptation strategy). This may be an adequate explanation for the criminality of some new offenders or rather 'crime-entrepreneurs'.
3. Crime as a routine activity connected with the daily way of life. It reflects the classical social background of crime, the crime which originates from a criminal subculture. The criminogenity of this milieu has been strengthened by the growth of various social problems accompanying the transformation of the post 1989 Czech society (criminality of Romanies, migrants, homeless people etc. Lubelcová, 1998).

The proportion of foreigners in the number of registered and cleared up crimes is not very high, but the number of *prosecuted* foreigners has been steadily increasing. If the citizens of the Slovak Republic are omitted the proportion of foreigners of the prosecuted offenders has increased from 2,3%

in 1994 to 3,7% in 1998. Even if the Slovak citizens are included, the portion of foreigners in the number of prosecuted offenders would still be significantly lower than in some neighbouring countries such as Austria and Germany. Nevertheless we can ignore neither the continuing increase of the number and of the proportion of foreigners (except Slovaks) of the total number of offenders, nor their share in some kinds of crime. For example, in 1997, the involvement of foreigners in robberies was 15,4 %, in murders 10,1 %, in rapes 11,2 %, in pandering 11,3 %, in frauds 15,5 %, in pick pocketing 21,5 %.

The main part of the criminal activities of foreigners was committed in 1998 by citizens of the following states: Slovak Republic (38,4% of all prosecuted foreigners, especially crimes against property), Ukraine (18,5%, but 24,5% of them were engaged in the violent crimes), Vietnam (9,4%, especially economic crime), Poland (5,4%), Bulgaria (4,0%), Germany (3,3 %), Yugoslavia (2,5 %), Romania (2,2 %), Russia (2,2 %). The citizens from the European countries constituted in this year 85 % of all prosecuted foreign offenders, the citizens from Asian countries 12,2 %, of Africa 1 %, of North America only 0,8 %. Crimes committed by foreigners have been concentrated mainly in the Prague region, North Moravia and in the frontier districts.

Regarding the foreign citizens convicted for crimes committed in an organised group during the last years (with the exception of Slovak citizens), most of them are citizens of the former Yugoslavia, former USSR, Vietnam and Colombia. The reasons for conviction were predominantly drug trafficking, blackmailing and robbery.

The source of the above mentioned figures is the statistics of the Police of the Czech Republic. This statistics does not include the special data on (cross-border) organised crime. But on the basis of qualitative analysis of police information and of the criminological research on organised crime, which began in 1993, we may formulate some characteristics of the cross-border organised crime in the Czech republic.

## The development of organised crime groups

Even if the influences of foreign crime groups would be disregarded, there was still sufficient potential for the emergence of domestic organised crime groups. Under the previous regime there existed some criminal groups with a certain level of organisation; there were also people who got rich in so-called shadow economy; there were people who covered and profited from such criminal activities and all of them suddenly got a chance to take advantage of the changing social conditions to carry on their activities in the new favourable situation, adopting quickly developing new opportunities.

The results of the 1997 expert inquiry among policemen, judges and state attorneys dealing with organised crime and the analysis of a few criminal cases and available information, lends evidence to the conclusion of the existence of Czech organised crime in the sense that there are a few groups composed of Czech citizens which manifest some of the distinguishing features of organised crime: groups at a certain level of organisation, structured and hierarchical which develop the systematic planned criminal activity in order to gain the maximal profit. The size of these groups is not very large and their criminal activities are rather specialised than versatile. Three types may be distinguished. Criminal groups of the first type develop their activities predominantly in drug trafficking, thefts and the smuggling of stolen cars. Criminal groups of the second type are involved in activities which are classified as *economic* and *financial* crime.[4] The third most widespread activity of Czech organised criminal groups has been organised prostitution, pornography and women trafficking and the organisation of illegal migration.

According to experts the members of Czech organised groups have two types of social or criminal backgrounds: there are members with *no* previous criminal records ('respectable' citizens), and members who were engaged in the so-called shadow economy already before 1989. In both groups young men prevail. These findings correspond to the data on the criminal situation in general (Scheinost, 1998).

Notwithstanding these findings, available evidence indicates that the major part of the criminal organisations operating in the Czech Republic are still of foreign origin. Some of the activities of foreign groups have been furthered by the existing backgrounds of their compatriots living in our the Czech Republic. Its history goes back to the era before 1989, when about 100.000 foreigners -workers, students, businessmen- stayed as legal residents in the

---

[4] The qualification these economic but criminal activities as organised crime is still disputed, particular by the perpetrators themselves who would rather consider it 'sophisticated business practice'.

CSFR. Their number decreased to about 35.000 in 1990 and then gradually increased again. Till the end of 1997 the number of foreigners who have obtained a permanent or long-term residence permit (i.e. beyond 180 days) in the CR. was about 210.000. Apart from the citizens of the Slovak Republic, the citizens of Ukraine, Poland and Vietnam are strongly represented in this group. In addition to this contingent of foreigners it should be reminded that every day about 1,3 million foreigners (including tourists) stay in the Czech Republic, i.e. more than 10% of the number of the Czech citizens. However, the number of foreigners that legally arrive in the Czech Republic significantly exceeds the number of those who leave the country. This difference also exceeds the number of residence permits. Most of those foreigners probably leave the Czech Republic illegally, but we may assume that a part of them stay behind illegally and represent a potential criminogenic risk. The increase of the number of people from abroad in the CR. was of course also influenced by the enormous migration wave using the Czech territory as a transit to the Europe Union or beyond.

The illegal migrants originated mainly from the Balkan countries and to a smaller extent from Asian and African countries. The special problem is represented by the Ukrainians entering the Czech Republic in search for employment, very often as illegal workers. Only a minor part of the migrants is interested in staying as refugees using the humanitarian care or asylum. Most of them want to leave the Czech territory as quickly as possible and to continue to the West. But certain number of them remain behind, constituting the ethnic background that may serve as a basis for foreign organised criminals. Criminal organisations of the same ethnic origin may search for and find helpers, aids, but very often also the first victims among their compatriots.

Cross-border organised crime is undoubtedly present in the Czech Republic and criminal organisations operating along multiple national links, with the leading unit or organisers outside the Czech Republic, have been identified and analysed.

Due to the fundamental change after 1989, the Czech Republic became much more attractive for the penetration of various forms and various groups of organised crime from abroad. During a relatively short time span the Czech Republic became an important link in the international network of drug trafficking, illegal migration, import and export of stolen cars and probably of money laundering as well. In addition, big criminal organisations from abroad probably try to use the Czech Republic as a basis for a further expansion of their activities. Therefore they refrain from carrying out overt criminal activities in this country, but they try to establish a kind of bridgehead using the legitimate means of investment, establishing companies and firms, purchase of the real estate etc. At the same time a few smaller organised groups coming from abroad began to develop their criminal activities in various crime markets like drugs and racketeering.

In the Czech Republic, we can observe activities of criminal groups from the former USSR (The Ukraine, Russia, the Caucasus area), of Chinese groups (differentiated according to the place of origin and dialect) and of Balkan groups (mainly from the former Yugoslavia, especially Albanians from the Kosovo region, and Bulgarian groups). To a lesser extent, the activities of Italian, Nigerian and Colombian crime groups have been recorded. A certain portion of the organised crime is committed by groups of Vietnamese, Arabs, and marginally also, by people of some other nationalities like Poles and Romanians.

The activities of crime groups from the former USSR can be observed at two levels. At a higher level the activities are carried out by members representing the connecting links of large criminal organisations. They are not themselves involved in any 'visible' criminal activity, but they have an interest in establishing contacts, legitimate companies, in investment and financial operations. At a lower level, we can observe the activities of smaller crime groups specialised in particular criminal activities including (violent) crimes: racketeering, organising prostitution and women trafficking, trafficking in arms, thefts, smuggling of cars and organising illegal labour rackets.

The Chinese activities are mainly focussed on the organisation of illegal migration of their compatriots, to establish possibilities for money laundering (network of restaurants, shops, trade companies) and trade contacts. The 'visible' criminal activities (racketeering, loan sharking, prostitution and relatively frequent violent conflicts) usually take place inside the Chinese community with a clear effort to avoid conflicts with the outside environment.

Groups of Albanians from the Kosovo region are mainly active in drug trafficking (heroin), in organising illegal migration, car thefts and smuggling, and in blackmailing and racketeering. Their organisations operate in various countries with links in multiple countries and 'supreme' leading units outside the Czech territory.

The activities of Vietnamese take place all over the Czech Republic and consist mainly in smuggling commodities and breaking trade mark regulations, usually brand piracy. The number of acts of violence within the Vietnamese community has been increasing. The effort to achieve an economic expansion is evident and confirmed, for example, by the investment in the Czech Republic, by establishing firms and companies concealing the Vietnamese capital.

The Italian activities whose linkage to the Italian organised crime (Camorra) is supposed to be limited to building up contacts and trade network consisting of legal companies.

Arabs have been mainly active in the Czech Republic in drug trafficking. However, even in those activities, the citizens from the former Yugoslavia have taken over the leading role and have reduced the Arabs to serve mainly as local dealers.

Nigerians emerged as relatively new participants on the drug market and their activities reveal a smartly operating organisation. At present they probably use the Czech Republic as a transit country. However, Nigerian criminal activities can also be observed in the economic field, particularly financial frauds.

Regarding Colombian drug cartels (especially the Cali cartel) the Czech Republic probably serves as a transit zone, where they try to establish a trade territorial connections. Recently, Bulgarian citizens have become involved in drug trafficking. Previously, Bulgarian crime groups in the Czech Republic had specialised in car thefts and smuggling (Macháek, Rumpl, 1997).

Organised crime in the territory of the Czech Republic manifests itself by a number of criminal activities, whose extent and frequency have been changing in time. The most frequent criminal activities of the organised groups (assessed by the police experts) are traditionally thefts and smuggling of cars, organised prostitution and 'white-slave' trafficking. A significant increase has been recorded in the field of production, smuggling and distribution of drugs. The crime connected with drugs appeared in 1995 at the top of the activities of the organised crime in the CR. and this trend was confirmed in 1996 as well as in 1998. In the recent period also the importance of tax, credit, insurance and bill of exchange frauds have increased (Cejp, 1998).

According to the available information from the Czech milieu, the core of all groups maintain their ethnic integrity. Usually ethnic mixing takes place at the lowest level of the organisation or group only, i.e. at the level of executive functions.

Some ethnic groups are more open to co-operation with other ethnic groups in their criminal activities, like people from the former Yugoslavia. Others, clinging to their cultural, historical and linguistic differences, strictly maintain their ethnic exclusiveness, like the Chinese and partly Vietnamese groups, that typically seek to attain a maximal isolation from the Czech environment.

In the groups of foreign origin, Czechs provide the 'upperworld' services for leaders of the groups, acting as advisers, lawyers, persons mediating contacts, straw men for companies and, most often, performing executive tasks as ordinary members of the criminal groups (couriers, smugglers, etc.). Czechs, however, are also sometimes in the position of customers, who buy the commodities and services supplied illegally by foreign groups (Scheinost, 1996).

## Cross-border organised crime trade

Cross-border organised crime trade activities have been very versatile. They involve trafficking in illegal commodities as drugs, in legitimate (taxed) goods and custom frauds, as well as trafficking in human beings. The trafficking in heroin provides a good example of the Czech situation. The Czech Republic is situated on the northern branch of the so-called Balkan route. This branch branches off in the Czech region into three destinations: Scandinavia, Great Britain and Germany. The ring leaders of the organisations involved in heroin trafficking is composed of Turks, but in the Czech Republic we encounter only the executives at middle level, who are Kosovo-Albanians. They manage the transport of heroin across the Czech territory and handle the distribution in this country (the distribution is sometimes also carried out by Arabs). The Czechs serve as dealers or couriers, but they show a tendency to rise to higher positions in the hierarchy. In addition there are also relatively independent Czech groups, which purchase heroin from Albanian suppliers and transport it to the West or distribute it on their own account. Other

Czech groups are involved in the production of the special Czech synthetic drug 'pervitin'.

Regarding the trafficking in legitimate goods we may presume the extensive involvement of Czech groups. The trafficking in object of arts (mostly stolen from Czech churches, museums and art galleries), the illegal import of alcohol (declared as another commodity in order to pay a lower tax rate and custom duties), frauds connected with import and export of so-called light mineral oil, abusing the differential custom and tax rates for light oil and for naphtha, are examples of cross-border activities of Czech groups in this field.

Illegal trafficking in human beings is one of the most important activities of the transnational organised crime in the Czech Republic. The research on the phenomenon of illegal migration showed that the number of illegal migrants are around tens of thousands per year. These figures include only the numbers of persons, who were detected and apprehended while crossing the borders. There is evidence that organised crime groups profit from this illegal migration by providing well paid services: forged passports and other travel documents, transport, accommodation, smuggling migrants across the border, etc.

The main part of the detected migrants consists of citizens from the Balkan countries. During the last four years the portion of apprehended migrants from other European countries significantly decreased in comparison with 1994, whereas the portion of people from Asia rapidly increased (*see the table*).

**Table 1**

| | **1994** | **1995** | **1996** | **1997** | **I-VI/1999** |
|---|---|---|---|---|---|
| | % | % | % | % | % |
| **European Countries** | 84,1 | 62,4 | 66,9 | 64,0 | 57,7 |
| **Asian Countries** | 11,4 | 33,2 | 26,2 | 30,2 | 40,0 |
| **African Countries** | 3,8 | 2,9 | 4,7 | 3,8 | |
| **Other Countries** | 0,7 | 1,5 | 2,2 | 2,0 | 2,3 |

Migrants from Balkan countries usually arrive to the Czech Republic by buses and trains via Hungary and Slovakia, but the illegal pedestrian traffic across the Czech-Slovakian border has increased gradually. The migration route from Asia leads across the area of the former USSR. Asian migrants arrive through the territory of Russia and Ukraine to the Czech Republic by plane or train (more rarely by other means of traffic), most often via Slovakia. This route is also used by some migrants from Africa, after they arrive in the former USSR.

The majority of migrants attempt to cross the Czech Republic to enter the Federal Republic of Germany (64,7 % of all apprehended migrants in 1997 were detected while crossing the borders from the Czech Republic to the Germany).

Only a few citizens from the former USSR (mostly from Ukraine) and a part of the migrants from China try to settle for some time as illegal workers in the Czech Republic. The greater majority of migrants remains in the Czech Republic until they are able to cross the western border (75 % of the migrants attached in 1997 crossed the borders within five days of their arrival to the Czech Republic).

Even though the volume of illegal migration in 1994 and 1995 decreased (in absolute numbers), compared to 1993, the proportion of migrant smuggling (i.e. organised form of illegal migration) has increased. Since 1996 the number of illegal migrants has been growing again.

The service of the smugglers or a smugglers organisation has mainly been used by the citizens of the former Yugoslavia states, Romania and those from Asia and Africa. In general, it is quite an exception when migrants from distant countries try to cross borders without smuggler's service. In addition the Asian migrants most often use forges or tampered documents.

Stricter measures (visas, organisational measures, reinforcement of frontier police, etc.) result in an improvement of the migration organisation. Uncontrolled, individual migration and individual smugglers has been replaced by organisations by now. These organisations are highly developed and their activities has been spreading worldwide.

Ring leaders of the international organisations tend to operate outside the Czech Republic, but lower level executive staff operates on the Czech territory, usually seeking a legal cover for their activities and either knows the Czech milieu or uses Czech contact persons. The Chinese tend to use Vietnamese in order to mediate the necessary contacts.

In these organisation or more precise in their units operating in Czech Republic Czechs citizens use to occupy executive positions as smugglers: drivers, persons providing transport and accommodation. In most cases they are low educated youngsters. Only a smaller part of the Czech aids come from the criminal milieu or have previously committed some crimes. This applies mainly to the above mentioned contact persons, who have the task to establish contacts with the 'organisers' belonging to other nationalities in the Czech milieu, including the recruitment of persons for the executive functions. The findings show that these contact persons are often middle aged.

Among the smugglers, a minority of people of other nationalities can observed too. The number of Slovaks increased, particularly involved in smuggling of people across the Czech - Slovak border. There are also Vietnamese smugglers (mostly used for smuggling Chinese people). The portion of Yugoslavian nationalities among smugglers decreased. Smugglers of non-Czech nationality are more specialised in the directions and routes of smuggling as well as in smuggling of people of a particular nationality (like the Vietnamese smuggling Chinese). The sums of money paid by migrants to the organisers range from hundreds to thousands US dollars or German marks, according to the type and complexity of the service.

Based on the research we may outline the probable structure of such an transnational smuggler organisation operating in the CR.

**leading staff** *supreme level*

Operating abroad.

↑

------------------- contact, control, „liaison officer" ---------------↓

within the CR.

**territorial organiser** *middle level*

↓

surveyor → contact person → co-ordinator middle-men

↓

transport → accommodation → smugglers executive level

The functions of surveyor and co-ordinator are probably present within larger organisations and may be combined with some other function. In the Chinese organisations there are Vietnamese at the executive level; only the function of accommodation provider is exclusively fulfilled by Chinese members.

It is likely that such a linear structure has mainly developed within organisations smuggling people from Asia. It is not quite clear whether the Balkan organisations have the similar linear structure or whether they have formed various local cells cooperating at an equal level. According to experts violence is considered the usual method to maintain the internal discipline or to solve conflicts arising from competition.

The forgery of documents and the attempts of corruption are often significant features of the activity of smuggler organisations. There is no evidence that human smugglers are involved in other kinds of organised cross-border crime (for example smuggling of drugs or illegal arms trafficking). Despite this specialisation one should not underestimate the possibility to use the established structures and the profits from the organised illegal migration for the other, possibly more dangerous objectives.

The occurrence of the organised illegal migration in the Czech Republic is expected to persist, its extent depending on the international situation, as well as on a increasing importance of the Czech Republic as the migration terminus. A development towards a more sophisticated organisation is also expected, together with potential connections with other forms of organised crime. It is likely that the control will remain in the hands of international organisations in which Czechs will less often occupy higher positions. These organisations will dominate the market and the individual organisers and groups will participate only on a minor scale (Scheinost, 1995).

Trafficking of women is also considered to be the widespread form of cross-border organised crime in this country. The increase of prostitution is considered to be one of the most important social problems for the Czech society. Prostitution itself has not been criminalised and a large part of the women involved in prostitution pursue still this activity without compulsion. However, as a result of the high profits a number of women who have been forced into prostitution, at least at the beginning of their prostitute career (by pimps, organisers or initially by their own social situation), has grown. Women involved in prostitution are abused to earn money for their 'protectors', pimps. This kind of prostitution is qualified and prosecuted by our Penal Code as *procuring*.

Organised procuring is usually committed by a groups of persons operating with a certain division of tasks: the tipper who looks for women and girls; the caller or 'recruiting officer' who contacts and recruits them often under false pretentions, the transporter (often a taxi driver); the procurer-pimp; the middleman who mediates the contact between customer and prostitute, etc. Czech street and road prostitution is largely controled by Romanies, some of whom have contacts abroad including the cross-border exchange of prostitutes. 'Indoor' prostitution is concentrated in night clubs and similar entertainment establishments, mainly managed by Czech owners, but sometimes with the participation of foreign capital. coming often from abroad, like the former Soviet Union or Germany. These night clubs employ usually Czech women, but there are also girls from Belarus, Ukraine and in one odd case Philippines. They are imported by organised foreign groups and delivered to the Czech brothel keepers. This is not a 'free service': usually the victims must also pay a part of their income to the purveyor as well to the owner of the nightclub.

The Czech Penal Code considers 'white slavery' (cross-border traffic of women for prostitution) a special form of procuring. The contemporary boom of this form of organised crime is caused by the substantial demand for 'cheap sex' in the developed countries and by the demand for the 'new faces' in the sex industry, i.e. for girls from Middle and Eastern Europe, apart from South America and Asia.

The Czech Republic has become the crossing point of the international white-slave trafficking between East and West. Some experts estimate, that since the beginning of the 1990s tens of thousands of women destined for prostitution in Western Europe passed the Czech territory. The Czech Republic does not only serve as the transit country for trafficking women from Russia, Belarus, Ukraine and Asia, but also as the source for exporting Czech girls and women. Well-organised and ramified groups from the former Soviet Union, China, former Yugoslavia, Poland as well as native offenders and people from Germany, Italy, Belgium, the Netherlands etc. are involved in this traffic.

Prostitutes who become victims of this traffic can be divided into two groups: the first group consists of women prostituting themselves voluntarily, consenting to being sent abroad. The second consists of women and girls who have been coerced into prostitution by physical or psychological violence. Most of them have been promised to work abroad as waitress, dancers, hostess, models etc. Some of them have even been kidnapped from their place of residence and transported to the place of destination.

Groups involved in the white-slave trafficking exporting Czech women abroad consist of about 5 to 10 members with similar division of tasks as mentioned above, enlarged with a seller having contacts abroad. This seller takes over the girls from procurers and 'recruiting officers' and delivers them to the purchaser - mostly a foreigner - who sends them to the place of destination. These groups may also employ persons providing the forged travel documents, the guards who look after the girls during transport, etc. (Trávníková, 1995, Milika, 1997).

## Conclusions

Before 1989 there were forms of crime bearing some features of organised crime but they took the shape corresponding with the previous political, economic and social system. Groups were mostly of domestic origin and their activities had rarely a cross-border character.

After the fall of the communist regime, the isolation was lifted and the borders opened simultaneously with the establishing of open market economy. The opened space was used for involving the Czech Republic into the international networks of cross-border crime and for developing sophisticated forms of organised criminal activities. Nevertheless the situation in the Czech Republic has developed to such a critical nature as for example in Russia or Ukraine, where Louisa I. Shelley speaks about 'political-criminal nexus' (Shelley, 1999), but it is obvious that the international cross-border crime uses this country not only as a logistic opportunity or as a transit country but also as the location for direct criminal activities. There are not only the groups and organisations from abroad that develop their cross-border criminal activities, but there are also the groups of domestic Czech origin involved in the international networks and crime markets. The speed of the process of formation and penetration of those groups and organisations was stipulated by the specific factors resulting on the one hand from the rapid transformation of our society and on the other hand from the lowering of social consciousness caused by the character of the previous regime. Recently we face the same problems with regard to the phenomenon of cross-border crime as the developed western countries.

## References

Cejp, M., *Expertízy k problematice organizovaného zloinu* (The expertise on the problem of organised crime), Prague, IKSP, 1998

Karabec, Z., *Úinnost legislativních zm_n ve vztahu k organizovanému zloinu* (The effectiveness of legislation changes in relation to organised crime), Prague, IKSP, 1998

Lubelcová, G., *Kriminalita v kontexte sociálnej transformácie na Slovensku* (Criminality in the context of social transformation in Slovakia), in:Radièová,I., Vieme èo odmietame a vieme èo chceme?, Bratislava, SPACE, 1998, pp. 131-134

Macháek, Z. and T. Rumpl, Zahrani_ní skupiny organizovaného zlo_inu a jejich aktivity naeském území (Foreign organised crime groups and their activites on the territory of the Czech Republic), in: M. Noina (ed.), *Mezinárodní organizovaný zloin v R*, Prague, Ústav mezinárodních vztah, 1997

Mileka, J., Obchod s lidmi (Trafficking in people). In: M. No_ina, (ed.), *Mezi-národnïorganizovaný zloin v R* (Transnational organised crime in the CR). Prague, Ústav mezinárodních vztahù, 1997

Mladá fronta Dnes (journal), 23.2.1994

Osman_ík, O., paper presented on the conference 'Penal Justice and Crime Control in the CR', Prague 13.-14.5.1996

Scheinost, M., *Nelegální migrace a pevadêství jako jedna z aktivit organizovaného zloinu* (Illegal migration and smuggling as one of the activities of organised crime), Prague, IKSP, 1995

Scheinost, M., *Trestná èinnost cizích státních píslušníkù v R a etnický faktor v organizované kriminalit* (The criminal activity of foreigners in the CR and ethnic factor in organised crime). Prague, IKSP, 1996

Scheinost, M., M. Cejp, J. Musil, I. Budka and I. Brabcová, *Výzkum struktury, forem a moností postihu organizovaného zloinu v eské republice* (Research on the structure, forms and recourse of organised crime in the CR), Prague, IKSP, 1997

Scheinost, M., *Organizovaná trestná èinnost obanù R* (Organised criminal activity of Czech citizens), Prague, IKSP, 1998

Shelley, L.I., The Political-Criminal Nexus: Russian-Ukrainian Case Studies, *Trends in Organised Crime*, 1999, Vol. 4, *nr.3*, 81-107

Trávníková, I., *Prostituce jako jedna z mo_ých aktivit organizovaného zloinu* (Prostitution as one of the possible activities of organised crime), Prague, IKSP, 1995

Válková, J., Jak je u nás bezpnì ? Hlavní výsledky výzkumu obtí trestných inù v R. In : *K problematice obtí trestných inù a výsledkm výzkumu obtí v eské republice* (What is the safety ? The main results of the research of victims of crime in the CR), Prague, IKSP, 1999

# Trafficking in women in Bosnia and Herzegovina

*Almir Maljevic*[1]

## Introduction: fertile grounds for crime entrepreneurs

Before anything is said about trafficking in human beings in Bosnia and Herzegovina, attention should be paid to certain features of the country that have had an enormous impact on the development and spread of crime in general. Bosnia and Herzegovina regained its independence in 1992 after the dissolution of the former Federal Socialist Republic of Yugoslavia. Unfortunately, the dissolution was followed by chaos, crises, and wars, which came to a head in the territory of Bosnia and Herzegovina. In addition to the almost unbelievable human losses, and the socio-economic damage that Bosnia and Herzegovina and its citizens suffered as consequences of the conflict, the 1992-1995 war also resulted in changes that created fertile ground for the development and spread of criminal organisations that challenged the state's capacity to combat crime in general.

Apart from trying to set up functional institutions of government, and to establish the rule of law, Bosnia and Herzegovina has also been going through a transition process – not only in the sense of a change from authoritarianism to democracy, but also in the sense of a change from a stringently controlled, to a free market economy. The disappearance of the absolute control over every feature of people's lives (including the economy and crime) that was exercised between the War and the early 1990s, allowed new forms of crime to emerge, driven primarily by the desire for illegal profit.

Moreover, in accordance with the terms of the Dayton Peace

---

1 Almir Maljevic is Academic and Research Assistant at the Faculty of Criminal Justice Sciences of the University of Sarajevo, Bosnia and Herzegovina.
This chapter is from: P.C. van Duyne, K. von Lampe, M. van Dijck and J.L. Newell (eds.), *The organised crime economy. Managing crime markets in Europe*. Nijmegen, Wolf Legal Publishers, 2005

Agreement,[2] Bosnia and Herzegovina was divided into two entities,[3] – each with extremely extensive powers and a high level of autonomy – and one district.[4] Though the powers of the central state extend to security issues – including the fight against criminal organisations, which have surfaced wherever opportunities have been favourable – the co-existence of two powerful entities has meant that the central state's control has always been weak. This problematic situation appears even worse if one considers that no fewer than 180 ministries are responsible for governing Bosnia and Herzegovina – thus providing fertile ground for all types of corruption, including corruption of the police and the judiciary.

In addition, until recently there was no state-wide agency of law-enforcement. This changed in 2000 when the State Border Service,[5] the very first state-wide law-enforcement agency, was formed. It established comprehensive control over the country's borders at the very end of 2002. This means that, due to the tensions that persisted in the aftermath of the 1992-1995 war, the institutions of government failed, until 2002, to establish any serious form of police or judicial cooperation, or to exercise adequate control over the country's borders. Another state-wide police force was established in 2004: the State Agency for Investigation and Protection (SIPA).[6]

In accordance with the country's constitution, prior to March 2003, legislative powers, including those relating to criminal matters, belonged almost entirely to the entities.[7] Given the differing political structures and philosophies of the two entities, this state of affairs resulted in the emergence

---

2 The Dayton Peace Agreement, which brought the war to an end, was signed on 14 December 1995. At the same time, in order to preserve Bosnia and Herzegovina as one country it contained very vague provisions defining very complex, completely decentralised, administrative structures

3 These are the Federation of Bosnia and Herzegovina – which is administratively and territorially divided into ten cantons with extensive powers, high levels of autonomy, and their own assemblies and governments – and the Republic of Srpska.

4 The Br ko District of Bosnia and Herzegovina

5 The Law on the State Border Service, *Official Gazette of Bosnia and Herzegovina*, no. 19/2001

6 The Law on the State Agency for Investigation and Protection, *Official Gazette of Bosnia and Herzegovina*, No. 27/2004. Among other things, trafficking in human beings falls within its jurisdiction.

7 The Office of the High Representative promulgated the Criminal Code of Bosnia and Herzegovina in January 2003. It has been published in the *Official gazette of Bosnia and Herzegovina*, No. 3/03 and it took effect on March 1st 2003

of two different approaches to a number of issues. This was true even during the early stages of criminal law reform and especially when it came to the implementation of standards prescribed by international conventions ratified by the state of Bosnia and Herzegovina.[8] As a consequence, the two entities had systems of criminal law that were incompatible, not only as far as the definition of certain criminal offences was concerned, but also in terms of criminal procedure, thus rendering judicial cooperation difficult.

The lack of unified political leadership, of harmonised criminal legislation, of state-wide law-enforcement agencies and of judicial and police cooperation: all this was of considerable assistance to crime entrepreneurs, who were able to develop and to extend their activities easily throughout the country and the whole region.

## Organised crime in Bosnia and Herzegovina

Due to the fact that very little serious research is available on the number of criminal organisations in Bosnia and Herzegovina, it would be highly speculative to say anything about their nature or extent.[9] Nevertheless, some research projects focusing on criminal activities that can be related to organised crime should be mentioned. Criminal activities that have been the subject of research projects in Bosnia and Herzegovina are corruption and trafficking in human beings.[10] Of course, this does not mean that other forms

---

8 From the very beginning the Republic of Srpska refused to acknowledge Bosnian and Herzegovinian legislation and implemented laws defined and applied in the neighbouring Serbia and Monte Negro. At the same time the Federation of Bosnia and Herzegovina strove to bring its criminal legislation into line with various international conventions, regional and bilateral agreements.

9 Most of the available research has been carried out by individuals interested in the field on the one hand (the results of such research being limited as a result of scarce financial resources) and by non-governmental organisations on the other.

10 Research on corruption has been conducted primarily by Transparency International Bosnia and Herzegovina using the well-known Corruption Perceptions Index, but also using the Study on National Integrity Systems. Using the same methodology in all cases, this is used to examine various institutions that should be combating corruption at a national level, by looking at the legal framework regulating the work of such institutions and the practical implementation of that framework. Meanwhile, the Association of Criminologists of Bosnia and Herzegovina is conducting research into the police and corruption, and is preparing research projects on corruption in the education system and in the judiciary.

of organised crime, such as illicit drug trafficking, money laundering, computer-related crime (Budimlić, 2003), child pornography, illicit trafficking of firearms (see Hajdinjak, 2002), cigarette smuggling (also Hajdinjak, 2002), or the smuggling of migrants, do not exist.[11] On the contrary, such offences have been recorded in abundance, but research into them has yet to be carried out. Hence there are no valid scientific indicators that can be presented here.[12]

The only organised criminal activity to have been the subject of systematic research so far, is the trafficking of human beings, or, more precisely, the trafficking of women. This chapter will present some of the core findings from this research.

Although this chapter focuses on human trafficking in Bosnia and Herzegovina, it goes without saying that this criminal activity extends to the whole region and beyond. Therefore, there is a need briefly to describe the wider Balkan-region context – within which the trafficking of humans in Bosnia and Herzegovina is just one instance. Owing to a number of local, regional and global factors (Nikolić-Ristanović, 2004, and 1998; Lewis, 1998; CSD, 2003), in recent decades the Balkans have become a centre for illegal trafficking in all kinds of substances from drugs (so called 'Balkan route', Wegner, 2004) and arms to cigarettes (Hajdinjak, 2002), but also for trafficking in humans (Ćopić, 2002). Humans, predominantly women and children seen as a commodity (Williams, 1999), are being sold in all geographical directions: this has led to the Balkan region becoming widely known not only as a source, but also as a transit and destination region (Albania, 2003; Bosnia and Herzegovina, 2003; Bulgaria, 2003; Croatia, 2003; The FYR Macedonia, 2003; Moldova, 2003; Serbia and Montenegro, 2003; Romania, 2003).

---

11 Although it is well known that Bosnia and Herzegovina lies at the heart of the (so called) *Balkan route* used for the trafficking of illicit drugs from East to West, the problem of drugs coming to and going through the country has never been researched!

12 Between January 2003 and June 2004, the State Prosecutor's Office initiated 79 investigations into allegations concerning the smuggling of migrants and 60 investigations into allegations of money laundering.

# Trafficking in women in Bosnia and Herzegovina

In order to obtain more insight into the phenomenon of trafficking in women in Bosnia and Herzegovina, the US Embassy recently financed the research project, "Trafficking in women in Bosnia and Herzegovina". The project was conducted by the Faculty of Criminal Justice Sciences at the University of Sarajevo under the supervision of Prof. Dr. Vladimir Obradović, from April 2003 until the end of the year.

The findings of the project are based on empirical data obtained from 691 respondents who were the victims of trafficking in Bosnia and Herzegovina in the period from 1999 to 2003. The sample included all recorded victims of trafficking in Bosnia and Herzegovina and was divided into two sub-samples: the first (N= 457) was used for social analysis, the second (N=238) for social- psychological analysis. Quantitative analysis was supplemented by a qualitative approach based on analysis of oral life-stories provided by the victims themselves, a number of semi-structured interviews conducted with five convicted traffickers, six taxi-drivers (transport providers) and *dancers* in night clubs, but also through participant observation during raids, and analysis of available police and judicial documents.

## Results

It is very difficult to say when the first cases of trafficking in women were recorded, as the activity was not defined as criminal in Bosnia and Herzegovina until 2003. Cases that could have been defined as trafficking in women, were prosecuted as prostitution or as cases of aiding and abetting prostitution. It is a plausible assumption that, although some isolated cases were registered earlier, trafficking really began to take off after the war began in the region. There is a strong belief that that its increase is to be explained, not only by the general causes described above but also by the growth in the number of foreign peace- keeping military forces in the country (Obradović, 2004; Nikolić-Ristanović, 2004). The increased numbers of foreign military personnel led primarily to an increase in the numbers of nightclubs and other establishments featuring *exotic dancers*. Due to the fact that most of these dancers were not residents of Bosnia and

Herzegovina, it was assumed that the women concerned were victims of trafficking, which, as born out by the very first anti-trafficking police action, 'Macro', in 1994, proved to be correct.

## Origin and routing of the victims

In his research, Obradović found that 93% of victims of trafficking were residents of Moldavia, Romania and The Ukraine. The fact that victims of trafficking came predominantly from these three countries, makes it plausible to assume that Bosnia and Herzegovina serves as a *destination* country with very well established routes for trafficking in women for sexual exploitation of various kinds (Obradović, 2004). These routes are the following:

- the majority (89,8%) travels on the route Moldavia-Romania-Serbia-Bosnia and Herzegovina and only 10,2% are sent on the route Moldavia-Romania-Hungary-Serbia-Bosnia and Herzegovina;
- the main routes for victims from *Romania* go through Serbia directly to Bosnia and Herzegovina (used in 94,2% of all these cases) or go from Romania to Hungary to Croatia to Bosnia and Herzegovina (5,8%);
- victims from *Russia, Belarus* and *Ukraine* come to Bosnia and
- Herzegovina through Romania and Serbia (58,6%) or through Hungary
- and Croatia (41,4%).

Accordingly, it can be said that almost all routes to Bosnia and Herzegovina are via Serbia. Therefore it is justifiable to assume that one of the main organised criminal networks involved in human trafficking in South Eastern Europe is to be found in Belgrade.

**Table 1. The national origins of victims of trafficking**

| | 1999 | 2000 | 2001 | 2002 | 2003 | Total N | % |
|---|---|---|---|---|---|---|---|
| Moldova | 7 | 97 | 80 | 109 | 10 | 303 | 44 |
| Romania | 3 | 65 | 89 | 92 | 4 | 253 | 37 |
| Ukraine | 2 | 31 | 15 | 32 | 4 | 84 | 12 |
| Russia | - | 2 | 6 | 11 | 1 | 20 | 3 |
| Byelorussia | - | 1 | 4 | 1 | - | 6 | 1 |
| Serbia and Montenegro | - | 2 | 6 | 6 | 2 | 16 | 2 |
| Bosnia and Herzegovina | - | - | - | 3 | 2 | 5 | 1 |
| Bulgaria | - | - | - | 1 | - | 1 | - |
| Hungary | - | 1 | - | - | - | 1 | - |
| Kazakhstan | 2 | - | - | - | - | 2 | - |
| **Total** | **14** | **199** | **200** | **255** | **23** | **691** | **100** |

## Recruitment

Considering human trafficking as an enterprise, the first question to be addressed concerns the ways in which the 'commodity' is obtained. The next table provides an overview of how the victims were 'recruited'.

Although almost one third of victims are recruited by someone they know, the figures in table 2 show that the majority of victims are recruited by people who, due to their active involvement in organised trafficking, victims define as traffickers.

Another finding that confirms the involvement of criminal organisations in human trafficking, is that a total of 71,6% of all journeys from the country of origin to another country were organised by known or unknown traffickers and only 10,3% by friends or acquaintances. If we assume that friends and acquaintances are not part of a criminal organisation (which may be entirely wrong), then we can suggest that in at least 71,6% of cases, victims were the objects of organised trafficking. The fact is that trafficking in women requires means of getting them out of a country, (forged?) travel documents, means of transport, temporary housing for the victim, and her sale on arrival at the pre- arranged destination. It is plausible to assume that these requirements (Escaler, 1998) are met by various criminal organisations.[13]

**Table 2. The 'recruitment' of victims**

| Recruited by | N | % |
|---|---|---|
| Acquaintances/friends, of whom: | 148 | 32,3 |
| Female friends | 92 | 20,1 |
| Male friends | 56 | 12,2 |
| Traffickers/unknown | 255 | 55,7 |
| Female trafficker | 16 | 3,5 |
| Male trafficker | 104 | 22,7 |
| Unknown female | 64 | 14,0 |
| Unknown male | 71 | 15,5 |
| No data/missing values | 55 | 12,0 |
| Total N= 458 | 458 | 100% |

When it comes to means of recruitment, it was found that in 59,6% of the cases, traffickers used friends and acquaintances to provide prospective victims with information about seemingly attractive work abroad, and that they did this themselves in only 17,9% of cases. Another result worth highlighting is that 8,7% of victims found the information concerning work abroad from newspaper advertisements.[14] One of reasons why this did not have consequences might be the fact that, for example, in Moldova in recent years, remittances from migrant labourers have become a very substantial part of the country's income. Migrants send home approximately $120 million each year, which is the equivalent of half the national income. Therefore, investigation of such advertisements seems an unlikely prospect (Trafficking in Human Beings in South Eastern Europe, 2003).

---

13 Aronowitz (2001) points out that, according to Europol, there are several indicators that point towards a high degree of organisation in trafficking. These are: the fact that women of different nationalities are smuggled together; the fact that a large number of persons are transferred over great distances; the large amounts of money that change hands; the fact that when things go wrong, legal assistance is immediately available.

14 This deserves special mention because one would have expected at least these 8,7% of cases to have been easily traced, investigated and prosecuted.

## Reasons for leaving home

The victim's journey is a long one, both in terms of time and distance. It is reasonable to ask why they do not try to escape and ask for help as soon as they became aware that something is suspicious or at least strange. There are several possible answers to this question. First, it is possible that they are treated well during the entire journey, appeased by deceiving and encouraging information about their future jobs or about good salaries. Second, some of the women are used to suffering at home at the hands of their husbands or partners; thus they may not perceive the violence or suffering to which they are subject while being transported as something that deviates unacceptably from what they are used to. According to IOM, more than 80% of Moldavian victims of trafficking had been subjected to domestic violence before their journeys began (Trafficking in Human Beings in South Eastern Europe, 2003). Third, it is possible that traffickers travel and cross transit-country borders by bribing police officials and border guards, so that victims have no chance to escape.[15]

**Table 3. Why did victims leave home?**

| Reasons for leaving | N | % |
|---|---|---|
| To work and earn some money | 221 | 92,9 |
| Tourism | 1 | 0,4 |
| Forced to leave her home | 1 | 0,4 |
| To escape from parents | 3 | 1,3 |
| Other | 12 | 5,0 |
| Total N =238 | 238 | 100 |

As the figures in Table 3 show, when asked about their reasons for leaving home, almost 93% of the victims said they had wanted to work abroad in order to earn enough money to make a decent living.[16]

Most victims (55,4%) were expecting (that is, they were promised) work as waitresses, shop assistants or something similar. A total of 23,6% were expecting to be employed in a factory, to work in a household or as baby sitters, while a total of 21% of victims assumed they would work as dancers

---

[15] During an interview, one of the convicted traffickers said that in order to cross a border without any difficulties, he usually paid €250 to a border guard.

[16] 55,9% of the victims agreed to travel to the former Yugoslav countries, 37,4% to Western Europe and only 6,7% to Greece, Turkey or Israel.

(16,4%) in nightclubs or as sexual workers (4,6%). Although only 4,6% of the victims openly declared that they were aware of the possibility that they would get involved in some kind of sex-related work, one wonders how many more, if any more, of the victims were aware that there was a risk of becoming involved in work of this nature.

**Table 4. Treatment of victims**

| Nature of treatment | N | % |
|---|---|---|
| Physical abuse | 116 | 25,4 |
| Sexual abuse | 41 | 9,0 |
| Threats/blackmail | 82 | 17,9 |
| Freedom of movement restricted | 49 | 10,7 |
| Good relationship/treated well | 125 | 27,4 |
| No answer | 44 | 9,6 |
| Total: N = 457 | 457 | 100 |

Given that 79% of the victims ended up in a business that they did not want to become involved in, it is interesting to see how they perceived the way they were treated by their *owners* or their co-workers. It should be noted that 34,4% of victims were abused either physically[17] or sexually.[18] In other words, more than one third of the women were subjected to serious violence. Another 17,9% was subjected to mental abuse. 10,7% was not allowed to move freely. 9,6% did not want to provide an answer, probably due to the fact that they were under stress and afraid to do so. Thus one can suggest that a total of 72,6% of victims was exposed to inhumane living and *working* conditions. At the same time, surprisingly, almost 27% of the women perceived their relationships with their *owners* as good. This may mean that they really were treated well – or that they were afraid to tell the truth.[19]

17 The most horrifying example of physical abuse recounted in the course of the research, was the case of an owner who shot a victim in the stomach nine times. She survived, though remains permanently disabled.

18 Sexual violence was usually perpetrated by violent and drunk clients, but also by *owners* whenever victims requested something (to visit their families, to see a doctor, to go shopping etc.).

19 There was one case, in which the victim stated in court that her *owner* treated her just like any father would treat his daughter!

## Revenues

Another interesting finding is that women are frequently sold more than once in Bosnia and Herzegovina. More precisely, 46,3% of those who responded (55,6% did not want to say how often they had been sold) said they had been sold once; 30% had been sold twice, and 23,7% had been sold three or more times. This means that almost every fourth woman, after becoming a victim of international trafficking, was re-sold at least once on the internal market in Bosnia and Herzegovina.

As far as the prices they were sold for are concerned,[20] these varied from KM 250-8000 (€127,9-4092).[21] As most of victims were sold for prices between KM 1500 (€767,3) (the first quartile) and KM 3500 (€1790,3) (third quartile), they were sold for an average price of KM 2643 (€1351,9). Since they had an average of four clients a day,[22] each paying an average price of KM100 (€51,15), their buyer made good on his *investment* within four to nine days. One of the outcomes was that *owners* usually had 5 to 17 women (with an average of 7) in their bars or clubs. If we multiply this by the average number of clients and the average price, we can conclude that owners' profits lay between KM 60.000 (€30.690) and KM 204.000 (€104.347) a month (an average of KM 84.000 (€42.967) a month).

## Clients

As far as clients are concerned, although the media portrayal and therefore the general population's assumption is that clients in nightclubs and bars are predominantly foreigners (foreign military personnel in particular), one of the most surprising findings of the research is that this assumption appears to be false.

20 57,3% of victims had no idea of the price they were sold for but the rest stated the exact amounts. Their answers are based on the amounts they had to *make up to (earn back for)* their *owners* because that is how much he told them he had paid for them.

21 KM 1,00 KM is equivalent to €1,955.

22 'Only' 15,0% of women had more than four clients a day.

**Table 5. Clients**

| Clients | N | % |
|---|---|---|
| Local men only | 119 | 66,5 |
| Local soldiers and police | 21 | 11,7 |
| "Internationals" and local clients | 12 | 6,7 |
| SFOR and local clients | 0 | 0,0 |
| All profiles | 27 | 15,1 |
| Total N = 179 | 179 | 100 |

As the figures in table 5 show, excluding the 24,8% (N = 59) of victims who were not willing to answer the question, it appears plausible that international clients, either alone or in combination with other types of clients, do not represent more than 21,8% of clients, whereas local clients account for no less than 78% of cases. In other words, only one in five is likely to be an *international* client. Therefore, it can be argued that the presence of international personnel in the country should not be seen as the primary cause of the increase in trafficking in women in Bosnia and Herzegovina.

## Victimisation characteristics

The research also focused on common victim characteristics. In order to do so, a total of 81 variables (situational, status-related or behavioural factors) were analysed by means of uni- and bivariate analysis, and appropriate techniques of multivariate analysis (factor analysis, regression analysis, cluster analysis, discriminant analysis, path analysis and logistical regression analysis were applied). It was found that 23 of the variables produced 11 factors – which in their turn explained 74,1% of the variance. Given that the research involved the collection of data from all recorded victims of trafficking in Bosnia and Herzegovina; given that the victims came from different countries, and given that victims of the same nationalities as those found in our sample are usually found in other countries in South Eastern Europe, it is plausible to assume that the characteristics found in the sample of victims in Bosnia and Herzegovina can be regarded as representative of those for other victims of trafficking in South-eastern Europe. The following factors were found to have the most significant impact on trafficking in women in Bosnia and Herzegovina.

The first factor (accounting for 16,4% of the variance) is victimisation by *owners* or clients. This is strongly connected to limited freedom of movement, physical or sexual abuse, and the denial of access to medical services.

The second factor (accounting for 9,9% of the variance) is the level of education, which correlates with sexual abuse and (not) being paid for providing sexual services. More educated victims are more successful in obtaining payment and in avoiding sexual abuse.

The third factor (accounting for 7,5% of the variance) concerns family relationships, which correlates with the quality of relationships, the economic status of the family, integrity of the family and physical or mental abuse.

The fourth factor (accounting for 6,7% of the variance) is a (dis)functional family.

The fifth factor (accounting for 6,1% of the variance) is a/an (un)known recruiter. This correlates strongly with the level of education.

The sixth factor (accounting for 5,8% of the variance) differentiates between victims on the basis of (not having) knowledge of possible involvement in sex- related work. This correlates with the type of job that was promised or expected and the presence of physical or mental abuse in the family of origin. The seventh factor (accounting for 5,0% of the variance) is abuse experienced in the family and it includes sexual, physical and mental abuse.

## Push and pull factors

The literature on trafficking in women (Aronowitz, 2001; De Ruyver and Niron, 2002) usually attempts to tackle the issue of so called *push* and *pull* factors that, depending on their impact on a situation and/or individuals, can facilitate the process of trafficking. The results of previous research carried out in the region have been described in the Stability Pact for South Eastern Europe Framework for Combating Trafficking in Human Beings.[23] The Stability Pact has identified the following *push* factors: unemployment, poverty, lack of education, gender discrimination and family violence; and the following *pull* factors: expectations of employment and a salary, for those

---

[23] The full text of the document can be downloaded from http://www.osce.org/attf/ attf_pa.pdf 27.02.2005.

involved in prostitution – high salaries, access to *western* material goods, improvements in social status and treatment, a glamorous life in Western Europe, demand for women for reproduction, demand for *exotic* prostitutes and a cheap labour force. In order to test the impact of *push* and *pull* factors related to trafficking in women in Bosnia and Herzegovina, multiple stepwise regression was carried out. The analysisshowed that a family's economic situation (poverty), unemployment and lack of education, viewed alone, do not represent *push* factors that facilitate trafficking in women in Bosnia and Herzegovina. However, the analysis showed that their impact significantly changes once family relationships are taken into consideration. In other words, unemployment and poverty do represent *push* factors, but only when a victim has problematic family relationships (e.g. due to alcoholism, drug addiction or a criminal environment).

As far as *pull* factors are concerned, the following factors were found to have the strongest impact: the kind of a job promised (expected), the way in which the victim learnt about the job (and who provided the information), who organised the journey and, for those who were aware of possible involvement in sex-related work, the potential client profile (foreigners).

These *pull* factors may explain why 27,4% of the victims (see Table 3) claimed to have a good relationship with their *owners*. It seems that traffickers are becoming aware that their *businesses* are likely to be more effective if they use their current *employees* as recruiters. Thus, they treat them well, pay them on a regular basis, allow them to see a doctor, allow them to go shopping and eventually allow them to travel home, where they are given the task of recruiting another woman.[24] In other words, it seems that the *business* is undergoing change. A further shift can be observed in relation to the location of prostitution: from nightclubs and bars to apartments and hotels.[25] These shifts towards more satisfactory working conditions may explain the decreased number of victims requesting assistance from the non-governmental sector.[26]

24 This was confirmed in an interview with one convicted trafficker. He stated: 'Today, there is a new practice. I send the old girl home. She calls after a few days saying she has two new girls. I send money for a train or a plane ticket and they travel to Romania or Hungary, where I pick them up'.

25 This was confirmed during the interview with one of the convicted traffickers.

## Conclusion

Despite the fact that only a few of the available findings on trafficking in women in Bosnia and Herzegovina have been presented here, some valuable conclusions can be drawn. First of all, Bosnia and Herzegovina serves as the destination country for women from Moldova, Romania and The Ukraine, as well as for women from other countries in the region, who arrive primarily via Serbia.[26]

Almost all women trafficked to Bosnia and Herzegovina are subjected to at least one form of abuse, including, but not limited to, sexual, physical or mental abuse. Their sexual exploitation provides their *owners* with enormous profits, which are apparently either invested in future trafficking or laundered and invested in legal activities (Adamoli et al., 1998). Although it is widely assumed in Bosnia and Herzegovina that international personnel, employed by a variety of humanitarian, governmental or non-governmental organisations, military or police forces, are the most frequent clients in night clubs and bars, and are therefore responsible for most of the demand for prostitution and trafficking in women, this study found most clients to be local people.

Anti-trafficking activities in the country, including problem-oriented police work, investigations, prosecutions and trials, together with legal reforms, have brought several changes in trafficking patterns. There are indications that some victims are now being treated much better than they were previously. As a result, they feel less exploited, and have even begun to serve as recruiters for their current *owners*. This is a possible explanation for the decrease in requests for help from victims as well as the geographic shift into private premises. These observations do not necessarily mean that the level of trafficking in women has decreased in Bosnia and Herzegovina. It should still be understood as a serious problem: it is one that has merely changed its appearance.

---

[26] It should not be argued that Bosnia and Herzegovina is not a source or transit country. On the contrary, it is defined as such in a number of studies (e.g. see Lehti and Aromaa, 2004).

## References

Adamoli, S., A., Di Nicola, E., Savona and P. Zoffi, *Organized crime around the world*. Helsinki, Heuni, 1998

Aronowitz, A., Smuggling and trafficking in human beings: the phenomenon, the markets that drive it and the organisations that promote it. *European journal on Criminal Policy and Research*, 2001, *vol. 9, no. 3*, 163-195

Budimlić, M., *Kompjuterski kriminalitet između teorije i prakse* (Transl.: Computer crime between theory and practice). Sarajevo, Fakultet krinalitičkih nauka, 2003

CSD, *Corruption. Contraband and organised crime in Southeast Europe*. Sofia. Center for the Study of Democracy (CSD), 2003

Ćopić, S., *Trafficking in human beings in the Balkan's post-war societies: legal reforms and practical issues*. Paper presented at British Criminology Society Conference 'Crossing Border', Keele, July 2002

De Ruyver, B., and N. Siron, Trafficking in migrants from a EU – perspective. In: De Ruyver, B., *et al.* (ed.), *Strategies of the EU and the US in combating transnational organised Crime*. Maklu, 2002

Escaler, N., *Keynote address. Report of the US-EU Trafficking in women seminar*. L'Viv, 9-10 July, 1998

Hajdinjak, M., *Smuggling in Southeast Europe: The Yugoslav wars and the development of regional criminal networks in the Balkans*. Sofia, Centre for the Study of Democracy (CSD), 2002

Korvinus, A. G., *Trafficking in human beings: first report if the Dutch National Rapporteur*. Den Haag, Bureau NRM, 2002

Korvinus, A. G., E.M.H. van Dijk, D.A.C. Koster and M. Smit, *Trafficking in Human Beings: supplementary figures. Second report of the Dutch National Rapporteur*. Den Haag, Bureau NRM, 2003

Lehti, M. and K., Aromaa, Trafficking in Women and Children in Europe. In: S. Nevala and K. Aromaa (eds.), *Organised crime, trafficking, drugs. Selected papers presented at the Annual Conference of the European Society of Criminology*. Helsinki, HEUNI, 2004

Lewis, R., Drugs, war and crime in the post-Soviet Balkans. In: V. Ruggiero, N. South and I. Taylor (eds.), *The New European Criminology: crime and order in Europe*. London/New York, Routledge, 1998

Nikolić-Ristanović, V., Illegal markets, human trade and transnational organised crime. In: P.C. van Duyne, J. Matjaž, K. von Lampe and J.L. Newell (eds.), *Threats and phantoms of organised crime. corruption and terrorism.* Nijmegen, Wolf Legal Publishers, 2004

Nikolić-Ristanović, V., War and crime in the former Yugoslavia, in V. Ruggiero, N. South and I. Taylor, *The New European Criminology: crime and order in Europe.* London/New York, Routledge, 1998

Obradović, V., *Trgovina ženama u Bosni i Hercegovini* (Transl.: Trafficking in women in Bosnia and Herzegovina), Sarajevo, Fakultet kriminalističkih nauka & US Embassy Sarajevo, 2004

UNDP, Albania Update on situation and responses to trafficking in human beings. In: *Trafficking in Human beings in Southeast Europe.* UNDP, 2003,

UNDP, Bosnia and Herzegovina Update on situation and responses to trafficking in Human Beings. In: *Trafficking in human beings in Southeast Europe.* UNDP, 2003

UNDP, Bulgaria Update on situation and responses to trafficking in human beings. In: *Trafficking in human beings in Southeast Europe.* UNDP, 2003

UNDP, Croatia Update on situation and responses to trafficking in human beings. In: *Trafficking in human beings in Southeast Europe.* UNDP, 2003

UNDP, Moldova Update on situation and responses to trafficking in human beings. In: *Trafficking in Human beings in Southeast Europe.* UNDP, 2003

UNDP, Romania Update on situation and responses to trafficking in human beings. In: *Trafficking in human beings in Southeast Europe*, UNDP, 2003

UNDP, Serbia and Montenegro, including the UN Administered Province of Kosovo, Update on situation and responses to trafficking in human beings. In: *Trafficking in human beings in Southeast Europe.* UNDP, 2003

UNDP, The Former Yugoslav Republic (FYR) of Macedonia Update on situation and responses to trafficking in human beings. In: *Trafficking in human beings in Southeast Europe.* UNDP, 2003

UNDP, *Trafficking in human beings in South Eastern Europe.* Sarajevo, UNDP, 2003

Wegner, W., *et al*, *Balkanski putevi droge i Bosna i Hercegovina*, Fakultet kriminalističkih nauka, Sarajevo, 2004

Williams, P., Trafficking in women and children: a market perspective, *Transnational organised crime*, Special issue on illegal immigration and commercial sex - The new slave trade, *vol. 3-4*, 1999

# Market regulation and criminal structures in the Bulgarian commercial sex market

*Philip Gounev, Tihomir Bezlov* and *Georgi Petrunov*[1]

## Introduction

Up until 1990 prostitution, as a social phenomenon, was almost completely absent in Bulgaria. Within less than two decades, between 25.000 and 30.000 Bulgarian women were annually involved in prostitution. Today the sex industry in Bulgaria is one of the main financial sources for organised crime (Bezlov *et al.* 2007). Furthermore, Bulgaria has become a major source of women trafficked for sexual exploitation to the EU, along with women from Ukraine, Romania, Russia and Nigeria (Europol 2008: 3).

The issue of involvement of Bulgarian women in prostitution came increasingly to prominence when some indirect data started to surface after 2001, indicating that the removal of visa restrictions for travel in the EU unleashed a large-scale export of women, possibly significantly increasing both the number of Bulgarian women involved in prostitution and the number that fall victims to trafficking.

Analysis of national data collected by UNODC (2009) shows that between 2005 and 2007, Bulgarian victims were amongst the *top five groups* of identified female victims of trafficking for the purpose of sexual exploitation in at *least thirteen* European countries for which there is data: Belgium, France, Germany, Netherlands, Greece, Poland, Slovenia, Czech Republic, Spain, Italy, Spain, Cyprus, and Croatia. Although the data from some countries are missing (France), some countries report only for some of the

1 The authors are respectively Research Fellow (philip.gounev@online.bg), Center for the Study of Democracy, Senior Analyst, Center for the Study of Democracy (tiho@online.bg) and Research Fellow, Institute of Sociology, Bulgarian Academy of Sciences (georgipetrunov@abv.bg).
This chapter was first published in: P.C. van Duyne, S. Donati, J. Harvey, A. Maljevic and K. von Lampe (eds.), *Crime, money and criminal mobility in Europe*. Nijmegen, Wolf Legal Publishers, 2009

years, or do not differentiate sexual and labour exploitation, it could be concluded that at least 300 victims were *identified* each year by government agencies or NGOs in the above countries. This indicates that possibly the actual number of victims is much higher.

If one uses the data on trafficked women as a proxy indicator to the number of women involved in prostitution, then the available data indicates that a small country like Bulgaria has become one of the biggest sources of prostitutes for EU sex markets. Estimates show that in total between as few as 8.000 (Petrunov 2009) or as many as 18.000 (Bezlov *et al.* 2007) Bulgarian women are involved European sex markets outside Bulgaria. In many countries (e.g. Belgium, the Netherlands, France, or Germany), the *absolute* number of detected victims often exceeds that of much larger source countries, such as Russia, Ukraine, China, or Nigeria. With the exception of Romania, (which is three times larger in terms of population) the number of Bulgarian women involved in prostitution in the EU exceeds that of any other East European country. Such disproportionate involvement raises the question as to what makes a country of 7,5 million inhabitants like Bulgaria a major source of women for EU's sex markets.

As other authors have already indicated (Vocks and Nijboer, 2000), and as is the case in Bulgaria, significant number of trafficked victims have been previously (voluntarily) involved in prostitution networks either in Bulgaria or abroad. Only, it is argued, after being 'exported' to work abroad, they fall victim to sexual exploitation.[2] This category is often overlooked by authors (e.g. Kara 2009), as the attention of past studies has focused on unsuspecting women from a different professional background as victims of trafficking for sexual exploitation.

Despite the significant number of journalist or policy reports on trafficking and prostitution in Eastern Europe (Beccucci 2008; Bruinsma and Meershoek 1999; Service Traité des Êtres Humains 2007), few have focused on linking the EU sex markets with those existing in the countries of origin. These analyses generally examine East European sex-trafficking operations or their operations in Western Europe, with little understanding of the market regulation mechanisms and criminal structures in the source countries in

2 What constitutes a victim is a contentious issue, and there are a range of legal definitions across Europe. In criminological terms there are also different degrees of victimhood – from being from a range of situations of physical abuse, to a range of unfair financial treatment, etc.

Eastern Europe. Some authors (Hughes and Denisova 2001: 52) have disregarded the link arguing that "prostitution is not a major activity of organised crime" inside the country of origin [The Ukraine].

This chapter aims to explain how the domestic sex industry in Bulgaria relates to the transnational prostitution networks in the EU. We argue that understanding the operation of transnational prostitution networks (or the trafficking for sexual exploitation) is only comprehensive if one understands the domestic prostitution market in the country of origin, as well as how it relates to the international market. The importance lies not only in analysing the links between the networks of criminal control but also in understanding the context and causes for women's involvement in prostitution; the mixture of cultural, social, economic and criminal factors. The analysis in this chapter focuses on the different segments of the domestic commercial sex market in Bulgaria. We explain how the methods of organised criminal control differ within the various market segments, and how women are moved through them: from street prostitution, brothels, elite prostitution, tourist resorts, or border towns to international markets.

International prostitution and sex-trafficking networks often overlap. The issue of victims is complex and there are various degrees to which a sex worker could be considered a victim depending on the level of coercion or deceit. Some authors (Jeffreys 2009, Petrunov 2009) argue that all women leaving their country to work abroad as prostitutes could be considered victims of trafficking for sexual exploitation. Petrunov (2009) takes this position based on the fact that almost all women working abroad do so for criminal structures or a pimp, and need to pay some sort of protection racket. The present paper focuses on the mechanisms of control in the domestic and foreign prostitution networks, while it ignores specific mechanisms of coercion and control of women who have been deceived and forced into prostituting themselves or held captive against their will.

## Methodology and sources

The present article draws on close to 160 semi-structured interviews that were conducted between 2007 and 2009 as part of two recent studies *Organised Crime in Bulgaria: Markets and Trends* (Bezlov *et al.* 2007) and *Key*

*Mechanisms of Money Laundering related to Trafficking of Human Beings* (Petrunov 2009).

Most of the interviews (about 140) took place in the context of the study on the trafficking of human beings for sexual exploitation. These interviews were face-to-face, and were conducted either by the authors of the present paper or through four social services non-profit organizations that work with street prostitutes on health related issues. In many cases the interviews went beyond a one-hour semi-structured interview. With some police officers, prostitutes, or pimps, a relation of trust was developed and numerous meetings were held. The sampling method of prostitutes and pimps was largely one of convenience, but an effort was made to have a wide geographic representation from around the country. In addition to Sofia, interviews were conducted in, Dobrich, Pleven, Pazardjik, Sliven, Blagoevgrad, Varna, Haskovo, Bourgas, Stara Zagora, Vratsa, and Yambol, as well as smaller towns (border or tourist), Botevgrad, Svoge, Sandanski, Bansko and Petrich, Borovets (a major ski resort) where larger prostitution networks were known to be present. Some of the respondents from public institutions (police, courts, prosecution) were officially appointed to be interviewed, following written requests by the authors. Additional investigators were then interviewed through personal connections that were established. In total, the following interviews took place:

- 37 law-enforcement officers: including the Head of Human Trafficking Department and an investigator in the same department, both at the Main Directorate Fighting Organised Crime in Sofia; three at the Sofia-city Directorate of Internal Affairs; five officers at district police departments (DPD); 22 officers across the country, including eight at Regional Directorates for Fighting Organised Crime; two DPD directors;
- Prosecutors: three at the Supreme Prosecution Office of Cassation, and eight outside of Sofia (in Sofia, Pazardjik, Plovdiv, Stara Zagora, and Haskovo);
- 12 investigators from the National Investigation Service; 19 representatives of the Commission for establishing of property acquired from criminal activity in Sofia, Plovdiv, Pazardjik, Haskovo, Blagoevgrad, Sofia-region;
- 37 prostitutes in Sofia, of which 12 were street prostitutes, five were former or present models, 11 working in 'club', three were working in bars; nine were working abroad;

- 57 prostitutes outside of Sofia, all of whom were working abroad; two transvestite prostitutes who were working abroad (in Plovdiv, Pazardjik, Blagoevgrad, Sandanski, Bourgas, Haskovo, and Botevgrad);
- Pimps: 14 in total: four of them working in Sofia; Most were low level, while three of them at the middle level, i.e. controlling a number of pimps (explained later in the paper);
- Others: two judges, two customs officers, two bar-tenders, five bouncers; seven non-profit organisation representatives in Sofia, Pazardjik, Plovdvi, Bourgas, Blagoevgrad, and Pleven.

For simplicity, below instead of listing the particular interviews, we indicate whether the source was law-enforcement interviewees ('LEI'), in which we include all officials (police, prosecutors, judges, customs) or market participant interviewees (MPI), in which we include, prostitutes, pimps, club owners, etc.[3]

## Social Factors and Prostitution

Similar to the factors listed by Vocks and Nijboer (2000) in their analysis of trafficking of women from East-Central Europe to the Netherlands, evidence indicates the same destructive cocktail of social and economic factors emerged in Bulgaria during the mid to late 1990s. These explain to a great extent the increased supply of women to the commercial sex sector as we will see below. Although, no single factor alone would provide an explanation, the interviews show that the combined effects of various factors was significant. Of importance were the following: a rise in unemployment, poverty, the disintegration of the educational system, the changes in the family structure, and in the change in attitudes to sex.

Poverty is one of the main factors that brought about a large number of women willing to enter the commercial sex business. In the interviews, the most commonly cited reason for entry into the profession (for both prostitutes and pimps) was unemployment and the lack of income to ensure even a minimal standard of living (MPIs). This finding is consistent with the rapid rise in unemployment that has occurred since 1990. For example, by

---

3 The multitude of interviews and the variety of texts make relating each single description or analytical point in the paper, a cumbersome and possibly distracting undertaking.

2001, the unemployment rate in Bulgaria reached 21%, its highest level since 1990. Significantly, within the female age group 15-30, in some regions of the country, unemployment reached some 50-60%. At the same time, visa restrictions for Bulgarians to the EU Schengen countries were lifted, with a resulting surge in emigration towards the EU. Income levels in Bulgaria were also amongst the lowest in Eastern Europe. At its lowest point in 1997, the average per capita income in the country fell to $30 per month. For the period 1997 – 2007, despite the improving economic situation and continuous economic growth and growing wages, average salaries particularly outside the capital Sofia remained between €100 and €150 per month.

Another set of factors relates to the crisis in Bulgaria's social institutions, particularly, education. Compared to other countries in Eastern Europe, for the period 1996-2000, Bulgaria had the highest school dropout rate among the 15-19 age group of about 38-39% on average. This can be compared with averages of 16% in Poland and 19% in Hungary and the Czech Republic (World Bank 2006; Ministry of Finance 2004).

Further to this, changes in Bulgarian family and society took place that were seen as conducive to the mass spread of prostitution. The 'nuclear socialist family' model that had been imposed before 1989 started to fall apart. Between 1990 and 2001, the proportion of children born out of wedlock increased from 12,4% to 42,1% of all newborns. The average age of marriage for women continually increased from 22 years in 1993 to 26 years in 2005, while divorce rates almost doubled between 1997 and 2004 (NSI 2003, NSI 2005).

With the end of Schengen visa restrictions in April 2001, Bulgarians wishing to work in the European Union gained an advantage over the rest of the Balkan states (in Romania, visa requirements were lifted in 2002) and the former Soviet Union countries. This access to the Schengen area, combined with soaring unemployment and extremely low income levels created an incentive for mass emigration. Whereas between 1991 and 2001, about 19.400 people left the country each year, in 2000-2003, the number of emigrants to the EU reached 100.000 per year. These new emigrants, however, had no legal right to work too, and as many suitable jobs had already been taken by other Central and East Europeans, they undertook a variety of illegal jobs in the (black labour) shadow economy. Many of the stories that we heard in the interviews were of women who started working as prostitutes after struggling for some time with a low-paid 'black' job. In this respect, the internet offered new opportunities for the anonymous search and offer of sex services.

Demand for sex, both in Bulgaria and the EU also needs to be considered. Growth in tourism or transit in commercial vehicles, both of which have direct effect on demand for paid sex in tourist resorts and on highways (see relevant sections below) was the greatest Bulgaria had ever experienced. For instance, between 2002 and 2004, the number of tourists visiting Bulgaria grew from 2,9 to 4,01 million visitors. Similarly, in the same short period the number of businessmen visiting Bulgaria grew from 180.000 to 270.000, giving surge to strip clubs (doubling as brothels) in the large cities. Before this period, international ski and sea resorts did not have prostitutes or strip clubs (i.e. brothels) before 1990 – they all do now.[4] The National Tourist Board (the largest tourist industry body) even publicly announced that is preparing jointly with the Ministry of Interior a draft legalisation of prostitution law (Petrov 2007).

Domestic demand has also been driven by changes in attitudes to sex in Bulgaria: porn (movies or magazines) or erotic dance clubs, both of which were banned during communism, exploded after 1989 and contributed to establishing a new sex culture where paying for sex was acceptable (Jeffreys 2009). The rise in demand for sex services across Europe was also a significant factor: in the largest market in Europe – Germany – in the beginning of the 1990s the numbers engaged in prostitution was estimated at least 50.000 to a maximum of 200.000 (Leopold *et al.*, 1993), but according to current estimates this number is now around 400.000 (Polzer 2007). In Great Britain, the Home Office indicated that there has been a significant increase in the size of the sex industry in recent years, estimating a market size of £1 billion annual turnover employing over 80.000 sex-workers. It further points to increased opportunities for sale and purchase of sex via sex clubs, the internet, or sex tourism (Home Office 2008). As Jeffreys (2009) shows, the increased demand for prostitution supports the trend towards industrialisation of commercial sex. Therefore, the increased supply of Bulgarian women to a large extent coincided with a growing demand for paid-sex in the EU.

---

4 For instance the third largest sea resort, Albena, listed on the stock exchange, and a majority owned by its CEO, has two strip clubs doubling as brothels.

## The prostitution market in Bulgaria

In addition to the socio-economic and value changes that took place in Bulgaria, a significant factor in the development of the sex market was the free-reign that organised crime has had in Bulgaria since 1990. The domestic, but in particular the foreign sex markets have provided one the most profitable criminal opportunities for Bulgarian criminals. Previous estimates have indicated that while the domestic sex market generates around €115 million per year, the Bulgarian prostitutes working across the EU generate at least €900 million per year[5] (Bezlov *et al*,. 2007: 139-140).

Within Bulgaria there are three strata of the sex industry – *street*, *club*, and *elite prostitution*. These three levels could be seen mostly in large cities but also have two important market locations – *tourist resorts* and *border towns*, both also meeting business demands. In addition a number of women use the internet or informal connections to work as amateur prostitutes. The latter aspect is described in detail in Bezlov *et al.* (2007: 141-143), and is not examined here, as the involvement of organised crime in amateur prostitution is much less pronounced. The largest market, though, is the international one: an estimated 70-80% of all prostitutes work (permanently or temporarily) abroad [MPI].

There are various ways in which these markets could be described. In the present chapter, we follow the typologies developed in Bezlov *et al.* (2007) and Petrunov (2009). There are three general ways in which participants in the above listed market segments are organised:

1. *Self-employed* – mostly observed amongst elite prostitutes, as well as amongst prostitutes working abroad that have managed to become independent. Amongst street prostitutes this is rarely observed. For example, Arsova (2000) shows that fewer than 5% of prostitutes surveyed in Bulgaria were working without a pimp.
2. *Partnership model* – a pimp with one or a few women, to whom he provides protection, and arranges infrastructure, including tackling administrative barriers in foreign countries. In this model pimps and

5 Depending on the assumptions made, this amount could be as much as €1,8 billion; Petrunov (2009) although estimating that 8.000 women work abroad as prostitutes, argues that their daily incomes are higher, concludes that they generate between €900 million and €1,3 billion. He argues that only 50% - 80% of the income is returned as profits, i.e. between €500 and 900 million.

prostitutes are partners, often intimate ones. These 'firms' often establish informal networks that are used to acquire market information (better opportunities) or protection from rivalling groups.

3. *Enterprise model* – in this model the prostitutes are hired as 'employees'. The employer could be the pimp or the brothel, or a legitimate business structure (massage parlour, bar, night-club). In this model, the 'employer' provides protection, provides the 'post', the clients, and any related infrastructure (transport, permits, housing). The enterprise model could be observed in all market segments. A 'firm' could consist of only a pimp and a prostitute, or a pimp with three or four women. A single owner running an enterprise with 10-15 prostitutes is already considered a big one.

What is common to all models is the reliance on the informal networks within the small towns around Bulgaria: informal networks of friends or family become the main way to recruit and control pimps *and* prostitutes, or to pressure women into prostitution, or to ensure the protection from law enforcement, politicians, or judiciary. Parts of these informal networks are culturally based while others, such as athletic schools (Bezlov *et al.* 2007: 14; Petrunov 2006: 305-307), 'boarding disciplinary schools', or orphanages, refer to a specific social phenomenon that exists in post-socialist Bulgaria.

Below we discuss the different market segments in an attempt to show how organised crime control mechanisms within each one function, and how the various levels are interrelated.

## Street and Highway Prostitution

Street and highway prostitutes only differ by the locations where they pick up clients, as well as by the specific occupations of their customers, mainly professional drivers in the case of highway prostitutes. In terms of their professional characteristics (reputation, practice, profits, clients, and level of protection), street and highway prostitutes occupy the lowest level in the stratification scale of prostitution. At the same time, this is the most conspicuous form of prostitution and most tightly controlled by the police.

There are several ways of recruiting street and highway prostitutes. One of the most vulnerable groups for recruitment is the Roma.[6] In some Roma families, there is a tradition of selling children to become prostitutes. All too often, the girls are resold from one pimp to another, with the price ranging from €250 to €500. Another method of recruitment is by kidnapping young women. These are mostly girls from broken families, from orphanages, girls who are vulnerable and cannot expect any help from family and friends. Lastly, some women enter prostitution on a voluntary basis, without being recruited by a pimp, but due to the need or desire for higher income.

Some women, enter this lowest level, after having started as elite prostitutes, but due to drug-habits or aging gradually move to brothels, and eventually to the street. Street prostitution could be used as type of punishment for brothel or on-call prostitutes (e.g. if they had tried to lie to their pimp).

The price of the service offered by street and highway prostitutes is usually negotiated with the customer and is in the range of 5 to 15 Euros[7] depending on the location, and above all, on the type of service requested by the customer.

What is particularly alarming in the case of street and highway prostitution is the fact that some of the girls are often very young, under 18 or even under 16 years of age. Furthermore, street and highway prostitutes are exposed to high risks and often fall victim to crimes, both on the part of the pimps and the customers. The victims rarely report the crimes to the police and do not seek legal protection.

According to our interviewees, with this type of prostitution, the pimps typically resort to two kinds of control. In the first type, the pimp supervises the girls at all times. He waits nearby and watches them; thus he sees each customer and immediately after the service, the prostitute hands over the money earned. Most of the time, the pimp gets 70% of the takings and the prostitutes keep 30%. Often, though, the women do not get paid for months, as they are in debt and need to pay-back for their 'post' arrangement, or having been fined for various reasons. The other form of control is exercised

6 The Roma are about 9% of Bulgaria's population and are dispersed across the country. All social and economic characteristics of the Roma minority point to the fact that they are the most disadvantaged part of the population. (UNDP 2003)

7 All prices quoted in the paper refer to the 2005 - 2007 period and do not reflect the 2008 inflation in prices, neither the fall in prices which started in early 2009 with the beginning of the economic crisis.

by setting a daily target amount that the prostitutes must earn, reinforced with sanctions, often involving the use of physical violence. The daily norm is usually 50 Euros and the pimp only comes by a few times a day to check on the girls and collect the money they have made. [MPI]

A single pimp usually has between two and six girls working for him, and sometimes even living with him. For a given pimp to work in a particular public place he needs to pay the police officers in the respective area, as well as a representative of the criminal ring operating there: all public areas identified in the interviews or through site visits were under the control of organised crime, and access to them was restricted only to pimps and prostitutes that pay these rings. The prostitutes related that they are allocated a daily amount, typically 10 Euros, to pay a racketeer who charges the fee for the particular location (e.g. Sofia). [MPI]

Each woman has a designated street location, a '*post*'. If the post is lost, it means less income, as she also loses the clients that know her. The new post is always a risk: it needs to have enough potential clients passing by, exposure to police patrols needs to be reduced.[8] Some street locations are highly controlled and organised. For instance, the Sofia ring-road[9] is serviced by 60 to 80 women brought daily from the nearby town of Botevgrad (60 km north-east of Sofia). The police control is somewhat impeded as the women reside permanently in a different town, which implies cooperation between police and prosecutor districts. Basically, the police in Botevgrad (which also lies on a major international highway) would push the women away from the Botevgrad district, and state in interviews that as long as the women work elsewhere, it is not their problem. The prostitution ring though is entirely operated out of Botevgrad [LEI].

The system of control is hierarchical, as there are several levels of pimps: (1) the pimp/guard/driver who exercises the immediate control and who often stays near to the work location; (2) pimps that control the various low-level pimps and deal with numerous women; (3) the ring-leader in Botevgrad; (4) a cashier that collects the money and is a middle man with (5)

8 Police patrols (on foot or by car) have fixed routes – therefore placing post on such routes is avoided.

9 As the ring road is one of the main places of street/highway prostitution in the country and in the capital, a number of interviews were conducted with prostitutes, pimps, and law-enforcement officers from Sofia and Botevgrad that were familiar with the situation.

one of the four or five big crime bosses in Sofia, who provide overall protection from law-enforcement or other crime groups.[MPI, LEI]

## Brothels (Club Prostitution)

This is the most common form of prostitution in Bulgaria, and could be described as mid-level between street and elite prostitution. It is encountered almost exclusively in the larger cities – Sofia, Varna, Plovdiv, Burgas or the tourist resorts. The interviews conducted showed that when speaking about 'clubs' the sex-workers had different types of sex-service locations in mind. They were referring either to (a) brothels in private apartments; (b) brothels operating under the guise of bars, nightclubs, strip bars, casinos, or restaurants, or (c) call girl /escort service;[10] These three categories differ only by their location, and the fact the last type does not offer on-site service. The first two (a) and (b) also offer call girls.

With club prostitution the pimps arrange the customers, rent the premises, and ensure protection from the police. They make sure the girls in their clubs go through medical checkups. They deal with the promotion of the establishment, running ads in newspapers, and, increasingly, on the Internet. Clubs use advertising not only to offer prostitutes but also to recruit them. Club prostitutes enjoy greater security than street and highway ones, both in terms of arrests and with respect to violence by customers and pimps. Few club prostitutes are resold by pimps, as is common practice for street prostitutes, and they are rarely forced to work. Most engage in this activity out of financial interest. Often they even approach the pimps themselves in order to work in their clubs and to secure their protection and support. The girls engaged in this type of prostitution are typically 18 to 30 years old. [LEI, MPI]

In a brothel there are usually three to four girls (on occasion as many as eight), a pimp and bodyguards. Sometimes they operate under the cover of massage parlours. In this way, the brothels sidestep the law, which neither explicitly bans, nor allows, prostitution. The hourly rates range from €15 to €35, with the price usually increasing by 50% for non-standard services. The

10 Law-enforcement respondents used more disparaging language calling all such establishment 'whore-houses'.

money is split 50 : 50 or 30 : 70 in favour of the pimp. In the big cities, there is an oligopoly model. In the capital, Sofia, for example, four to five owners control all brothels. [MPI]

Some brothels operate under the cover of strip-dance bars or nightclubs, with the prostitutes officially employed as dancers or waitresses, and the pimp acting as the manager. Almost all erotic/strip clubs in Bulgaria operate as brothels, although not all dancers in these enterprises are necessarily prostitutes. In some of the more luxurious establishments of this type, the prices exceed those for the private apartment brothels, and could reach €50 to €100.

## Elite Prostitution

Whereas street prostitutes are regarded by pimps as 'commodity' and those in the brothels as 'workers', the so-called elite prostitutes rank highest in the stratification scale. Its importance lies in the fact that in addition to being a lucrative business, it is used as a corruption instrument by organised crime or oligarchs to gain influence over politicians, magistrates, and representatives of multinational corporations. The elite prostitution is organised around modelling agencies, often owned by influential businesswomen, wives and girlfriends of 'oligarchs', organised crime figures, or former 'violent entrepreneurs' (Bezlov *et.al* 2007: 9).

The modelling agencies that offer elite prostitutes are primarily engaged in normal business activities, such as providing models for fashion shows, advertising campaigns, TV shows, promotions, film productions, or magazine photo shoots. Only some of the models that work for these agencies engage in prostitution. They are hired as models, but the boundaries between their modelling and escort-related duties are blurred, and they easily make the transition to paid sex services. Such a mixture of duties has also been described in Russia and The Ukraine (Belyi and Volkova 2008).

The elite prostitutes in such agencies are informally organised in two layers: a core permanent staff and a periphery of part-timers/temps. The first group gets the most lucrative assignments and has close relations with the managers and owners of the agencies. The 'peripheral' group engages in escort-type work at corporate functions or private parties, encompassing company events (e.g. office openings, presentations, trade shows). They are often hired by bars and discos to simply hang around and make the place more attractive to wealthy customers. However, with this job the girls are often not required to provide sex services.

The agencies invest significant resources in recruiting the core group, most often through beauty pageants held in larger towns. These events are preceded by an active advertising campaign throughout the surrounding villages or towns. The main target group consists of girls aged 15-16 but there are many older participants, as well. The selected girls have to move to the agency's 'modelling school', with all expenses covered by the agency. The transition from professional modelling to paid escort services and ultimately paid sex takes place on the basis of this economic and social dependency on the agency. Coercion and violence are seldom ever applied.

In addition to the modelling agencies a small nationwide network of pimps are also involved with 'luxury' prostitution. These pimps could rather be described as 'impresarios'. They are concentrated in several big cities around the country, but work independently connecting wealthy clients either to individual prostitutes or to modelling agencies. The agencies, though, have a major advantage, as they have access to international markets: international fashion shows or beauty pageants provide opportunities to reach extremely wealthy customers abroad.

Stories about girls provided for luxury yacht parties in the Mediterranean, or for cruises in Greece, Italy, and Spain often surface within political and business elites. Models for temporary work are also 'borrowed' from former Soviet Union countries, mainly from Ukraine, or nearby Serbia, if demand suddenly surges. One interviewee recounted the story of the foreign managers of a Bulgarian telecommunications operator who hired for an occasion several dozen girls from the 'luxury pool' of four agencies, while additional women were brought in from Serbia.

The rates of elite prostitutes start from € 250 per hour. They are typically engaged for the whole night rather than on an hourly basis. That is why the price can exceed € 1000. The split of the earnings are 50/50 or less for the prostitute.

## Resort Prostitution and Sex Tourism

One separate segment of the prostitution market is related to providing sex services to foreign tourists. In many respects this is a separate market, as it is limited to several resorts and three border towns, while the customers are largely foreign tourists.

Tourist resort prostitution is marked by seasonality and a migratory process: in summer prostitutes move from the big cities towards the Black Sea resorts – Sunny Beach and Golden Sands; and in winter they move towards the ski resorts – Borovets, Pamporovo, and Bansko. Three border towns Svilengrad (near Turkey), and Petrich and Sandanski (near Greece) serve cross-border sex-tourists. At all these locations the general market structure (street/brothel/elite) described in the preceding sections still exists, but the prices are twice as high.

Prostitution in the resorts is almost entirely under the control of individuals or networks of the former violent entrepreneurs [*sylovi groupirovki*], such as Club 777 or SIC[11], with the prostitutes and pimps operating as 'employees' of the respective ring. Resort prostitution can be a key factor contributing to a recent trend of Bulgaria evolving into a general sex tourism destination. This may be due to two circumstances: the 'product' is delivered straight to the tourist clients and some hotel owners have also interests in that business.

## International markets: the 'export' of women

The domestic market, as noted above is much smaller and less profitable than the West European one. Its organisational structures are closely related to the ones associated with the export of women (and men). In the early 1990s the first Bulgarian pimp networks were formed in Hungary and the Czech Republic which became the first destinations for export of prostitutes. The geographic proximity, higher profits, and easier access (visas were still needed for Western Europe) made them attractive. Bulgarian pimps made use of the foothold (in terms of local connections, knowledge, travel channels, even

11 For more in violent entrepreneurs see Bezlov *et al.* (2007), CSD (2004), Tzvetkova (2007), Gounev (2006), Petrunov (2006).

'infrastructure', such as sharing apartments) put in place by Bulgarian car thieves, burglars, and smugglers [LEI, MPI].

The first cases of 'exported' prostitutes often concerned women accompanying migrant criminals looking for a better life. Many were not prostitutes in Bulgaria but out of necessity or lured by the higher incomes became involved. Once it was realized that risks were low and profits high, some criminals started to specialise in aggressively recruiting girls from Bulgaria. Bulgarian prostitutes worked mostly in locations close to the borders with Germany and Austria, where sex tourism was most active and profits were higher. By 1993-94, the first groups of pimps and prostitutes started to settle in more liberal countries like the Netherlands and Belgium, or in countries bordering Bulgaria such to Macedonia and Greece. In the mid 1990s, prostitution networks gradually expanded to Austria, Germany, Italy and Spain. [LEI, MPI]

With the removal of visa restrictions to Schengen countries in 2001, number of Bulgarian prostitutes working abroad sharply increased with Belgium (see figure below), the Netherlands, Spain, Italy, Germany, and Greece becoming the main 'export' destinations.

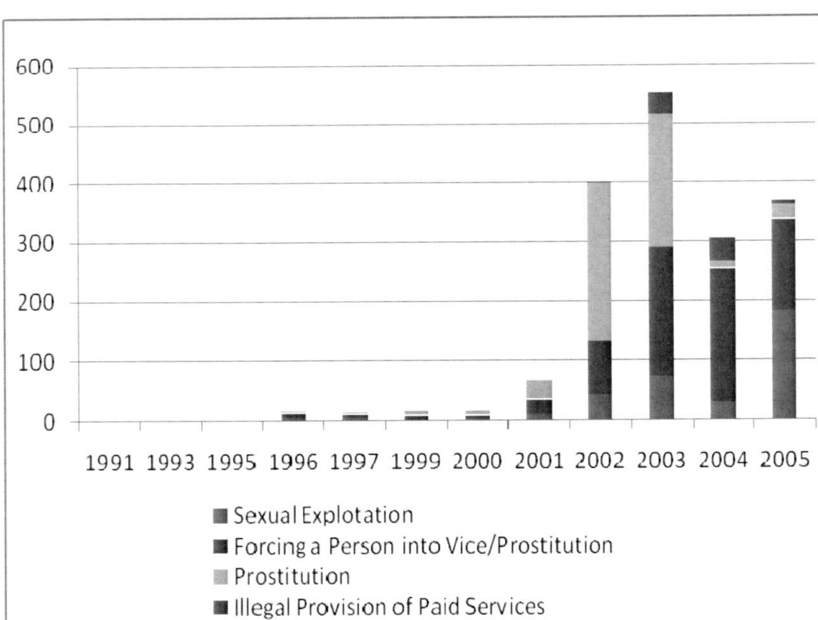


*Figure 1. Belgium: Registered crimes committed by Bulgarians (Source: Federal Ministry of Interior, Belgium)*

One of the key characteristics of the export business was that prostitution rings from particular towns in Bulgaria exported women to particular countries, often even to 'sister' towns abroad. In many respects, the partitioning of West-European territories (see below) is conditioned by the need to maintain constant communication with the towns/regions where the pimps come from. The Bulgarian source locations are usually either a single larger town or several smaller towns, as women are recruited from surrounding villages and small towns. Based on interviews [LEI, MPI] and other sources (Belgian Police, 2007: 27-46, Bulgarian National Anti-trafficking Commission 2008: 32) the following known 'sister' cities are:

- Sliven – Belgium/Holland (Brussels/Groningen)
- Blagoevgrad – Spain/Italy/Greece (Barcelona/Canary Islands/Milan)
- Pazardjik – France/Belgium/Spain/Germany (Brussels/Marseille/ Bordeaux /Cologne/Milan
- Gabrovo – Spain (Valencia)
- Rousse – Italy/Spain/France (Charleroi)
- Pleven – Spain (Madrid)
- Varna region (incl. Razgrad and Dobrich) to Germany/Czech Republic/ Scandinavian countries.

Little is known about the backgrounds of this geography of prostitution migration to provide a specific explanation. One underlying reason for such territorial distribution is that the locally established criminal structures in Bulgaria engage in a range of other criminal activities in the respective regions in Western Europe: drugs trafficking/burglary/car-theft/currency or credit card fraud. Therefore, it is plausible that the foreign localities of these criminal activities determine the migration of prostitution rings. Such synergies facilitate remote control of prostitutes and pimps in the respective foreign markets.

The analysis of the export flows shows that the *eight* cities and towns with an established sex-industry are the main supply sources for export of prostitutes to the EU. They function as 'wholesale export distribution centres' that concentrate women and pimps from the entire country, willing to work abroad. For example, cities such as Varna and Bourgas (situated respectively nearby the resorts of Golden Sands and Sunny Beach) concentrate prostitutes from all over the country who come, particularly, in the summer months. Varna, in particular, attracts women and pimps from the nearby towns of

Dobrich, Shumen, and Silistra. In southern Bulgaria, Plovdiv and Pazardzhik attract women from Asenovgrad, Haskovo, Kardjali, Smolyan, or Dimitrovgrad. Prostitutions rings based in the towns of Sliven and Pleven recruit women from the surrounding villages and smaller towns. The markets in these cities are also related to each other and supply and demand are balanced. For instance women are transferred from the towns to the ski resorts in the winter, and then to sea resorts in the summer. Supply is even fine-tuned, as women could work during the week in a nearby city and transferred for the weekend to the resorts to meet weekend demand.

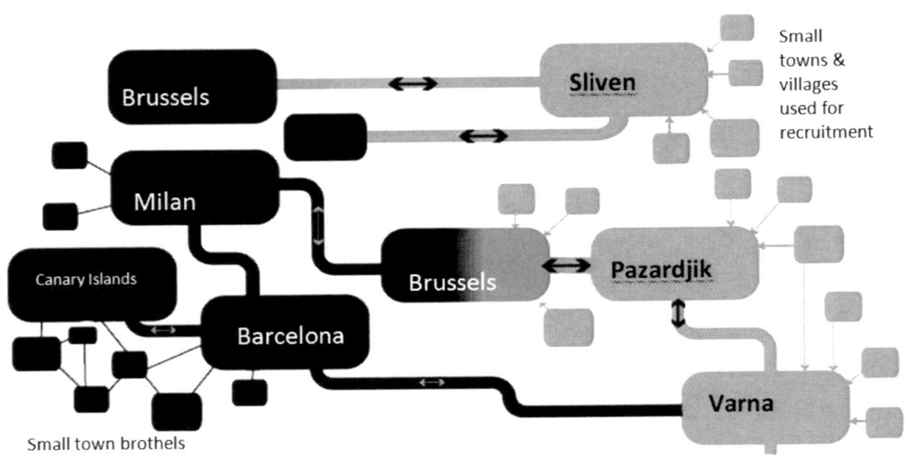


*Figure 2. Connecting domestic and foreign markets – a sample scheme*

Large cities also function as intermediary export centres: a girl to be exported from Dobrich to Strasbourg, Mannheim, or Oslo works for some time in Varna and Sofia, while waiting for a place to be arranged. This model of inter-connected prostitution rings and markets makes it possible to ensure control of the pimp networks that recruit, export, and money-launder the proceeds. The roles of the various players in the market are detailed in the next section.

In the past year (2008), with the increased movement and contacts that pimps and criminal networks have established in Western Europe, even direct export from smaller towns has become possible [MPI]. The capital or the larger cities like Varna or Sliven that served as 'export' centres could be losing their significance to pimps and prostitutes in smaller towns. They would still remain important, though, as their local markets or established networks will continue to provide the main supply of women to work abroad.

## Organised crime and control of the prostitution market

Organised criminal control is observed in all segments of the prostitution market. In Bulgaria, prostitution without the involvement of pimp networks or of club owners is practically impossible. Despite the fact that the sex-market could be described as gray or illegal, corrupt local law-enforcement and municipal authorities have regular interactions with this business. Therefore, they could play an important role in the regulation and organisation of the market. In addition, the methods of control differ across ethnic lines, as Roma and Turkish-Roma often run family based prostitution rings (Belgian Police 2007).

Shelley's (2003) description of the organisation of criminal control in the prostitution market has been adapted in Bezlov *et al.* (2007) and Petrunov (2009) to be of three types:

- a *hierarchical* model: one boss uses controls a large number of prostitutes and controls them through several levels of intermediaries and pimps, using violence and extortion.
- a '*natural resource*' model: a boss who imposes a protection racket on the self-employed, the small and family businesses.
- an *entrepreneurial* model, when the criminal bosses act as entrepreneurs at some or all stages.

*The hierarchical model*

This model could be described as one in which a local boss controls the major pimps and through them, part of the pimp networks in a given area. The boss operates usually at a town or regional level. For instance, in Sofia there it is known that there are four such bosses: in Varna there are two, in Bourgas three and in Sliven four bosses. The role of the boss is to protect the network from rivals and law-enforcement. Each pimp pays his dues to a local town/regional boss.

As the present research project could not effectively reach beyond the mid-level of the rings to elucidate their operations and the related finances, it is difficult to speak about a single business model of the hierarchical prostitution ring. There are many factors that influence the earnings sharing arrangements with the different players: the market segment (street/club/elite), the particular foreign market (risks in countries might differ depending on legality/other market participants); size of the ring (larger hierarchical structures with many levels need different control mechanisms); place where the ring is headquartered in Bulgaria (in smaller town corrupting the local police, government administration or judiciary might be a necessity; in the capital or bigger cities with several prostitution rings, these corruption arrangements are less clear).

At the first level, the prostitutes share 50 to 70% of their earnings with the person authorised to collect the money at the particular location or town (the supervising girls, pimps, 'cashiers', club owners, etc.). The people at this lowest level control leave a share to themselves, and that varies between street prostitution or club owners. The rest of the money goes to the next level. Depending on the size of local-regional market a different number of layers exist, however, as at the national level six to seven individuals receive shares of the profits from the lower levels.

The key to the efficient operation of this system is the use of violence. In addition, in all major 'supply towns', one observes a symbiosis between prostitution ring leaders (and pimps at all levels) and the local authorities, police, prosecutors and even judges. [MPI]

*The natural resource model*

In this model (Shelley, 2003) the boss treats the prostitutes and their pimps as a local 'natural resource' that he simply exploits. Whether they work independently or in small partnerships/firms and networks, the boss extorts money from them and in return provides some protection from rivals and authorities. The boss could exploit these 'natural resources' regardless of whether he runs his own prostitution ring. Again the payment arrangements of this model are fluid and vary between towns.

*The enterprise model*

This has developed in recent years with the increased internationalisation of prostitution networks. Within an enterprise framework criminal entrepreneurs do not rely structurally on violence and threat but on market forces and economic logic. Abroad, where the Bulgarian criminal structures have little control over the local markets or impact on local law enforcement and judiciary, the girls working within an enterprising prostitution ring often receive higher and more stable income than those who try to work independently. Therefore, there are strong incentives for the women to remain within the system.

## Roles and actors in international prostitution networks

The main roles within the system of control and operation of the sex-industry are laid out below. Some of variations of the functions exist in the cases of trafficking, but often the same individuals may operate in both systems.

Below we focus only on the specific roles and responsibilities related to the *international* component of prostitution networks. As with the case above, many of these roles would also overlap in networks that traffic women. Some mixture of responsibilities could be observed in smaller networks, when one person takes on several roles. Here again, we do not examine the ethnicity-based differences in the roles that could be observed amongst Roma, Turk-Roma, or Bulgarian networks.

The roles are the following.

*'New flesh hunter'*

This is a person recruiting girls in Bulgaria for the purpose of working abroad. Unlike the cases of trafficking, here, the job offer (usually) makes it quite clear that the work involves prostitution. With smaller prostitution rings, the hunter and the pimp are often one and the same person. It is believed that 'hunting' requires special skills and talent: "to judge a woman in just a few minutes whether she would bring sufficient earnings, and will not create problems" is not easy [MPI].[12] The majority of 'hunter' recruits only in Bulgaria, but recruitment amongst girls that are already abroad is also known. The girls who work regular jobs are recruited in prostitution when they are offered rooms for which they cannot pay or a better job, for which they need to pay in advance to get it, giving them loans or gifts. One scheme is to recruit their friend or even a boyfriend, who eventually begins to act as their pimp.

'*Racketeers*' and '*bodyguards*'

The racketeer takes a percentage of the earnings and makes it extremely difficult for women to work without pimps. In exchange they protect the girls. In brothels, clubs, call girls and any non-street prostitution 'bodyguards' are used to protect the girls, as well as performing the role of drivers and cashiers.

'*Mules*'

The role of the 'mules' has changed significantly in recent years. Before 2007 they were guides who took the sex workers to the targeted respective country, usually by minivan, in which case they were often the drivers, but sometimes by regular coach lines when the guides accompany the girls. After 2007, when Bulgaria joined the EU, and borders controls were further diminished, they were probably used only in cases of trafficking. In other cases the prostitutes appear to usually travel on their own.

*Supervisors*

Supervisors ('Madam', 'first girl') are usually promoted prostitutes watching how much money each girl working for a given pimp network is making, whether she reports all her earnings, if she is making unauthorised calls, if she has any risky customers.

---

12 As one of the most successful pimps interviewed stated 'to break' (change the motivation) of a girls that does not have money-problem, and which is pretty, and which has all the chances of having a nice husband and family, you need to be really good. Only the real professionals in the industry could to this". [MPI]

*Pimp*

Pimps work at up to three to four different levels, depending on the complexity of the prostitution ring. At the lowest level, they are the person who picks up the girls upon arrival and assigns them to the prostitution locations agreed in advance. This low level pimp *might* interface with someone at a higher level who controls several lower pimps. This person, who is also primarily based in Bulgaria, is the one that makes the prearrangements and usually sells the 'posts' (e.g. window display/bar post) to the new market entrants coming from Bulgaria. They could also be engaged in coordinating the recruitment and shipment of additional women to pimps already functioning in the international market. He is authorised to manage a certain number of girls himself, to keep records of the payments by smaller entrepreneurs gravitating toward the structure, and to collect the protection racket from the small independent businesses. [MPI; LEI]

*Money carrier*

Although money transfer systems, like Western Union, remain the most common way to repatriate profits and to pay those further up the chain of control, drivers of minivans or bus-drivers that transport prostitutes are occasionally used for moving money

*Investors/launderers*

These functions are often performed by trusted businessmen and lawyers responsible for investing and legalizing the repatriated funds. Depending on the size of the structure, they may serve one or more organisations. The role of money laundering and the investor has proven quite important (Petrunov 2009) for the remote control over pimp networks. Many pimps working within hierarchical networks are forced into laundering their money through the network's money-launderers. [MPI]

*The boss*

At the very top of the organisation is the boss, based in Bulgaria and who controls the other participants in the scheme. Prostitution is typically just one of his businesses, and all individuals that were identified as 'bosses' have legitimate enterprises. The main towns identified in the beginning of this chapter that work as 'export centres', have one or more such bosses. They are not concerned with day-to-day operations. The person(s) in charge of the international dimension is the higher level 'pimp-boss' described above.

While in small towns/regions, one observes a monopoly or oligopoly (one to three big bosses and about a dozen small ones) in large towns, and in particular in Sofia the highest levels are difficult to describe. The networks and hierarchical structures are controlled by groups of people, one could describe as 'syndicates': they take control over the sections of the local market, including an entire resort for example, or the export.

## Conclusion

The present chapter has examined the various levels of the prostitution market in Bulgaria. The described structures and functioning of the domestic and foreign markets of the sex trade in many respects provide a static picture of the state of Bulgarian prostitution. Yet the processes in this country have been evolving dynamically during the period after 2001 and since the accession to the European Union in January 2007, thus many of the outlined characteristics and mechanisms have been undergoing changes.

The main contribution of this work is that it demonstrates how the prostitution market in the source country and destination markets interrelate. The importance lies in the interrelated methods of control and overlapping networks for recruitment of women.

The 'geographic patterns' of prostitution rings are important from the law-enforcement or policy point of view. They allow one to narrow the analysis focusing on the towns and regions where these rings recruit and operate. The analysis shows that the local criminal elite in small (by European standards) towns has monopolised and has made prostitution a mass and, to a large extent, socially acceptable phenomenon. It shows how social, economic, and in some cases cultural factors contribute to a situation, where many woman feel that prostitution has become an inevitable, but economically sound choice.

The described mechanisms of organised crime control also explain why to a large extent Bulgarian organised crime does not get involved (or does to a very limited extent) in the control or trafficking of women that are not Bulgarian. For instance, women from Ukraine or Moldova, both of which are a major source of trafficking victims in the EU are geographically close and have fairly sizeable ethnic Bulgarian minorities in Bessarabia. These could theoretically become involved with Bulgarian prostitution rings or fall victim to trafficking, yet there is no evidence that this has taken place.

Many questions and issues elaborated in this paper still need to be studied through more empirically based research. The social and economic conditions that have contributed to the increasing willingness of Bulgarian women to enter into prostitution need to be examined in a more systematic way. The ethnic and cultural difference between Bulgarian and (Turkish) Roma run prostitution networks are not well understood. Specific studies based on observations in destination countries do not exist yet, and information as to how Bulgarian prostitution networks relate to local markets in destination countries still suffer from being based solely on accounts of law-enforcement sources or only Bulgarian market participants.

Prostitution will continue to be a priority area of activity for organised crime groups in Bulgaria. Even though sex-industry revenues fell due to the economic crisis in 2008-2009, few other criminal areas remain as lucrative for the Bulgarian criminal. While major illegal drugs routes have by-passed Bulgaria, domestic demand for drugs and stolen cars in Bulgaria remains modest. Further, with the collapse of the real-estate market, prostitution is likely to remain a key area of organised criminal activity.

The mutual penetration and interaction between local and international organised crime structures will intensify. Prostitution rings are likely to remain associated with other criminal activities, as they provide good inroads into underworlds of foreign criminal markets, such as drugs or car-theft.

## References

Arsova, T., *Prostitution and sex workers in Bulgaria: Analysis of the situation and the risk with regards to HIV/AIDS/STDs*. Sofia: Health and Social Development Foundation, 2000

Belgian Police, *Image annuelle 2007 (chiffres 2005/2006): Exploitation sexuelle et exploitation au travail*, Brussels: Belgian Police, 2007

Beccucci, S., New players in an old game: The sex market in Italy. In: D. Siegel and H. Nelen (eds.), *Organised crime: Culture, markets and policies.* New York: Springer, 2008

Belyi, M. and N. Volkova, N., Beauties and beasts: in Russia the modeling business looks ever more criminal, *Noviye Izvestia,* 2008, 27.10.2008

Bezlov, T., P. Gounev, G. Petrunov, E. Tzenkov and M. Tzvetkova, *Organised Crime in Bulgaria: Markets and Trends.* Sofia: Center for the Study of Democracy, 2007

Bruinsma, G. and G. Meershoek, Organised crime and trafficking in women from Eastern Europe in the Netherlands. In: P. Williams (ed.), *Illegal migration and commercial sex. The new slave trade.* London and Portland: Frank Cass, 1999

Bulgarian National Anti-trafficking Commission (2008) *Report on the activity of the national commission for combating trafficking in human beings for 2007,* (http://antitraffic.government.bg/)

Center for the Study of Democracy, *Partners in crime: The risk of symbiosis between the security sector and organised crime in South-East Europe,* Sofia: CSD, 2004

Dencheva, R., G. Spirov, K. Gilina, D. Niagolova, G. Pehlivanov, N. Tsankov, Epidemiology of syphilis in Bulgaria, 1990–1998. *International Journal of STD & AIDS,* 2000, vol. 11, 12: 819–822.

Europol, *Trafficking in human beings in the European Union: A Europol perspective,* The Hague, 2008

Gounev, P., Bulgaria's private security industry. In: A.Bryden, and M. Caparini (eds.), *Private Actors and Security Governance,* Lit & DCAF, 2006

Home Office, *Tackling the demand for prostitution: a review.* London: Home Office. 2008

Hughes, D. and T. Denisova, The transnational political criminal nexus of trafficking in women from Ukraine', *Trends in Organized Crime,* 2001, vol. 6, *No. 3 & 4, Spring /Summer 2001*

Jeffreys, S., *The industrial vagina.* New York: Routledge, 2009

Kara, S., *Sex trafficking: Inside the business of modern slavery.* New York: Columbia University Press, 2009

Leopold, B., E. Steffan and N. Paul, *Dokumentation zur rechtlichen und sozialen Situation von Prostitutierten in der Bundesrepublik Deutschland, Schriftenreihe des Bundesministeriums für Frauen und Jugend.* Band 15, 1993

Ministry of Finance, *Overview of Public Expenditures: Education - State, Problems, and Opportunities*, 2004

National Investigation Service. 2005. *Genezis, razvitie i projavni formi na organizirana prestapnost v Balgaria*. Sofia, 2005

National Statistical Institute, *Status, trends and issues of the birth rate in the Republic of Bulgaria*, Sofia: NSI, 2003

National Statistical Institute, Statistical Yearbook. Sofia: NSI, 2005

Petrunov, G., Organized Crime and Social Transformation in Bulgaria. *European Journal of Sociology/Archives Europeennes de Sociologie/Europaeisches Archiv Fuer Soziologie*, 2006, vol. 47, 2: 297-325.

Petrunov, G., *Key Mechanisms of money laundering related to trafficking of human beings*, Sofia: RiskMonitor, 2009

Petrov, K., *Ministry of Interior and the National Tourist Board to work jointly on a draft legalisation of Prostitution Law*, Mediapool, 13 February 2007

Polzer, W., German prostitution law has failed, no reduction in crime through improved legal status. *Journal Chretien*, 24 January 2007 (http://www.spcm.org/Journal/spip.php?article5939)

Sarang, A. and J. Hoover, *Sex work, HIV/AIDS, and human rights in Central and Eastern Europe and Central Asia*. The Central and Eastern Europe Harm Reduction Network, 2005

Shelley, L. Trafficking in women: The business model approach. *Brown Journal of International Affairs*, 2003, vol. X, Issue I

Service Traité des Êtres Humains, *Exploitation sexuelle et exploitation au travail*. Bruxelles, 2007

Tzvetkova, M., Aspects of the evolution of extra-legal protection in Bulgaria (1989–1999), *Trends in Organised Crime*, 2008, *11*, 326–351.

Trud Daily, *Petkanov counts 4611 prostitutes*, Trud Daily, 31 May 2003.

UNDP, *Avoiding the dependency trap*, UNDP, 2003

UNODC, *Global Report on Trafficking in Persons*, 2009.

World Bank, *A policy note, Bulgaria – Education and skills for the knowledge economy*, 2006

# Trafficking in humans and illegal economy in war and post-war society

*Vesna Nikolić-Ristanović*[1]

## Introduction

Socio-economic changes related to globalisation and neo-liberal capitalism, instability of social status and overall insecurity exist in almost all contemporary societies. In addition, all countries worldwide are facing recession and increasing unemployment, but also the expansion of irregular and illegal markets and the incorporation of informal economies into formal ones (Ruggiero, 2001:64; European Commission, 2007). The distinction between legal and illegal activities became in general less clear and visible than before.

However, the speed and accumulation of change and related difficulties in everyday life of people are especially emphasised in transition societies and in the societies affected by war. The overall social disorganisation resulted from war and transition is followed by the disorganisation of economic relations, so that the former legal economy is replaced with an informal, i.e. illegal one.[2]

---

1 Vesna Nikolić-Ristanović is director of the Victimology Society of Serbia and professor at the Faculty for special education and rehabilitation and Police academy in Belgrade. E-mail:vnikolic@Eunet.rs
This chapter was first published in: P.C. van Duyne, S. Donati, J. Harvey, A. Maljevic and K. von Lampe (eds.), *Crime, money and criminal mobility in Europe*. Nijmegen, Wolf Legal Publishers, 2009

2 It is necessary to make distinction between two types of illegal economies, i.e. criminal markets (Van Duyne, 1996: 341): illegal trading in goods and services that are themselves forbidden, i.e. whose trade is strictly forbidden (e.g. drugs and people) and illegal trading in otherwise legal goods and services (e.g. goods such as cigarettes, liquor or petrol and other scarce goods during embargo in Serbia in 1990s). This latter form of crime market is sometimes called informal market or informal (hidden or shadow) economy (UNDP, 1998: 4; Ruggiero, 2000: 66). The hidden economy is the part of the larger context of the shadow economy, which is expanding not only in developing, but in developed countries as well. For example, in most of OECD countries, shadow economy was far below 10 per cent of GDP in 1970, while in 1990s it increased in some of them, such as Belgium,

During a war, an informal economy offers not only scarce goods but also various jobs related to the functioning of the illegal market. In this way the illegal economy compensates for the (non-existent or inefficient) formal economy. However, the same situation may continue to exist in a post conflict period as well, and its duration usually depends on the speed with which institutions are repaired, and trust in them regained.

Structural factors related to war and its aftermath play a significant role in the development of various illegal markets, including illegal labour and identity documents markets, as well as in trafficking and smuggling of humans. This is directly related to overall criminalisation of war-affected societies as well as to the status of anomie resulting from war (Nikolić-Ristanovic, 1998). The existence of a shadow economy, which frequently develops during war, in combination with economic mismanagement and corruption that can occur during and afterwards, is also one of the main contributing factors to long-term loss of a clear distinction between legal and illegal economic activity.

All of the above-mentioned factors create conditions for recruitment of both victims and offenders of trafficking in humans. In spite of that, trafficking in humans is often treated as an isolated phenomenon, independent of its close connection with structural problems. These frequently take the form of poverty; an increasing gap between rich and poor; unemployment; social exclusion; as well as gender discrimination and other forms of violence against women and children (Nikolić-Ristanović, 2005: 14; Aromaa and Lehti, 2007).

The impact of these factors on victimisation is identified and explored in a number of academic works, while their impact on criminalisation is almost completely neglected and under researched.[3] As a consequence, the connection between structural victimisation and criminal actors is hidden. Simplified pictures call for simplified solutions which are rarely effective. Without required nuance, no prospect for effective solution of the problem is likely to emerge. Thus, in order to improve understanding and help develop more efficient programs against trafficking in humans, it is necessary that the

---

Denmark, Italy, Norway, Spain and Sweden to almost 20 per cent of GDP (Schneider & Ernste, 2000:41, 44).

3 This may be the consequence of the fact that so far research has dealt primarily with victims, while research interest only recently shifted toward traffickers. As a consequence, available knowledge about traffickers is in general very poor.

relationship between structural victimisation and criminal economic activities is explored.

From the above perspective, this paper aims to explore the relationship between structural victimisation and criminal behaviour of traffickers. This work aims to answer the following questions:

1. What causes people, who once used to be law abiding, to look for jobs/income within the informal economy?
2. How does acceptance of a job within the informal economy lead people to self-criminalisation by in particular, becoming involved with smuggling and trafficking in humans?
3. What is the impact of war and transition on the above two questions?

The points raised in the previous sections and questions raised above are relevant for most countries in the Balkan region, but in this chapter I will address them for the Republic of Serbia. By analysing the conditions under which individual choices and motivations are created in war and post-war societies, the intention is to contribute to a better understanding of trafficking in humans in Serbia. This work will consider their actions both as a form of organised and professional crime, as well as a strategy for survival. This latter especially includes exploration of criminalisation factors which are seen to be directly connected with difficulties resulted from war. These may include international economic sanctions, slow reestablishment of trust and rule of law, transition from communism to neo-liberal capitalism, as well as with their gender implications – gender inequality and gender-based violence.

Taking as a starting point research findings from a study of the illegal economy and trafficking in humans in Serbia, during and after the ethnic wars in 1990s, it will be argued that traffickers committing these crimes view their actions as part of normal economic activity, which can be considered as a continuation of long-term illegal activities that are largely accepted as coping (economic) strategies during and after the war.[4]

---

[4] Similarly, the close connection between the conflict and criminalisation of the economy in Bosnia is also stressed by Lalic, 2007:85, and Andreas, quoted in the same work. The economic heritage of the conflict affects also post conflict reconstruction. In addition, the transition had an impact as well. Although institutions were eroded earlier and informal economy existed before the war as well, in Serbia as well as in other transitional countries, it became dominant within economy when void was filled by the destruction of one system and the development of another (Marinković, 2006).

The analysis is based on earlier research into the impact of war on crime in general (Nikolić-Ristanović, 1998), and, especially, on work that dealt with the impact of war on trafficking in humans as the form of illegal market, where people are treated as commodities (Nikolić-Ristanović, 2003).5 In addition, part of the findings from the Victimology Society of Serbia research "Male victims of trafficking" are included. These are, based on life story interviews with 11 traffickers (6 men and 5 women) and 11 victims, as well as on interviews with 82 professionals, on reports on trials and criminal files. Life history interviews focused on the exploration of life stories in changing social circumstances (course of life interviews). Both traffickers and victims were interviewed in prison. Traffickers were imprisoned for trafficking and smuggling of men and/or women, while victims were imprisoned because of illegal border crossing or illegal stay in Serbia (Nikolić-Ristanović, 2009).[6]

The general theoretical perspective of this analysis is an economic approach to the explanation of crime, as well as an understanding of organised crime as criminal enterprise, which represents the counterpart of

5 In my earlier research I dealt with trafficking in humans as an illegal market from the perspective of victims (victimological perspective), while the focus of my interest in this paper is moved to the perpetrator, i.e. to trafficking of humans as an illegal labour enterprise (criminological perspective). However, both perspectives are connected by structural victimisation and its impact on both victimisation and criminalisation in postconflict and transitional societies.

6 The sample included the perpetrators, convicted individuals who, at the time of the data collection, were serving their prison sentences in the Penal- Correctional Institute in Sremska Mitrovica and the Penal-Correctional Institute for women in Požarevac and who agreed to be interviewed by researchers. The sample also included the potential victims of male trafficking (adults and minors, domestic citizens and foreigners), who, in the period in which we conducted the phase of data collection, were in prison in Subotica, serving sentences related to the administrative offences of the unlawful crossing of the state border, and the unlawful stay in Serbia. The questionnaire for interviewing the potential victims as well as the questionnaire intended for interviewing the perpetrators are similarly designed, and as such they were used to conduct the life history interviews, along with the monitoring of the changes in the course of their lives that occurred as a result of the social changes (especially transition and war). This is how we wanted to obtain a deepened understanding of the social factors that influence the exposure to the victimisation and the criminalisation by male trafficking as well as of their mutual interconnectedness.
Using the life story approach, the questions were designed in such a way as to enable us to investigate how the family situation, gender socialisation, economic transition, i.e. the crisis and the war, as well the social marginalisation can influence men becoming victims of trafficking in people. Also, this approach enabled us to identify the critical phases in one's life route of both the victims and the traffickers in the moments when the important choices/decisions were made and also to obtain a more complete picture of male trafficking in Serbia and the recommendations about its prevention. The data obtained in this way were analysed using qualitative analyses.

legal enterprise. Trafficking in humans is thus explored primarily from the perspective of the labour market and as a form of criminal enterprise, where job, status and power distribution is organised in a similar way to the organisation of legal enterprise. This perspective questions prevailing policy approach to trafficking in humans in post-war societies, which prioritise criminal law as an appropriate solution.[7] I will argue for alternatives that may tackle and minimise sources of recruitment of both victims and traffickers. The paper concludes with identification of possible social responses that could provide alternatives to, or even supplement, the usual criminal sanctions.

## Trafficking in humans as an illegal economic activity

Recognition of the economic features of criminal behaviour started during the late 1960s in the USA. Gary S. Becker's study 'Crime and Punishment: An Economic Approach', considered to be one of the earliest studies of crime from economic perspective. He explored crime as the result of rational calculations by the offender related to opportunities for earning income (legal and illegal) and amounts of profits as well as to the probability of being arrested and punished (Becker, quoted by Schloenhardt, 1999:204). After Becker's pioneering work, many studies explored crime from the same economic point of view. A crucial objective of the economic analyses of crime is understanding crime as an illegal economic activity, and perpetrators as "*rationally and normally calculating people maximising their preferences subject to given constraints, like the rest of us.*" (Sullivan, quoted by Schloenhardt, 1999: 204).

On the basis of the analyses of crime in the USA in the 1970s, Smith suggested the crime and its various manifestations could be positioned in "*a taxonomy of all economic activities.*" According to him, "*the spectrum of economic activity ranges from legal to criminal activities, from legitimate to illegitimate businesses*" (Smith, quoted by Schloenhardt, 1999: 204), while organised crime has an important place in the latter ones. The major goal of organised crime is to maximise economic gain, in a way that profit goes into the hands of those who stand back and are not directly involved in committing the

7 E.g. US Department of State Trafficking in people reports and policies in Balkan countries.

crime. In that regard, the aim of organised crime does not differ from the aim of commercial organisations (Schloenhardt, 1999: 206). As has been well observed by Savona, "*crimes are to criminal organisation as legal activities are for legal enterprise*" (Savona, quoted by Schloenhardt, 1999: 206). Thus, as noticed by Schloenhardt (1999: 207), "*a drug trafficker can be described as a wholesaler in the illegal market, while the migrant trafficker may be seen as the illegal counterpart of a migration agent*".

As a result of the constant growth in the number of economic studies on organised crime, there is a high level of agreement within criminology that the economic analysis of organised crime was very successful in clarifying goals and organisational and operational characteristics of criminal organisations. In order to understand criminal organisations, economic theories started by viewing them as organisations functioning within illegal markets. They also explored the similarities and differences between legal and illegal economic activities (Schloenhardt, 1999: 205, 206). Thus, the analysis of organised crime as an enterprise and labour market are developed.

## Trafficking in humans as criminal enterprise and labour market

In the literature about organised crime there is an assumption that its economic activities can rather be described within the conceptual framework of the criminal enterprise than by using the conceptually unclear notion 'organised crime'. (Van Duyne, quoted by Naylor, 2004: 5). Existing knowledge about human trafficking shows that it has various organisational structures. The relationships among members and the management of a criminal enterprise can be vertical, i.e. hierarchical (corporative model), but in contemporary societies more often it is horizontal (network model).

Criminal enterprises can include smaller or larger groups of people, can be of a local or international character, but it can also have a form of 'family business' (Nikolić-Ristanović *et al*, 2004: 160). Very often, these organisations, apart from trafficking in humans, are involved in other criminal activities as well, particularly drug trafficking. In addition, some associates may act as independent individuals who perform individual tasks *ad hoc* or, less often, on a permanent basis. Schloenhardt calls these individuals amateur traffickers. They usually act in border areas, using their own boats, taxis and lorries. However, this author warns that, in spite of the individual and local nature of their functioning, many of these traffickers work for big organisations which act at an international level (Schloenhardt, 1999: 215).

Research shows that, similarly as with legal enterprise, division of labour is a key characteristic of a criminal enterprise as well. Moreover, when a criminal enterprise is in question, the division of tasks and functions assumes a protective role: if it comes to arrest and investigation, only small units of the organisation are exposed (Schloenhardt, 1999: 217). So far research has identified two key positions for the members of a criminal enterprise, bearing in mind the job they are performing, and education and skills they possess:

- distant managers/investors – competent persons who invest in trafficking in humans and supervise its overall functioning. These individuals are usually not known to persons from lower levels or to trafficked persons;
- persons on the lower levels who deal with various criminal activities and come in direct contact with victims. These individuals generally do not have or have only low levels of education and experience and are mainly hired *ad hoc*, not on a permanent basis:
  - persons who recruit and transport victims,
  - guides and crew members responsible for transfer of migrants,
  - persons who rent their own flats or houses for temporary accommodation of migrants etc. (Schloenhardt, 1999:218).

Apart from the above-mentioned findings, surveys of trafficking in males, carried out in Serbia, found evidence of a third group of individuals being those on the middle managerial level. This clearly makes the criminal enterprise even more similar to a legal enterprise. In essence, the distinction between entrepreneurs, managers and experienced but non-educated workers, which are identified on the basis of the analysis of interviews with traffickers, is very much in accordance with Taylor's review of legal and illegal labour markets and other financial possibilities in market societies (1999:230).

Managers/investors are rarely arrested and punished, mid level managers a bit more often, while those on the lowest positions are the most exposed to arrests and punishments. Bearing in mind that there is no contract, the order among 'employees' is maintained by the use of threats, intimidation and violence. Also, important to the functioning of a criminal enterprise, is that the entire business is secured from outside. This appears to be achieved through the use of violence and intimidation against witnesses and victims, as well as through corruption of state officials (Schloenhardt, 1999: 209, 210).

Up to date surveys hardly shed light on the method of recruitment. This can be with respect to both the employment of members of a criminal enterprise for trafficking in humans, as well as to the process of establishing contacts and interactions between the person who offers and the one who accepts and commits the crime. However, studies of some other forms of organised crime, particularly drug trafficking, provide a proper theoretical basis for the analysis of trafficking in humans from the perspective of the (illegal) labour market. In this regard, especially, an important contribution is made by critical criminologists such as Ian Taylor and Vincenzo Ruggiero.

Ruggiero and Taylor, starting from the analysis of organised crime from the labour perspective,[8] pointed out to the impact of neoliberal capitalism as providing an enormous increase in employment opportunity from within the "*hidden, parallel and semi-legal economies*" (Ruggiero, 2001: 11), as well as in the increased flexibility and informality of work (Taylor, 1999: 163, 228;). It is also important to stress these authors' emphasis on the connection between employment in the informal (grey, hidden) economy and looking for a job or possibilities for investment, either in the purely criminal economy, or in both the licit and illicit one.

Ruggiero, in particular, points out the proximity that exists between the informal and the criminal economy, as well as at the blurring of boundaries which distinguish them, often influencing both simple workers and investors periodically to shift from one 'dirty economy' to another. Consequently, Ruggiero identified continuity between the irregular, hidden, semi-legal and openly criminal economies, discovering at the same time "*scandalous normality*" of criminal markets, which "*reproduce the most repulsive aspects of legitimate ones*" (Ruggiero, 2001: 11, 12). Myths about hierarchically organised professional criminal enterprise that involve life criminals are increasingly replaced by empirically confirmed facts about its "*essentially local, opportunistic and entrepreneurial character*" (Van Duyne, 1996).

---

8 This analysis relates mainly to studying professional criminals. Ruggiero reminds that this perspective takes into consideration skills which are necessary for dealing with specific criminal activity/job and can be useful for identification of important elements of its organisation (Ruggiero, 2001: 16).

Taylor noticed the connection between economic changes that brought about a significant increase of unemployment, thus producing "*the emergence of a mass underclass population of unemployed young men in a permanent position of marginality vis-a-vis the Fordist labour market of opportunity and routinely seduced by the alternative opportunities of local hidden economies of illicit activity . . .*", on the one hand, and the emergence of new criminal syndicates in Europe and North America, on the other hand. Many of those new criminal syndicates emerged only in areas affected by long periods of intensive and deep crises connected to changes in the local economy (Taylor, 2001: 169). As a consequence, employment within local 'economies of crime' often is the result of the efforts of the individual to adapt to worsening of material wellbeing, i.e. to find appropriate strategies to survive the change (Taylor, 1999: 228). As a consequence, acceptance of a job within criminal enterprise in these circumstances often is being rationalised and justified by the use of different techniques of neutralisation.

Pugh (2005), who researched the links between Balkan post conflict economic difficulties and crime, suggests that economic crime can be categorised into three types of shadow economy: (1) organised mafia and trafficking, (2) corruption, fraud and nepotism in business and public life and (3) survival shadow economies (including black markets in employment and trade) of the population at large. Pugh also contends that because of the institution of neo-liberal economic policies (in Bosnia and Herzegovina), the dependence on shadow economies is integral to survival among poor populations.

For the analysis of trafficking in humans as a criminal enterprise as well as a possible source of 'jobs', it is of special importance to stress the contradiction between two possible causal explanations ('causality of contraries') of organised crime, which was suggested by Ruggiero. On the one hand, this author pointed out that the lack of resources and legitimate possibilities for employment, and even the need for belonging to a collective have important places among factors that lead to joining organised crime on the lower levels of its structure. However, as he noticed, this etiological explanation can explain only crime committed by 'soldiers' in the organisation – thus by those with the lowest level of education, with the least experience and power – but not criminal entrepreneurial knowledge of the organisation as whole. This latter can be better explained by something completely different: "*through the availability of resources, access to markets and to political mediators*". In this respect, the following question raised by Ruggiero in relation to drug trafficking can be almost identically be raised in relation to trafficking in humans: "*How can we explain the general causes of drug-related offences, if for some these offences amount to the search for a basic income, while for others they are part of strategies for the valorisation of an income they already have?*" (Ruggiero, 2001: 9). One of the rare comprehensive explanations applicable to both types of criminals is the seduction of crime concept developed by Katz, which suggests the influence of emotional processes that seduce people to deviance, with quality of dynamics differing by social position (Katz, 1988: 321).

## Structural victimisation, hidden economy and the trafficking in humans in Serbia

### The impact of war and transition

Poverty, rise in unemployment, the lack of trust in institutions and a strict taxation policy in post-communist and war-affected societies force numerous people to look for jobs in the informal sectors that are, along with the connected job markets, on the rise in many transitional societies. The informal sector often offers better-paid jobs than the formal one, making it the most significant source of income for a part of the population (Nikolić-Ristanović, 2003: 7). On the other hand, the development of the informal job market means that increasing numbers of people (both men and women) are relatively unprotected and open for exploitation in their job positions (inadequate salaries, prolonged work hours, lack of any sort of rights, etc) (UNICEF, 1999: 6).

All of the aforementioned conditions became worse with the armed fighting that was happening in the territories of the former Yugoslavia, "*when criminalized paramilitary and government security troops invested in, sponsored or took part directly in the criminal markets*" (Lewis, 1998: 217).

As a result, war zones became seedbeds for organised crime related to illegal trade of drugs, fuel, weapons, human organs and human trafficking (Nikolić-Ristanović, 1998: 466). Economic sanctions imposed on the Federal Republic of Yugoslavia and sanctions that Greece imposed on Macedonia also contributed to the development of the informal economy in the entire region.

During the war, the informal economy offered jobs and commodities that could not be found through the legal market. The economic and financial crisis in Serbia with galloping inflation, which was a consequence of the war and international economic sanctions, enabled the criminalisation of the entire society. This was evident in the fact that virtually the entire population became involved with some kind of illegal activity. This was particularly the case in terms of their involvement in the hidden or informal economy.

In another words, the enormous inflation and the impossibility of legally earning a wage forced many people to smuggle and sell on the black market scarce goods or to give in to some other illegal activity as a way to survive (Nikolić-Ristanović, 1998: 462). The hidden economy encompassed those who made profit from the wars, criminalised businessmen employed in large export-import jobs and connected with the ruling elite but it also encompassed the petty or street economy in which "*thousands of poverty stricken ordinary individuals were trying to make money in order to survive*". (Bolčić, 1995: 153). Such stratification that emerged because of the war and which continued to exist in the post-war period, greatly contributed to the determination of the role of the looser/victim or the winner in the structure of the society that emerged. With that, their role in the closely connected criminal economy was also decided.

The hidden economy offered 'temporary alternative employment' to those who were otherwise nominally employed in legal companies (in which more often than not, they were not getting paid or the paycheque was insufficient to make a living). Also, it offered many types of jobs which were not available in the legal job market at that time. In short, people who took the jobs in the sphere of the grey economy were for the most part honest citizens who were forced into this arena as they were unable to find legal jobs. As observed by Bolčić (1994:143), everyday life became a fight for survival, which did not leave much space for thinking about the legality of one's deeds. Moreover, the extent of the people's involvement in the illegal activities and the benefit that the state elite derived from this were so big that it was no longer in the interest of the authorities to punish the perpetrators.

This led to the complete anomie and social disorganisation, and generated a further rise of crime and other forms of deviant social behaviour.[9]

All of the afore mentioned enabled the development of all types of criminal markets and organised crime which, similar to other developed and undeveloped countries alike, serve as a survival strategy for some and as a method of capital accrual for others.[10] Economic hardships related to the war continued to exist in the post-war society as well. Related to this, illegal markets played an important role in the post war economy, despite the re-establishment of the formal economy and the heightened openness of the citizens to the idea of conformity.

After the war, some of the criminals who were connected to the ruling elite used privatisation to legalise their activities and used the profit made for investments in legal jobs and privatised enterprises. The other part continued with their criminal economic activities or moved on to other activities that were more profitable and carried less risk, such as trafficking in humans. They continued to get rich in the sphere of the illegal economy and they began to take on the role of the 'employer' within it: arrangers/investors and managers.

The lowest level are marginalised, war-stricken individuals and those with the lowest socio-economic status who are forced, in order to cope with economic difficulties and problems related to migration, to continue to look to the informal markets for cheap commodities and documents that they could not get legally. Research conducted in the majority of the post war societies point to the particular vulnerability of the war participants regarding the aforementioned (Nitzschke, 2003:1). Under the above given conditions, these people came into a situation to ask for, or accept the job in the sphere of trafficking in people. Closely related to this category of traffickers, the available data on trafficking in humans as a form of organised crime in Serbia and in other countries alike, points to the existence of a relationship between structural victimisation caused by war, the development of the informal economy and the risk of criminalisation of the law abiding citizens but who have since then turned to illegal activities (Studdard, 2004).

---

9 Similar situation is in Bosnia and Herzegovina (Lalić, 2006).

10 See more about this in Ballentine and Nitzschke (2003).

## Lessons from the survey on male trafficking in Serbia

The survey on male trafficking in Serbia (see footnote 6) produced detailed information about mid- and low-level traffickers' roles in criminal enterprises.[11] Men from lower levels performed the role of recruitment and transfer organisers, while both men and women were mid level night bar (brothel) owners. On the lower organisational levels, men were recruiters, drivers, guides, or they rented houses or flats for migrants to stay in temporarily during transfer, while women were mostly involved in recruitment.

The results of the survey show that traffickers who perform tasks at these lower levels in the criminal enterprise commit trafficking as the part of the continuing search for a job in the informal market. On the other hand, those who are on higher levels use to do that as the part of maintaining a stable and diversified criminal career.[12]

Mid-level traffickers were hired by the main organisers or were small-scale entrepreneurs/brothel owners, while those from the lower levels mainly answered that they used to get *ad hoc* job offers from those from mid level. According to the answers of convicted traffickers, no one from the low level had any long term arrangement. Men received offers from mid level 'managers' whom they knew as friends, acquaintances and/or their legal or semi-legal employers. All women were involved in human trafficking by their partners or husbands, who played a similar (low level) or more important (mid level) role in trafficking network.

All traffickers-men whom we interviewed had in common that they were all involved in the last Balkan wars (as soldiers or as policemen). Interviewed men-traffickers who were engaged on the lowest level had problems with physical and mental health, which were a direct consequence of the war, while this was not the case with the ones at the middle level.

The beginning of employment in the informal sector for the trafficker from the lowest category is related to the war in the following ways:

---

11 Unfortunately, those from the highest level were not in prison, i.e. available for interview by the time the survey was conducted.

12 Similar is found by Ruggiero (Ruggiero, 2000).

- during the war, upon being wounded and becoming a refugee (for example, they started to be involved in re-sale of smuggled commodities in order to survive)
- after the war, when they are faced with economic problems related to the war and taking refuge (for example, the beginning of the work: 'off the books').

Completely opposite to that, traffickers from the higher levels saw war and the post war circumstances as an opportunity for developing their criminal activities and for quick enrichment – for fulfilment of their 'American dream.' They had been involved in various forms of illegal trade, mostly drug trafficking and human trafficking/smuggling for a long time and on a permanent basis – as a stable and main job. They became involved in such informal/illegal activity at the beginning of war (illegal trade on war affected territories, opening bars in Kosovo after KFOR[13] arrived) – after coming in from abroad, after loss of a job in the police forces, or by shifting into a new type of trade that fitted the new social circumstances. Their main motive for getting involved in trafficking in people was a bigger income.

Some of the human smugglers in Serbia, as told by our interviewees, had luxurious houses and otherwise were very wealthy. One of the convicted smugglers, interviewed for our survey, for example, said: "*I am financially secured, at least for the next 10 years. I have €30.000 in a term account in a German bank, as well as income from my wife and my mom's pension in foreign currency.*"

It is not unusual that some of the mid level traffickers are criminals who, during the 1990s, returned to Serbia from emigration in Western Europe, either voluntarily or upon the deportation because of their criminal record. This is when they joined the war and various illegal market activities on the territory of the former Yugoslavia. Some of them first started with drug trafficking, shifting later to trafficking in humans.[14]

Although rarely, women also have higher positions in trafficking business, especially as managers ('madams') or brothel and night bar owners. In this case, the war can also have an impact on women shifting their economic position to earn money in this way. One such woman, convicted for trafficking women for sexual exploitation in her night bar/brothel in Serbia,

13 The Kosovo Force (KFOR) is a NATO-led international force responsible for establishing a safe and secure environment in Kosovo

14 For similar see Logonder, 2008: 78.

explained that she started to smuggle alcohol during the war in Croatia, and opened a night bar in Kosovo immediately after the arrival of the KFOR. She considers that all she ever did was trade, which was exactly what she was trained for in school. She used to work together with her father, whom she described as 'good merchant'. She also said that she had made a big profit, had acquired a lot of real estate and a stable financial situation.

The Serbian survey findings also suggest that those who were low level traffickers during the war advanced and acquired managerial or higher positions. As a result, they themselves were able to recruit young people, especially drivers, who found themselves to be in an unfortunate economic situation. One of convicted traffickers said that previously he used to work for other employers as a driver and through renting and subletting the flat, but later on he started to make direct deals with people on both the Croatian and Albanian sides.

With the women on the low level, the war did not play a significant role in upward mobility but instead the gender marginalisation, partner violence and transition played a significant role. Women began working in the illegal economy under the coercion of their partners, but in some cases, their first encounter with the informal economy was related to the transition and opening of the borders of Eastern Europe (i.e. smuggling of commodities). The partners who got them into human trafficking had either the same or a higher position than they had (they were usually recruiters or coordinators of the recruiters' network).

Our respondents/convicted traffickers continued to look for jobs in the informal and criminal economy in the post conflict period as well. On the one hand, this could be explained by the lack of distinction between licit and illicit behaviour and the associated habits they formed to look for jobs informally. On the other hand, the wider social and economic context in Serbia also furthered this tendency because of the insufficient availability of legal jobs and income. This was compounded by both the slow recovery of ruined institutions and the lack of citizens' trust in those institutions. Moreover, the economic situation in Serbia is still extremely difficult since the negative consequences of transition have been added to the serious consequences of war affecting the living standard and overall everyday life of people (Nikolić-Ristanović, 2008), as well as corruption of the ruling elite.

Interviews carried out for the purpose of the survey on trafficking in men in Serbia suggest firm patterns of transporting migrants through the territory of Serbia, especially Albanians from Kosovo and Albania, and earning money in this way. It seems that trafficking in humans is a very important source of labour and income for a large number of people, especially for those living in areas near the borders. In addition, Serbia is obviously recognised as a territory where illegal activities are facilitated by weak police control and widespread corruption, and this is why this route is chosen, although it is often a longer and roundabout way.

One of our respondents from the police gave the example of the village from the south of Serbia where about 80 men are involved in smuggling and trafficking of humans, while their relatives operate in other areas. They are the part of criminal groups with firm cohesion as they are all in some kind of kinship. On the other side, in the north, people are renting houses for smuggled and trafficked migrants to stay in, sometimes housing more than 20 of them at the same time. This 'business' seems flourishing in border areas in Serbia and may in some degree be comparable with the situation with drug trafficking in Latin American countries, such as Columbia, after the demise of cartels, which involved large part of population (Decker, Townsend Chapman, 2008: 60).

When it comes down to people hired in human trafficking on the lowest level, the influence of structural victimisation is evident also from the findings which suggest instability of employment and 'doing everything and anything', as well as the existence of economic hardships immediately prior to taking the criminal job in the sphere of trafficking in humans. As stressed by our interviewee, a police inspector from the border area, traffickers are most often persons "*who used to do all sorts of things – smuggling of merchandise, cigarettes, cattle, etc. Thus, jobs where the income is quick and risk is small.*"

Mainly, as was the case in the aforementioned research carried out in other countries, they tended to accept *ad hoc* jobs offered to them by the people they knew. Some traffickers also used to have either part-time or even full time legal jobs, apart from being involved in criminal jobs. Traffickers who are on the lowest level do not make any profit (for example: women who do not get any money or are forced to hand it over to their partner) or they make very little money (€ 100 – 300).

The impact of structural victimisation and the informal economy in dealing with trafficking in humans is shown in its most drastic form in the case of children who are hired to guide illegal migrants, sometimes being of their own age, through the border between Serbia (Kosovo) and Albania for symbolic amounts of money (e.g. € 20).

It is also interesting to look at how traffickers perceive their own criminal activity. At the time of crime commitment, traffickers from the lowest level, did not consider their activity in the frame of trafficking in humans to be criminal but instead, that they were only doing their job. Traffickers from this group are low educated people, with problems in verbal expression, who sometime also have mental and physical health problems. They thought that they were doing what was normal, that they were helping other people migrate or get a job, which points to different neutralisation techniques used by them to rationalise their actions. As Goffman (quoted by Nordstrom, 2007: 155) says, they downplay their sense of wrongdoing, using psychological defence such as: "*Everyone does it, it's not really bad, I'm not involved in criminal activity . . .*" And this keeps the entire system running (Nordstrom, 2007: 155). Finally, in accordance with that and with their total socio-economic positions, they are either likely to blame those they worked for, people close to themselves who got them in touch with the 'employer' or the victim for being mistaken about the true nature of the job, the age of the victim and similar. They also tended to deny victimisation of those they trafficked, while they are more likely to look at themselves as the true victims and not as criminals.[15]

In contrast, traffickers from higher levels see themselves as criminals who cannot resist temptation. They leave the impression of educated persons, speak eloquently, describing details and seem proud of what they had achieved so far, of their skills and business. They say that they earned a lot of money, and feel financially secured for the future.

They did not make much of an effort to rationalise their behaviour, but spoke more about their effort to avoid arrest. They tend to think that punishment is deserved. Some of them thought that they should be charged with a more lenient offence such as procurement ("*it is criminal but not trafficking*"), but there were also some who were even happy for not getting harsher penalty.

---

15 For similar regarding people involved in various types of illegal markets, see Nordstrom, 2007: 207.

## Instead of conclusion: toward a holistic approach to structural victimisation and criminalisation in post-war society

As the previous analysis shows, the connection between scarce legal jobs, the hidden economy and dealing with trafficking in humans is evident. As pointed out by Marinković, there are an enormous number of jobs which are neither legal nor illegal, or which often shift sides. Moreover, informal economy, black labour market, organised crime and corruption are closely connected and it is very difficult to make a clear distinction between jobs in informal economy and those belonging to the category of organised crime, including trafficking in humans (Marinković, 2006: 28, 37).

The perpetrators of trafficking in humans who take up the lowest levels in the criminal enterprise are usually those who were victimised on several different levels, relating to the place they hold in the social, economic and gender structure and also to their experiences during the war and the consequences they suffered. Their acceptance of a job related to trafficking or alternately smuggling of humans is motivated by economic reasons and it is mostly a part of a continuation of the job search in the informal job market. It is for that reason that they, unlike the 'real' traffickers-criminals, are not aware of the illegality of their job, or they tend to neutralise its illegality. With that, their capability to escape arrest is lessened, making them prone to arrest and punishment.

The statistical data on convicted[16] traffickers in Serbia in the time period of 2003-2008 show that out of the total 262 accused individuals, only 47 of them were convicted.[17] Recent analyses of verdicts in trafficking cases showed that the largest portion of the convicted persons are the recruiters and transporters, the ones on the lowest level while the lesser part of them are the middle, i.e. the managerial level (Copic, 2009). With regards to this, the situation in Serbia does not differ significantly from the one that exists in other countries regarding trafficking in humans (Kelly, 2002: 45; Markovska

---

16 Humans trafficking is criminal offence from 2003 in Serbia, and humans smuggling from 2005. Between 2003 and 2005 smuggling cases were treated as trafficking, but now trafficking is mostly connected with women, and smuggling/illegal migration with men/entire families.

17 Data of Statistics Bureau of the Republic of Serbia, http://webrzs.stat.gov.rs, retrieved at 10 June 2009.

and Moore, 2008), but also regarding illegal markets, such as drug trafficking.[18] In other words, those who are the most responsible and those who take the most of the profit have a higher chance of remaining out of the hands of the law.

Looking at the big picture, those with the least power and those who are the most marginalised are at the same time those who are the most prone to repression. Traffickers who are on the lowest level in criminal business are most often also those who are arrested and incarcerated. On the other hand, traffickers from higher levels only rarely are arrested, and even more rarely convicted. This can be explained from the social constraints within the business. Remaining silent about the 'business' in the case of arrest is especially appreciated and is awarded with 'career development' As said by one convicted trafficker, "*when you become known, everyone calls you, especially if you do not squeak. I did not squeak and since then they had more confidence in me.*" If it happens that these traffickers are convicted, the conviction have much smaller impact on them comparing to low level traffickers, since the challenge of making profit is usually bigger than fear of arrest and conviction.

However, not only the arrest policy but also the sentences passed to traffickers do not reflect the position and share of power and profit within criminal enterprises. Thus, penalties, which are in general lenient (imprisonment from several months to six years, and conditional sentences), are not proportional to the responsibility, influence, power nor the realised profits by the perpetrators. Those at the lowest level and those who make the least money are sentenced similarly or equally as heavy as the ones on higher levels who made a bigger profit. If we look at imprisoned traffickers interviewed for the male trafficker's survey, we can see that they got following sentences:

1. Mid level traffickers:
    a. Men: one year and six months, and six years imprisonment;
    b. Woman: four years imprisonment.

---

18 Ruggiero, for example, stress that social panic connected to international war against drugs in 1980s led to increase of incarceration rate of users and small dealers, who became the part of a "carceral social zone", similarly as other marginalised, poor and underemployed, in whose economic activities legality and illegality are interlinked. „Prison discipline lowered their social expectations, turning the majority of them into routine criminal workers", with drug users being treated as "criminal reserve army", as "the poor of the era of forced industrialization were redefined as the reserve army of labour." (Ruggiero, 2001: 24).

2. Low level traffickers:
   a. Men:10 months, three years, five years imprisonment;
   b. Women: one year and six months, two years, three years and 10 months, four years imprisonment.[19]

The words of a woman who was convicted for working for her husband as a recruiter of girls for trafficking are very illustrative of the disproportionate sentences: "*He got six years, and me four. For him it is too little, for me it is too much.*"

Thus, we could ask ourselves, like Liz Kelly did: what would be the appropriate punishment for those who get the least in the criminal business? (Kelly, 2002: 57).Considering that for those traffickers, committing a criminal act has an importance of normal economic activity, which is related to the long-lasting legal and semi legal activities which were widely present as economic strategies of survival during and after the war, I think that it is important for criminologists and the general public to question the current approach to human trafficking in Serbia and surrounding countries.

In other words, the approach which deals with the perpetrators solely through repression ought to be re-evaluated. Repression, meaning criminal law enforcement, besides the short-term useful effects, in the long run deepens the already existing social exclusion and marginalisation of these individuals. With that, as pointed out by some authors, some changes along the lines of a strategic reconstruction and a sudden move to the formal economy, without taking into consideration the useful social function which hidden economy is known to play in transitional societies, one risks ignoring the hidden entrepreneurs. It would hurt those who became dependent on the hidden and survival economy in conflict and post-conflict societies (Nitzschke, 2003: 14).

Keeping the aforementioned in mind, it is my belief that the business of trafficking in humans in the post-war society has to be closely tied with dealing with the aftermath of war, including the said war economy. In that sense, it is necessary to adopt a holistic approach that joins the two problems together and has as its priority long term measures, such as the development of democratic institutions, the concept of a rule of law and, especially, measures of social policy, based on social solidarity, empowering support and

---

19 This is confirmed in recent analyses of 37 cases of convicted traffickers in Serbia (Copic, 2009)

social inclusion. This last one includes the increase in the number of legal jobs and better access to jobs for marginalised groups in general, and particularly for war victims and participants, as well as programmes for providing employment for the said groups. That is how the decrease of the source of victims and perpetrators alike as well as the commencement of a lasting and positive peace could be influenced.

With that, the mechanisms of restorative justice can also be usefully applied, considering that findings of the research in trafficking of men in Serbia show that the traffickers on lowest levels are still not aware of the consequences that their actions have caused or that – if aware – they still have a tendency to deny the consequences of their own criminal activity on the victim. Very illustrative in that regard are the words of the above-mentioned woman, who was convicted for trafficking (recruitment of girls):

> "*When once I am out of prison, I would like to go to see these girls, to ask for their forgiveness. Thanks God, this was only attempt. I realised that something like that may happen to me as well. No penalty can punish you as you can punish yourself. The girls were victims of course. They wanted to sell them. I realised what I did only here, in prison. Then I was not able to think about consequences and their situation. Now I started to think how it would be if I were on their place. If something like that happened to me, I would forgive. I would feel better if I go to talk with them and if they can forgive me.*"

Closely related to this is the need to raise awareness of those belonging to the vulnerable population, especially war veterans and refugees, not just about the risks of victimisation but also that taking of a job in the hidden economy can make them a part of a criminal group and can lead to harmful consequences for other people.

Particular attention must be given to areas close to borders, whose marginalised population is particularly prone to the risk of inclusion in the illegal network. Moreover, the regional approach to the fight against organised crime and consequences of the war and war economy is necessary (Studdard, 2004: 2).

## References

Aromaa, K. and M. Lehti, Trafficking in human beings: policy problems and recommendations. In: P.C. van Duyne, A. Maljević, M. van Dijck, K. von Lampe and J. Harvey (eds.), *Crime business and crime money in Europe. The dirty linen of illicit enterprise.* Nijmegen, Wolf Legal Publishers, 2007

Ballentine, K. and H. Nityschke, Beyond greed and grievance: Policy lessons from studies in the political economy of armed conflict. New York: International Peace Academy, 2003
http://www.ipacademy.org, retrieved on 25 October 2008.

Bolčić, S., O 'svakodnevnici' razorenog društva Srbije početkom devedesetih - iz sociološke perspektive (About everyday life in ruined society of Serbia at the beginning of 1990s - from sociological perspective.) In: M. Prošić-Dvornić (ed.) *Kulture u tranziciji*(Cultures of transition), Beograd: Plato, 1994, 143.

Bolčić, S., Izmenjena sfera rada. In: S. Bolčić (ed.), *Društvene promene i svakodnevni život: Srbija početkom 1990-tih.* Beograd: Insitut za sociološka istraživanja Filozofskog fakulteta u Beogradu, 1995, str. 153

Copic, S., Trgovina ljudima u Srbiji: kaznena politika sudova u funkciji kontrole kriminaliteta. (Trafficking in humans in Serbia:courts penal policy in the function of crime control). In: L.Kron, (ed.), *Crime control and European standards: the situation in Serbia,* Belgrade: Institute for Criminological and Sociological Research, 2009, 323-341

Decker, S. and M. Townsend Chapman, *Drug smugglers on drug smuggling: lessons from the inside*, Philadelphia: Temple University Press, 2008

Duyne, P.C. van, The phantom and threat of organized crime. *Crime, Law and Social Change,* 1996, *no. 4*, 241-377

EC, Undeclared work in European Union. *Special Eurobarometer,* 2007, 284/Wave 67.3

Katz, J., *Seductions of crime: a chilling exploration of the criminal mind – from juvenile delinquency to cold-blooded murder*, USA: Basic Books, 1988

Kelly, L., *Journeys of jeopardy: A review of research on trafficking in women and children in Europe.* IOM Report, 2002

Lalić, V., *Trgovina ljudima u Bosni i Hercegovini* (Trafficking in humans in Bosnia and Herzegovina), Banja Luka: Defendologija, 2007

Lewis, R., Drugs, war and crime in the post-Soviet Balkans. In: V. Ruggiero, N. South and I. Taylor (eds.) *The New European criminology: Crime and order in Europe*. London and New York: Routledge, 1998, 216-230

Logonder, A., Who is 'Yugo' in 'Yugo-mafia'? A comparative analysis of the Serbian and Slovene offenders. In: P.C. van Duyne, J. Harvey, A. Maljević, K. von Lampe and M. Scheinost (eds.), *European crime-markets at cross-roads: extended and extending criminal Europe*, Nijmegen: Wolf Legal Publishers, 2008, 63-97

Markovska, A., C. Moore, Stilettos and steel toe-caps: Legislation of human trafficking and sexual exploitation, and its enforcement in the UK and The Ukraine. In: P.C. van Duyne, J. Harvey, A. Maljević, K. von Lampe and M. Scheinost (eds.), *European crime-markets at cross-roads:extended and extenging criminal Europe*, Nijmegen: Wolf Legal Publishers, 2008, 121-151.

Marinković, D., Shadow labour market as an obstacle to strengthening the competitiveness of companies. *South- East Europe Review for Labour and Social Affaires*, 2006, *no. 4*, p. 31-43

Nikolić-Ristanović, V., War and crime in the former Yugoslavia. In: V. Ruggiero, N. South and I.Taylor (eds.) *New European Criminology*, London: Routledge, 1998, 462-480

Nikolić-Ristanović, V., Illegal markets, human trade and transnational organised crime. In: P.C. van Duyne, M. Jager, K.von Lampe and J. Newell *Threats and phantoms of organised crime, corruption and terrorism*, Wolf Legal Publishers, Nijmegen, 2004, 117-139

Nikolić-Ristanović, V., S. Copić, B. Simeunović-Patić, S. Milivojević and B. Mihić, *Trafficking in people in Serbia*. OSCE: Belgrade, 2004

Nikolić-Ristanović, V., Trgovina ljudima u Srbiji: između moralne panike i društvene strategije (Trafficking in humans in Serbia: between moral panic and social strategy). *Temida*, 2005, *no. 4*, 5-15.

Nikolić-Ristanović, V., *Male trafficking in Serbia*. Belgrade: Victimology Society of Serbia, 2009

Nitzschke, H., Transforming war economies: Challenges for peacemaking and peace building. New York: International Peace Academy, 2003 http://www.ipacademy.org, retrieved on 25 October 2008.

Naylor, R.T., *Wages of crime: black markets, illegal finance, and the underworld economy*. New York: Cornell University Press, 2004

Nordstrom, C., *Global outlaws: crime, money, and power in the contemporary world.* Berkeley and Los Angeles: University of California Press, 2007

Pugh, M., *Liquid transformation in the political economies of BiH and Kosovo.* Draft Paper for TD10 International Studies Association Honolulu, March, 2005

Ruggiero, V., *Crime and markets: Essays in anti-criminology.* Oxford: Oxford University Press, 2001

Sykes, G., and D. Matza, Techniques of neutralization: A theory of delinquency. *American Sociological Review*, 1957, *vol 22*, p. 664 - 70

Studdard, K., *War economies in a regional context: Overcoming the challenges of transformation.* New York: International Peace Academy, 2004, http://www.ipacademy.org, retrieved on 25 October 2008.

Schneider, F. and D. Ernste, *Shadow economies around the world: Size, causes, and consequences.* IMF Working Paper, International Monetary Fund, 2000

Schloenhardt, A., Organised crime and the business of migrant trafficking: An economic analysis. *Crime, Law and Social Change*, 1999, *32*, 203-233.

Taylor, I., *Crime in context*, Cambridge:Polity Press, 1999

UNICEF, *Women in Transition.* The MONEE Project CEE/CIS/ Baltics, Regional Monitoring Reports, No.6., Florence: UNICEF International Child Development Centre, 1999

# Stilettos and steel toe-caps
## Legislation of human trafficking and sexual exploitation, and its enforcement in the UK and The Ukraine[1]

*Anna Markovska and Colleen Moore*[2]

## Introduction

In recent years, trafficking in human beings has thrived as a lucrative criminal enterprise, and although not a new phenomenon, governments, enforcers and lobbyists have escalated their actions to combat it. The Ukraine has become one of the leading suppliers of human beings in the global human trafficking market. At the same time the United Kingdom has become a popular destination country in Europe. Both countries have sought to respond through legislation and more focused policing methods. However, the scale and nature of trafficking in human beings for sexual exploitation (TfSE)[3] is escalating in both countries. There are difficulties in attempting comparative research. Culturally, historically and legally The Ukraine and the UK do not share many common traditions, but in relation to recent legislation on trafficking and its implementation, some shared themes can be identified. It is not straightforward to contrast legal or social policy implementation or processes in different countries, but without attempting to make comparisons, we may preclude some deeper grasp of the issues.

---

1 The authors would like to thank Nicky Padfield, Petrus C. van Duyne and Olga Biletska for their very helpful comments on earlier drafts of this paper. The faults that remain are all ours.
This chapter was first published in: P.C. van Duyne, J. Harvey, A. Maljevic, K. von Lampe and M. Scheinost (eds.), *European crime-markets at cross-roads. Extended and extending criminal Europe*. Nijmegen, Wolf Legal Publishers, 2008

2 The authors are lecturers in Criminology at Anglia Ruskin University, Cambridge, England.

3 This is the acronym that has been adopted by the Home Office in the UK

The authors have attempted to examine the responses of The Ukraine and the UK, but acknowledge that contrasting legal definitions and legislation has problems due to different interpretations and applications of the law. Who or what drives particular legislation? Who implements it? Who ensures that legislation is effective and who is accountable? The defendant's right to a fair trial must be ensured, whilst ensuring that the complainant is suitably represented in all cases. Difficulties arise in many trafficking cases, due to the questionable 'victim status' of the complainants. In addition, justice has to be seen to achieve parity and political approval. The final hurdle in this debate, relates to polarised perspectives on the business of prostitution itself. The vast majority of women in all levels of prostitution do not choose to be in the profession for any reason other than to escape poverty, and would arguably prefer another type of employment, if available. There exists a tension between the level of support and legislative response directed towards 'rescuing' the 'internationally-trafficked, foreign' prostitute and the 'locally-cultivated' sex worker. The trauma suffered by trafficked prostitute women is magnified against that of 'prostitution' *per se*, as containing 'shocking abuse', devastating health implications, physical abuse and post-traumatic stress disorder, which is also true for many women globally who have been trafficked from one street corner to another. The impact of this polarised perspective is apparent in the legal discussions before and during trials.

Those concerned about the horrors of trafficking and sexual exploitation may be blinkered to some of the other effects (or indeed, intentions) of related legislation. Support measures (crack-downs) that are presented as mechanisms to cull people-trafficking, may confirm the public's perceived fears of immigrant as 'other', which can add to the moral panic that is popularised through the media[4] and political[5] agenda. Much of what is known about TfSE is contested. Subsequently, major disagreements within the anti-trafficking, lobbying world have developed. Although activists may be seeking similar ends, they often have distinct agendas, both politically and ideologically (Ditmore, 2005; Miko, 2005).

---

4 See, for example Rogers, (2008) "The Shocking Truth About the Vice Trade: Girls of fourteen working as sex slaves" in *The Daily Mail*, 25th January, 2008 or Hickley, M. (2008) "Hundreds of girls rescued from traffickers in Britain are snatched back and forced into prostitution" in *The Daily Mail*, 4th January 2008, which suggests that "up to 25.000 women and girls are trapped in a modern form of slavery – smuggled into the country, threatened with violence and forced to work as prostitutes".

5 See, for example Branigan, T. (2008) "Tories attack government for lack of action on trafficking" in the Guardian, January 4th, 2008

Despite their common interest, activists and lobbyists may hold diametrically opposed views about whether prostitution itself is inherently *trafficking in persons.*

Unreliable and uncorroborated assertions have led to confusion as to even the scale of trafficking in the world. For example, the UN has estimated that between 700.000 and 2 million women are trafficked across international borders annually (up to 4 million, including domestic trafficking), the majority of which are exploited for sexual purposes (UNPFA, 2008). According to the International Organisation of Migration (IOM) around 500.000 women are sold annually to local prostitution markets and "100.000[6] individuals have been trafficked from The Ukraine for various forms of exploitation since 1991" (IOM, 2007). Pyshchulina (2005) has suggested that "420.000 women have been trafficked [from The Ukraine] in the last few years alone" and the US Department of State (2004) maintains that between 600.000 and 800.000 people worldwide are trafficked across borders each year. Many of these estimates have been queried (Jordan *et al*, 2005, di Nicola, 2007) due to the absence of valid research or evidence therein. Statistics about trafficking are unreliable, due to the clandestine nature of the activity, but also because many countries cannot maintain accurate data (Jordan *et al*, 2005; di Nicola, 2007). What statistics do exist are 'slippery', due in part to the variability of the definitions used to identify who constitutes a 'trafficked-person' and the criminal networks that are responsible for the trade. In addition, in this chapter, statistics illustrating cases and prosecutions in The Ukraine and the UK must be acknowledged as limited, due to differences in recording procedures, interpretations of seriousness and of 'success'. International researchers report large numbers of unrecorded cases and dramatic increases in recent years. Indeed, TfSE is not amenable to traditional forms of data collection or social research (Kelly, 2000) although Kelly has estimated that up to 4.000 women had been trafficked into the UK by 2003. To sum, there are still no accurate estimates available either nationally or internationally (di Nicola, 2007).

The trial processes and subsequent sanctions imposed that follow the much-hyped 'crack-downs' on human trafficking in The Ukraine and the England & Wales[7] are difficult to interpret. Pakes, (2004) has pointed out the importance of 'pre-trial justice', the relative secrecy in which it often takes place and the far-reaching nature of the decisions that can be made at that stage. Available

---

6 All numbers in this paper are in European decimal notation.

7 Operation Pentameter; Operation Pentameter 2; Operation Radium (Cambridgeshire)

conviction data does not offer insight into 'plea-bargaining' or subsequent convictions on 'lesser' charges applied to the defendant at the prosecution stage (Lewis, 2008). Nor do they provide information on the impact that the proceedings had on the victims. In the UK, the first Operation Pentameter[8] in 2006, 'freed' 88 women and teenage girls from brothels and massage parlours leading to 232 arrests[9] (Avenall, 2008; BBC, 2007). However, many 'released victims' are deported, despite the government's assurance that they intend to ratify the Council of Europe Convention on Action Against Trafficking in Human Beings (the "Council of Europe Convention"), which they signed in March 2007. The Convention advocates (*inter alia*) that each signatory 'shall adopt such legislative or other measures as may be necessary to assist victims in their physical, psychological and social recovery' (Chapter III, Article 12.1); and that each signatory shall provide *in its internal law* a recovery and reflection period of at least 30 days, when there are reasonable grounds to believe that the person concerned *is a victim*. These articles are relevant because deportation remains one the main ways that victims of trafficking can be returned to their countries of origin from the various countries they have been transported to. Out of 46 cases considered in one Ukrainian study, 16 of the women were repatriated (Shvab, 2007). Furthermore, despite pledges of co-operation, through Interpol and Europol, there is arguably little evidence of close working-relationships – especially with the countries where levels of police and judicial corruption are so closely aligned with the levels of sexual exploitation therein. Law enforcement officers in The Ukraine and the UK complain about delays and inadequate responses from international organisations, such as Interpol (Shvab, 2007).

In the following sections, we will evaluate the impact of recent legislative changes in the UK and The Ukraine on human trafficking for sexual exploitation. We contrast and compare them, whilst acknowledging the difficulties in equating two very different countries. We also highlight differences between the UK and Ukrainian legal systems, including sentencing, victim

---

8 Operation Pentameter 1 (P1) was a police-led, multi-agency campaign against trafficking for sexual exploitation. It was the first operation of its kind and involved police and partners across the United Kingdom. Its primary aim was to rescue victims of trafficking for sexual exploitation (TfSE). Preparation began in 2005 and the live operational phase ran between February and May 2006. In total, 88 women were rescued as a result. The operation was intended to shift the policing focus from victim escapees (reactive) to active identification/rescue (proactive). (Avenall, 2008)

9 "New Crackdown on Sex Trafficking", BBC, October 3rd, 2007. Accessed at http://news.bbc.co.uk/1/hi/uk/7024646.stm

support and repatriation. Although the definitions of 'trafficking' within the two countries are now relatively coherent, differences in data collection, analysis and the respective legal systems make it complicated to determine the reality, both for trafficked individuals and traffickers. The Ukraine has been identified as a country with an endemic level of corruption, which adds further complexity. This chapter also considers the possible impact of corruption within law enforcement agencies on the treatment of traffickers.

## Definitional and national 'translations' of trafficking in women

Crossing borders in the twenty-first century, other than for reasons of tourism, is often an attempt to improve quality of life (Spencer, 2007). Spencer (2007) has provided a useful analysis of the gaps that remain in our capacity to disentangle many of the issues that surround trafficking. Despite the recent surge of interest in and research on trafficking and immigration, there still exists a dark area, when it comes to distinguishing between: migrant workers; willing trafficked-migrants; smuggled migrants; unwilling trafficked victims and victims of sexual exploitation (Ditmore, 2005; Kempadoo, 2005; Anderson and O'Connell Davidson, 2003). Judgements are further muddied by the entrenched attitudes that societies and governments exhibit towards sex-workers, which promote the idea that prostitution is a social *problem*. The position of the prostitute woman as a 'problem' to society has been well documented, and aligned with political and social policy developments (see Scott, 2005 for a very good analysis). Despite this, the demand has magnified along with its provision, and the clientele that clearly endorse and capitalise on prostitution.

The way women are viewed in relation to sex work attributes to a general ambiguity. A woman who willingly becomes a prostitute is barely tolerated, and she is rarely viewed as a 'real' or 'innocent' victim, regardless how she is treated by her customer, pimp or trafficker. Sex-workers have been portrayed as victims (of circumstance, predators or drugs), yet they are still characterised (at least through many legal battles) as untrustworthy, disreputable and suspicious. This problem is augmented further when women involved in sex work are called as witnesses in legal trials. Through the underground nature of their trade, sex-workers are associated with all kinds of illicit behaviour, as well as sex, which, in turn, can be used against them should they report further victimisation. Further complexities that affect sex work in the 21st Century can be identified in the economic transition experienced in the former Soviet Union and Eastern Europe, adding to the conditions in which prostitution and human trafficking can flourish (Miko, 2005; Surtees 2008). Many people have been attracted by the opportunities of a better life abroad, providing traffickers with lucrative exploitative prospects.

Numerous definitions have been proffered to aid in our understanding of what constitutes human trafficking[10], and they can shift in emphasis (Di Nicola, 2007; O'Connell Davidson, 2003; Kelly, 2000). TfSE has been addressed separately in many countries. However, defining such trafficking is further complicated by the fact that such 'abuses' can vary in severity, covering a continuum of experience (Anderson, 2007). Between those transported and forced to work under threats of violence or death, and trafficked people who are complicit in their arrangements lie an endless realm of accounts and experiences (Anderson, 2007). This definitional conundrum is further complicated, in that often the 'definers' are those who provide victim services or enforce the law (Spencer, 2007), frequently operating from polarised (and sometimes contested) perspectives. In addition, the judgement of 'innocent' or 'engaged' (Ditmore, 2005, Anderson, 2007) can be arbitrarily applied, depending on the (re)actions of the police, the prosecutors or immigration officials. Relying on legal definitions, can limit research directions and prevent the research community from producing new and helpful knowledge (Di Nicola, 2007). As researchers, we aim to go beyond official definitions, whilst still bearing them in mind in order to unravel what happens in practice.

England and Wales, and The Ukraine have adopted distinct 'definitions' of human trafficking, which we will contrast. In 1998, The Ukraine became the first country of the Former Soviet Union to make human trafficking a separate criminal offence. Changes were made to the existing Criminal Code, introducing article 124-1.[11] This Ukrainian definition of human trafficking was inconsistent

---

10 See, for example The European Commission, 1996, EUROPOL, 1997, Escaler, 1998, Global Alliance Against Traffic in Women (GAATW), 1999, The Coalition Against Trafficking in Women (CATW), 1999, Kalayaan, 1999 & the United Nations 2000.

11 Article 124-1, 1998 defined trafficking in human beings as "an open or secret capture of a human being, committing him or her to any other illegal contract concerning legal, or illegal, consensual or otherwise, crossing of the Ukrainian state border, or without crossing, for further sale or other transfer with the aim of sexual exploitation,

with contemporary international developments as there was no clear legal definition within the article. For example, the law did not accommodate for different *types* of human trafficking. Article 124-1 mentioned 'sexual exploitation', 'pornographic industry', 'servitude' and 'exploitation of labour' with little contextualisation. In order to begin the criminal investigation according to article 124-1, it was necessary to establish the *intention* of sexual exploitation, or similar crimes.

A new Criminal Code was adopted in The Ukraine in April 2001, introducing Article 149, "Trafficking in human beings or other illegal agreements about humans".[12] Under this legislation, a conviction will result in imprisonment of between three and eight years. Part II of Article 149 makes provision for actions "committed against a minor, or several persons, or repeatedly, by previous arrangement between a group of persons, using one's official position or by a person on whom the victim was financially or otherwise dependent". Upon conviction, this crime is punishable by imprisonment of between five and twelve years. Part III of Article 149 makes the provision for those previously outlined actions "which have been committed by an organised group or which have been connected to illegal trafficking of children abroad or failing to return them to The Ukraine".[13] Upon conviction, this crime is punishable by imprisonment of between eight and fifteen years. Amendments to Article 112 "Under Investigation" transferred the authority for the investigation from Prosecutor's Office[14] to the police. The Ministry of Internal Affairs is now responsible for investigating criminal cases and, where appropriate, cases are passed on to the Office of Prosecutor General. The case is admitted to court if the prosecutor is satisfied that "there is sufficient evidence to substantiate the charges brought against a suspect, and that the correct procedures have been followed" (Lucenko, *et al*, 2005). This rule can prove problematic, as when the prosecutor is not

---

use in the pornography industry, taking part in criminal activities, servitude, adoption for commercial purposes, using in armed conflicts, exploitation of labour".

12 Article 149, 2001 defines trafficking in human beings as "the sale or other paid transfer of a human being and committing him or her to any other illegal contract concerning legal or illegal, consensual or otherwise, crossing of Ukrainian state border, for further sale or other transfer to another person (persons) with the aim of sexual exploitation, using in pornographic industry, taking part in criminal activities, servitude, adoption for commercial purposes, using in armed conflicts, exploitation of labour".

13 Or with the goal of taking organs or tissues for transplantation from the victims, or forced donation, or if these actions have caused grave consequences.

14 Under Article 124-1, The Prosecutor General of The Ukraine was the only department to authorise and conduct criminal investigations in trafficking cases.

satisfied, the case is returned to the police for 'additional investigation' which in reality is rarely possible.

Since 1999, The Ukraine has arguably made a number of serious attempts to legislate against TfSE and to establish a coordinated response to the problem. However, the first wide-ranging programme adopted in 1999, and the comprehensive approach that followed in 2002, failed to attract funding to support the initiative. Consequently, it failed to provide coordinated and practical responses to trafficking, thus leaving the laws 'without teeth'. It might also be argued that the main drivers of the adoption of the human trafficking legislation in The Ukraine were non-governmental organisations (NGOs) working on behalf of women's interests, and politicians keen to introduce legislation to comply with international conventions. Parallels may be drawn with the establishment of Ukrainian money laundering legislation, where non-compliance may damage a country's reputation and business interests.

In 2002, the Ukrainian Cabinet of Ministers established an action plan to address trade in human beings. It also addressed the issue of cooperation *between* agencies in the country. In 2003, the question of rehabilitative centres for the victims of trafficking reached the agenda of the Cabinet of Ministers, and in 2004, The Ukraine ratified the United Nations Convention Against Transnational Organised Crime and its Protocols (see footnote 15), which it had signed in 2001. To ensure compliance with international legislation the Ukrainian national legislation has been adjusted. However, whilst The Palermo Protocol described both domestic and international trafficking, the Ukrainian side focused on the facilitation of movement across the Ukrainian border for the purpose of exploitation, identifying the concept of trafficking in the context of organised crime (Lucenko, *et al*, 2005).

By February, 2006, both the UK and The Ukraine had ratified the UN Protocol to Prevent, Suppress and Punish Trafficking in Persons, Especially Women and Children.[15] So far, England and Wales has passed three separate

15 Article 3 of the UN Protocol, 1996 stipulates that: "Trafficking in persons" shall mean the recruitment, transportation, transfer, harbouring, or receipt of persons, by means of threat or use of force or other forms of coercion, of abduction, of fraud, of deception, of the abuse of power or of a position of vulnerability or of the giving or receiving of payments or benefits to achieve the consent of a person having control over another person, for the purpose of exploitation. Exploitation shall include, at the minimum, the exploitation of the prostitution of others or other forms of sexual exploitation, forced labour or services, slavery or practices similar to slavery, servitude or removal of organs".

pieces of legislation relating to trafficking in human beings[16]: section 145 of the Nationality, Immigration and Asylum Act, 2002[17] legislates against "Traffic in prostitution"; section 57, 58 & 59 of the Sexual Offences Act, 2003[18] has legislated against "trafficking into the UK -", "trafficking within the UK -", and "trafficking out of the UK - for sexual exploitation" respectively; and section 4 of the Asylum and Immigration Act, 2004[19] has legislated against "Trafficking people for exploitation" generally. All of these newly defined crimes carry a maximum penalty, upon conviction on indictment of fourteen years imprisonment. In the years since these pieces of legislation have been passed the scale and response to TfSE by the police and media[20] has far surpassed the scale of successful convictions or prevention strategies. There is also recent evidence that the focus on trafficking and exploitation has diverted attention away from some of the other effects of such intensive policing, such as speedy deportations of illegal immigrants who refuse to testify against their traffickers.

The two countries in question have approached the definition and legislative focus from very different perspectives. In The Ukraine, the emphasis has been on contractual agreements, the age of the victim, number of victims and abuses of 'trust'. In contrast, the UK has chosen to identify 'trafficking' and its specified intent (prostitution or exploitation) as the main area of focus. Already, these variable approaches highlight the problems that arise when attempting to contrast the process and outcomes of these charges, as played through the system. Even after identifying numbers (of prosecutions, trial or convictions), the type of case involved, the relevant legal issues and the measure of 'success' will vary due to

---

16 Until 2002, there was no specific human trafficking law. Prior to the enactment of the Nationality, Immigration and Asylum Act 2002 prosecuting authorities could proceed against traffickers by using laws criminalising some of the constituent elements of trafficking, such as kidnapping, assault, rape, or immigration offences like facilitating illegal entry (Gilbert, 2007).

17 Available to view online at http://www.opsi.gov.uk/Acts/acts2002/ukpga_20020041_en_1

18 Available to view online at http://www.opsi.gov.uk/Acts/acts2003/ukpga_20030042_en_1

19 Available to view online at http://www.opsi.gov.uk/ACTS/acts2004/ukpga_20040019_en_1#pb1-l1g4

20 News stories, such as the following, "*Police, launching an operation to liberate women forced into prostitution, revealed there were up to 100 brothels in the county, many operating as "sex prisons" for women lured from abroad with false promises of a better life. Six victims of the evil trade have already been rescued, including a pregnant 16-year-old from Uganda, and have told of a grim existence, threatened with swords and baseball bats by their captives and too terrified to try to escape*" (Cambridge Evening News, 17th, August, 2007).

the different classifications of what constitutes 'trafficking' itself within each country.

## The Ukraine: scale and nature of human trafficking for sexual exploitation

In The Ukraine in 2007, 454 and 267 victims of sexual and labour exploitation were identified, respectively (IOM, 2007). This data may not be a true interpretation – indeed, most likely it is an under-representation. It is noteworthy, that 34% of the victims were men, and that the proportion of men claiming to be the victims of trafficking has increased from a level of only 16% in 2004.[21] Anecdotal evidence suggests that most of the victims of slave labour come from Russia, where recruiters often claim to be able to provide well-paid work in Moscow. Shvab (2007; see footnote 23) suggests that in the majority of trafficking cases, the recruiters are often acquaintances or friends and know the victim well. Some recruiters specifically target those in difficult financial circumstances (Shvab, 2007). "A friend of my older sister offered me a job in Moscow to earn 'lots of money'. I didn't ask how much money would earn or what I needed to do", explained one victim of trafficking" (*Ibid*).

Levchenko (2007) maintains that in recent years the merchandise of human trafficking in The Ukraine 'got younger'. More women aged 15 to 19, are trafficked to work in the sex industry, suggesting an increasing problem with trade in children (*Ibid.*).[22] In addition, the 'workload' of recruiters seems to have changed significantly during the last few years, in order for the business to be more profitable (Levchenko, 2007). Now, as well as finding their victims and preparing all the necessary official papers, recruiters appear to have expanded their remit to that of 'trafficker': moving the victims abroad and transferring them to the buyers for payments. Shelley (2007) cites an American example where a Ukrainian was in charge of a significant trafficking network in Los Angeles, including recruiters, entrepreneurs and managers. Levchenko (2007) has also suggested that the relaxation of the visa regime for citizens of the EU, Canada and the USA in 2005 will contribute to increased levels of sexual exploitation in

21 Men are more likely to be the victims of labour exploitation and it has been suggested by one Ukrainian NGO that 70% of new cases of trafficking is of this type.

22 More 'victims' aged 30 to 50 are trafficked to provide servile, domestic work, and to work in illegal factories.

disadvantaged children. Law enforcement agencies have already identified cases of child sex tourism in The Ukraine with the perpetrators coming from France, Sweden, the USA and elsewhere (*ibid*). It seems that the predictions were correct, and the UK is experiencing similar trends, since the accession of many central and eastern European countries into the EU.

## Legislative Response in The Ukraine

Although attempts have been made to improve the legislation in The Ukraine, a number of problems still persist. Shvab (2007)[23] has identified problems with Article 149. Firstly, trafficking was only considered to be a crime if undertaken outside of Ukrainian borders. Without proof of 'recruitment', 'transfer', or 'crossing the state boarder' the crime could not be proven. Those who helped the traffickers to 'recruit', apply for a passport or to buy travel tickets for the victims, could be considered merely as witnesses, thus avoiding prosecution. The main perpetrators of the crime usually reside abroad, leading to difficulties relating to prosecution in The Ukraine. In particular, Shvab (2007) notes lengthy waiting-periods for confirmation on the perpetrators' identities from Interpol, resulting in the commencement of the trial without important information from abroad. Frequently, in extra-national cases, the legal action was not even considered under article 149. Instead, Article 302 of the Criminal Code of The Ukraine "Establishing and running of the place to sell sexual services and soliciting" was applied. Similar results have been identified in the UK, with defendants pleading guilty to charges that carry much reduced penalties upon conviction. Further difficulties have arisen through the necessity to prove the 'transfer-for-payment' of the victim from one individual to another. Even with proof of payments, such as Western Union receipts, it can be difficult to prove *intention* of monies exchanged. One officer working on trafficking cases commented that the majority of judges understand the definition of 'paid transfer' literally, and demand the receipts in cases where the victim was present during 'the transfer' (Shvab, 2007). Such examples illustrate that there are some

[23] Shvab (2007) conducted some major research on the issue of human trafficking, analysing a sample of criminal cases on trafficking, discussing the problems with the different criminal justice agencies involved, and victims of trafficking.

significant obstacles to achieving satisfactory outcomes, even when a substantial case has made it as far as the prosecution stage.

Proving the *intention* of exploitation of another individual is also problematic. Shvab (2007) has highlighted that the majority of regional courts in The Ukraine have failed to pursue any cases under charges of trafficking *with the aim* of exploitation. Most cases opened concern the transportation of people under false documents, or the absence of appropriate licenses. Apart from the problems with the law and its application, Shvab (2007) has also identified concerns with the pre-trial investigation stage. The main problem is the absence of adequate resources[24] and problems with international cooperation. In The Ukraine, the majority of defendants prosecuted under Article 149 tend to be 'recruiters', and they normally present the weakest link in trafficking cases. As mentioned before, the main perpetrators often live abroad, requiring official requests for information, with associated delays. It is possible that the Ukrainian judiciary may not have appropriate experience of trafficking be able to deliver the appropriate sentence in all cases. Also, corruption may complicate individual cases. Interestingly, Shvab (2007) mentioned that both the police and victims of trafficking identified the corruption of judges as a possible obstacle to a fair trial, potentially leading to complications in sentencing. Not surprisingly, no specific examples were specified.

## Prosecution and sentencing in The Ukraine

In The Ukraine, the Prosecutor General's Office is responsible for: ensuring the legality of investigation; approval for the detention of suspects; the protection of the rights of all participants, including suspects, witnesses and victims). It is difficult to prove cases under Article 149, and such cases are not encouraged by the Office of Public Prosecutors, instead, prosecutions are steered under Article 303, part 2 on Prostitution and Pimping. These findings are corroborated by Lucenko, (2004) who found that in the period from 2001-2004, and Shvab (2007) in 2007, that Ukrainian prosecutors have avoided using the human trafficking legislation to prosecute offenders, which may be preferable to no conviction at all.

---

24 One Head of Department mentioned that his department received 10 litres of petrol for the three months of the investigative work (Shvab, 2007).

**Table 1.**
**Numbers of defendants charged and the articles of the Criminal Code of The Ukraine (connected to prostitution) in 2002**

| Type of offence committed | Article of the Criminal Code of The Ukraine | Convictions |
|---|---|---|
| Maintaining brothels and procuring | 210, part 1 | 5 |
| Establishing or maintaining brothels and procuring | 302, parts 1 & 2 | 105 |
| Prostitution, coercion or recruiting into the business of prostitution (1) | 303 | 53 |

*(Source: Lucenko, et al, 2004)*

Further obstacles are encountered due to the fact that the Ukrainian legislation permits only two months to complete the required pre-trial investigation. Given this time frame, it can be almost impossible to collect sufficient evidence to build a successful case. Law enforcement officials who fail to comply with the deadlines can be subject to reprimand, so there is "fear among prosecutors of losing a case because of too little evidence" (Pyshchulina, 2005). The success rate is usually determined according to the number of cases *opened* in any given period. As we know, human trafficking cases are often complex cases with multiple victims, involving a number of officers using different indicators. Therefore, *success* rates may not reflect the effectiveness of the department. Low conviction rates for sexual offences are common in most jurisdictions, so the Ukrainian decision to focus on other sexual offences may be based on utilitarian considerations.

**Table 2.**
**Human trafficking criminal cases 1/01/2003- 31/12/2003**

| | |
|---|---|
| Criminal cases opened in 2003 | 104 |
| Criminal cases opened before 2003 and pending | 130 |
| Criminal cases brought to court 2003 | 59 |
| The number of cases completed in 2003 with the offenders convicted (verdicts) | 11 |
| Criminal cases under investigation by the end of 2003 (unfinished) | 20 |
| Criminal cases closed under art. 6 of Criminal Procedure Code in 2003 | 6 |
| Criminal cases dropped under art. 206 of Criminal Procedure Code (adjourned in 2003) | 80 |
| Total number of people under investigation | 160 |
| Total number of victims | 413 |

*(Source: Lucenko, et al, 2004)*

Table 2 demonstrates that the total number of human trafficking cases (opened and pending) in 2003 was 234, only 59 reached the court, and less than 5% of these cases resulted in a conviction.25 In the first six months of 2003, seven people were convicted under the old Article 124, and 13 were convicted under the new Article 149 (see footnote 12). However, Lucenko (2004) points out that the actual number of cases is unclear, and (as in later examples from England and Wales) it is difficult to ascertain under which article these cases have been prosecuted. By focusing on convictions in the region of Lugansk from 2000-2003, Lucenko *et al.* (2004) has drawn attention to suspicions of court leniency towards offenders. In 2002, out of 19 criminal cases filed in Lugansk, 16 reached the court and only eight resulted in conviction. None of the convicted had charges complying with those proposed by Section 149 of the Criminal Code. In all cases, the appeal successfully challenged the original terms of sentencing ranging from one to five years imprisonment, to two to three years of suspended sentence (*Ibid*). Shvab (2007) considers an example of a case where the judge originally sentenced a trafficker to eight years imprisonment, but upon appeal significantly reduced the terms. Such outcomes left police investigators involved to question the decision of the appeal, as well as to suggest corruption and bribery as a possible explanation. Court leniency may be an indication of corruption although the evidence is difficult to gather. Despite this low conviction rate in both countries, and the problems associated with variable definitions and prosecution charges, successful convictions of TfSE still appear proportionately higher in England and Wales than in The Ukraine.

It seems that there is a series of events that contribute to these trends. Firstly, the pre-trial investigation is often not conducted properly due to the lack of resources and qualifications (such as specific training on the issues of trafficking), then, when the case reaches court, the judges may have their own agenda either in terms of indicators of the successful work of the criminal justice agencies, or reclassifying the offence to make sure that the case prepared is sound and stands a strong chance of conviction. The victim's willing participation is also crucial to a fair trial. It is thus important to understand why victims often do not want to cooperate with the authorities to achieve this judicial goal and sometimes neglected part of the process.

25 It is not possible to disaggregate cases of human trafficking from those involving sexual exploitation at this stage.

## The position of the victim

The treatment of victims and witnesses in The Ukraine is regulated by legislation concerned with "Protection of victims of crime and witnesses during criminal investigations" adopted in 1994. Unlike in England and Wales, victims of crime have a formal right to obtain protection during any criminal investigation. The law is rather declaratory, however, and may be difficult to implement in practice, due to the financial cost involved. Research conducted by Anti-Slavery International (2002) suggests that "mechanisms for witness protection are hardly developed in general . . . and more often applied to court officials, not witnesses or trafficked persons". Moreover, Shvab (2007) has highlighted further problems for victims of trafficking, relating to disrespect from the general public and the investigative teams, who confuse stereotypes about people who willingly work in the sex industry with those who have been trafficked.

There is a long tradition of criminalisation of the sex industry in The Ukraine. Prior to the implementation of the Criminal Code of 2001, prostitution was not considered a criminal offence in The Ukraine.[26] However, despite protests from many agencies, Part 1 of Article 303[27], "Prostitution or committing or introducing the individual to the Business of and Coercion or Enticement into Prostitution" allowed for prosecution of anyone *systematically* involved in prostitution. Changes introduced in 2006 removed 'criminal' responsibility for individual involvement in prostitution. It is important to emphasise the role of the decriminalisation of prostitution in The Ukraine. Shav's (2007) study suggested that prior to 2006 many traffickers used the criminal standing of prostitution to prevent their victims from going to police. To comply with international law, The Ukraine introduced changes to the Criminal Code, 2001 and 'reversed' its decision to use criminal sanctions against prostitutes. From 2006, prostitution has been considered under the Administrative Code of The Ukraine under 'administrative' misdemeanours. Criminal charges cover such aspects of prostitution as soliciting, introducing somebody to prostitution and coercing them to work as a prostitute, which is broadly similar to the UK.

---

26 It was considered under the same categories as youthful antisocial behaviour and drinking alcohol in public places.

27 Of the Criminal Code of 2001.

In addition, Shvab (2007) identified lack of confidentiality[28] and minimal qualifications of the prosecution lawyers as potentially damaging for victims. Experienced lawyers are often comparatively expensive, thus only available for the defence of the traffickers, who have the means to pay and very often the victims are not aware of the help provided by NGOs. As table 3 demonstrates, since 2007, law enforcement agencies have begun to inform victims about the activities of NGOs in the country, with the result that in that year, 237 victims applied for help.

**Table 3.**
**Victims of trafficking who asked for help from different organisations**

| Organisations | 2001 | 2002 | 2003 | 2004 | 2005 | 2006 | 2007 |
|---|---|---|---|---|---|---|---|
| International migration organisation | 95 | 108 | 42 | 45 | 86 | 66 | 16 |
| Non-governmental organisations | 129 | 205 | 440 | 552 | 727 | 824 | 786 |
| Law enforcement agencies | 30 | 15 | 28 | 9 | 9 | 16 | 14 |

*Source: International Organisation for Migration, 2008*

NGOs may be best equipped to assist the victims of trafficking, as in The Ukraine the enforcement agencies are comparatively poorly-funded and often not sufficiently trained to deal with assisting victims. The NGOs working on projects financed by either international organisation or governments may be better positioned to provide legal consultation, including funding prosecution lawyers. Another potential explanation of poor take-up is the low level of trust in the law enforcement agencies, as well as high levels of corruption (KIIS, 2007). A number of these issues are not specific to The Ukraine, and may resonate in the UK, as many victims bring with them entrenched stereotypes of their homeland criminal justice agencies. Such stereotypes include: threats from traffickers[29]; a reluctance to discuss personal details; a long and arduous judicial process; the

28 In one case the victim was informed about the dates for her trial through the village council. Although the trial process is necessarily transparent, the stigma that is often attached to the status of the victim is very difficult to bear. These issues are also volatile in the UK, where it is now a crime under the Sexual Offences Act, 2003 for the name of a victim in a sexual offence-related trial to be divulged.

29 Relating to revenge, making details public, etc.

excessive length of the trial; the absence of trust in the police; a lack of understanding of victims' rights, indeed that they are the victims at all; unwillingness to spoil a 'relationship' with traffickers in case the victim wants to travel abroad in the future, which further complicates their status as a 'victim'; and the long tradition of criminalisation of prostitution in The Ukraine. Interestingly, several law enforcement officers interviewed by Shvab (2007) also suggested that compensation received by the victims from the traffickers may be an obstacle to conviction, as the victim may withdraw the case even when offered a comparatively small reward. Despite these issues, the number of human trafficking criminal cases registered by the Ministry of Internal Affairs cases filed under the Human Trafficking law continues to rise (Lucenko, 2004; Matiyashek, 2004 and IOM (2007) which suggests that the government is achieving some measure of success.

**Figure 1.**

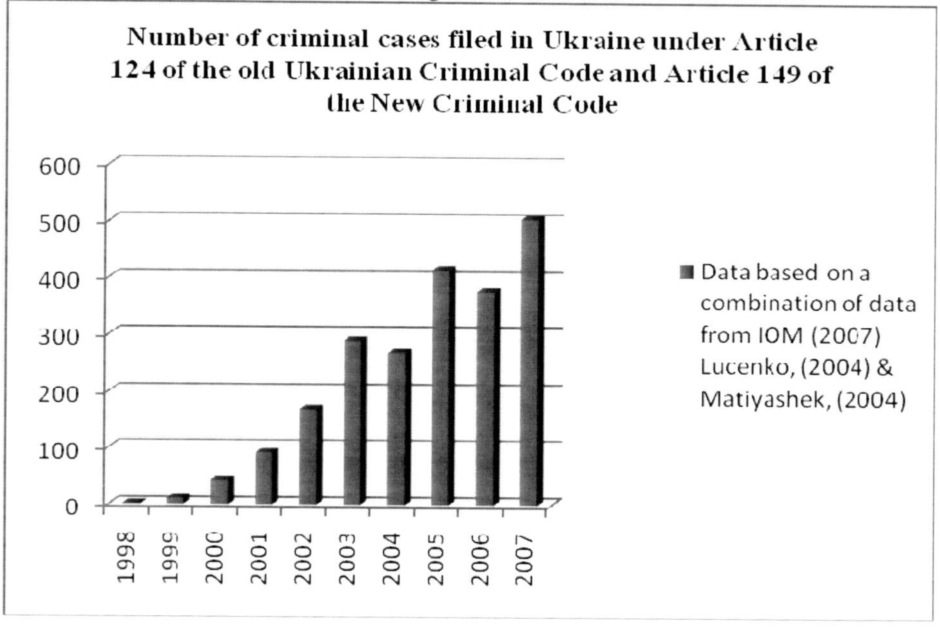


*Source: IOM (2007), Lecenko (2004) and Matiyashek (2004)*

Changes introduced to Article 149 in 2006, might help explain the rise in the number of reported cases from 376 in 2006 to 504 in 2007. These changes include a number of significant issues. Firstly, the physical transportation of an individual *outside* of the boarders of The Ukraine is no longer a precondition for the definition of trafficking. So, the law now permits trafficking cases within the country to be heard. There are also improvements related to the actual definition of trafficking (including the definition of recruiting, transporting, hiding, transfer to another person and receivership of a person). In addition, it is helpful that the term 'exploitation' is now defined, and that trafficking in small children and underage children has been differentiated.

## The UK: The scale and nature of human trafficking for sexual exploitation

As already suggested, there are widely varying estimates as to the scale and nature of TfSE. As a result, a wide and ambiguous range of figures can be found in research reports around the world, with little regard paid to the estimation criteria used to gather them (Van Dijck, 2005, cited in di Nicola, 2007). Added to this, are the difficulties that arise when attempting to understand official statistics and information relating to offender and victim characteristics. Nonetheless, there is a consensus that, from the information available, trafficking into the UK occurs on a scale that merits serious attention by the authorities.

Most thriving businesses escalate due to demand, and TfSE appears to be one of the biggest growing 'organised criminal' industries[30] (Roberts, 2006). What constitutes 'organised crime' is contested, however. As Spencer (2007) illustrates, 'gangs' may be small family affairs, and the costly national response to the 'transnational threat' may be misdirected. The IOM (2005) conducted research on the question "Is trafficking in human beings demand driven?" and found a causal link between labour-protections and trafficking: "In both sex and domestic work, the absence of effective regulation is one of the factors that help to create an environment in which it is possible and profitable to use un-free labour" (Anderson & O'Connell Davidson, 2005). The UK is primarily a destination country for victims of sexual exploitation, rather than a transit country in trafficking routes (as in the case of The Ukraine), which suggests that there is an existing demand for their services there.

---

30 According to police and lawyers, up to 80% of 'off street' prostitution- in massage parlours, peep shows and brothels – in places such as Glasgow and London, involve women from Eastern Europe and the Baltic states.

Not a great deal of research exists which focuses on the expansion through demand-debate. However, Anderson and O'Connell Davidson (2005) have suggested that "personal characteristics, including linguistic capacities can matter a great deal to those who buy sex . . ." This premise was corroborated during a recent trial in England, where the Latvian complainant described all of the men she was sold for sex with as being Russian or Latvian-speaking. In the area in which she had been put to work, there is a large and growing Eastern European migrant population, which facilitated meeting demand. The complainant claimed to have been trafficked for sexual exploitation within England, after having come to England legally, to find legitimate work. Here we find again the backgrounds with which such migration has been connected, (poverty, lack of sustainable livelihoods, structural inequities in society and gender discrimination) though they are not necessarily causes in themselves. However, they do exacerbate vulnerability of marginalised and disadvantaged groups (Sanghera, 2005). In her statement to the police, the complainant stated that she had initially been sold as a sex worker in Latvia, when she was eighteen years old (eight years previously). Such revelations can further confuse the decision-makers[31] in the legal process, as during the cross-examination of witnesses, their 'character' comes under close scrutiny. If it is revealed that they have had previous convictions, previous encounters with the law, or that they have attempted to conceal something that may be relevant to their case (such as having previously worked as a prostitute), they can be discredited, and in some cases, this can mean that the case is dismissed. For example, in 2005, during a trial where the complainant failed to acknowledge her past, the presiding judge stated "she dishonestly and persistently stuck to her assertion [that] she had never previously been a prostitute, but there has now been incontrovertible evidence that her assertion is wholly untrue". Directing not guilty verdicts, he said because the Russian (complainant) had been proved a liar on that point, it would be difficult to be sure she was telling the truth on other issues. This case illustrates the precarious position that a woman who has a history of sex work can find herself in, should she complain about her working conditions. In this case, because she had previously worked as a prostitute –about which she lied– she was not believed when she claimed she was trafficked and forced into prostitution against her will.

Added to these problems are other potential obstacles to successful outcomes for the trafficked-exploited person, such as: their age, their status within the

31 Such as the jury.

country (which may be undocumented), their colleagues or peers who may be engaging in illegal activities (Sanghera, 2005), and language barriers during police questioning. All of these additional issues can be barriers to justice. Furthermore, there is a considerable gap that exists between the demand-driven phenomenon and the intervention strategies proposed (rescue, repatriation, rehabilitation and prevention, as well as exploration into options for legal employment) within England and Wales. When a woman is identified as a potential victim of TfSE, she is faced with a range of disagreeable prospects, such as testifying against her trafficker and making police statements, which may implicate a wide range of other people, and result in criminal chargesfor herself and in deportation. She is transformed simultaneously into both a victim and a criminal (Sanghera, 2005). Many women choose to 'disappear' or opt for immediate deportation, only to return and take up sex work in alternative and possibly safer environments. These issues highlight further the problems that can be associated with successful prosecutions of traffickers, when the 'victim' was once a willing prostitute, but is now unwillingly working in certain, undesirable conditions.

In England and Wales there are a handful of refuges where women seeking support can turn. Since 2003, the Poppy Project, funded by the UK Government[32] has, offered thirty-five beds to 'suitably' abused women. There are a number of criteria that women must agree to before they are given refuge at the Poppy Project, namely that they are encouraged to co-operate with the authorities (agree to testify against their abuser, give information to law enforcement agencies for intelligence purposes or agree to be a witness in court) (Poppy Project, 2008). They have to have been trafficked to the UK, and forced to work as a prostitute in the UK in the three months prior to the date of referral. According to the English Collective of Prostitutes33, "the fear of arrest and being detained and deported is the single biggest obstacle to coming forward"; a fear that will arguably be aggravated by criteria posited by the Poppy Project. These fears are comparable to those expressed in The Ukraine, as cited earlier in the chapter. One victim in The Ukraine is recorded as stating "The traffickers told me that if I go to the militia they would first open a criminal case against me, as I was a prostitute. And only after that would they think about the traffickers themselves. But who is going to seriously listen to me if I am myself a criminal?" (Shvab, 2007).

32 The Government pledged £2,4 million over 2 years in 2006.

33 BBC News, 2nd October, 2006, "A Tiny Drop in the Ocean", accessed at http://news.bbc.co.uk/1/hi/uk/5365412.stm

Appalling levels of violence mean that women often deny they have been trafficked when 'recovered' in raids by the police or refuse to disclose their experiences. This applies particularly when, in contravention of Home Office guidelines on gender, they are questioned by men, using male interpreters (Roberts, 2006). In October, 2005, when 'Cuddles', a Birmingham massage parlour was raided, police discovered 19 women, six of whom were illegal immigrants, who they transferred to Yarl's Wood immigration removal centre to face deportation within days. Immigration officials claimed that none of the women indicated that they were trafficked into the UK (Roberts, 2006). It is not surprising that the women failed to disclose their circumstances in such an intimidating environment.

If the women were not trafficked at all, those cases should not be made with human trafficking in [other] discussions. Adams (2008) has expressed concern for the very motives underlying government scrutiny, suggesting that trafficking "is being used to target and deport immigrant sex workers." There is little evidence that a distinction is made between genuine victims and immigrant sex workers – especially since so few make it to court, and to date, no information pertaining to the status of the 88 'rescued' victims through Operation Pentameter 1 has been forthcoming. The Poppy Project has claimed that although 99% of women who are trafficked tend to be refused stay in the UK, about 80% of women win their cases on appeal (Hibbert, 2007). This figure, however, is based on those women who admit to having been trafficked, pursue their cases and have the support of the Poppy Project. Therefore the data seems not to include those women who are deported quickly, and who do not fit the Poppy Project selection criteria.

## Discussion of legal responses to trafficking & related offences in England & Wales and The Ukraine

Following the first Operation Pentameter[34] in 2006 in the UK, 232 arrests were made, of which 134 resulted in charges.[35] It has not been made public what specific charges were brought following these arrests. By examining national judicial statistics published through the UK Ministry of Justice for 2005 and 2006,

[34] See footnote 7 for more information.
[35] Ministry of Justice, 2007.

it is possible to identify some trends relating to specific crimes. For example, there were 33 and 43 "Trafficking for Sexual Exploitation" crimes recorded, respectively in 2005/6. Bearing in mind that some charges recorded in 2004 may not reach court until later, there still exist a large incongruity between arrests and subsequent convictions (12 and 15 respectively) under identifiable categories. Furthermore, appeals can alter published criminal statistics from year to year. As a result, it is very difficult to present a complete picture of the success or otherwise of criminal procedure relating to TfSE to date. It is hoped that by highlighting these difficulties, it will become possible to address them in the future.[36] Based on such confusing information, it is difficult to appreciate how the allocation of police activity, publication of statistics and prevention programmes can be effective.

The majority of police forces in England and Wales have limited knowledge of, and thus give restricted attention to, trafficking,[37] and there is a danger that this unintentionally creates a climate of toleration for trafficking of women into and within the UK. Styles of policing reflect 'cultural, religious, economic, political and historic realities' (Fairchild & Dammer, cited in Pakes, 2003) and comparing police activity or 'success' in either country can be problematical. In addition, as in The Ukraine, establishing 'intent' to traffic, until the crime is committed is problematical (Sanghera, 2005: 16).[38] Even when police and prosecution services successfully bring a case to trial, all kinds of barriers exist to conviction, as demonstrated above. In 2006, 43 charges of Trafficking for sexual exploitation were brought in the UK, but only 16 made it to court under these charges. It is possible that some of the trafficking charges were discarded, at the pre-trial stage, to align with guilty pleas or stronger evidence relating to exploitation of prostitution[39], and this may explain why the convictions relating to convictions for procuration or exploitation of prostitution (as shown in figure

---

36 When the authors requested more comprehensive data from police in the UK, under the Freedom of Information Act, we were informed that such information is not held on local police systems (email correspondence, Cambridgeshire Constabulary, 2008). We are still pursuing the data.

37 The government in the UK have pledged to address this deficit in 2008 (Avenall, 2008).

38 Although through Pentameter 1, one trafficked-girl was intercepted and rescued by police and never reached her destination.

39 Such as Causing or inciting prostitution for gain (*Sexual Offences Act 2003 Sec 52.* 24/18). Controlling prostitution for gain (*Sexual Offences Act 2003 Sec 33A (53.*24/19). Keeping a brothel used for prostitution (*Sexual Offences Act 1956 Sec as added by Sexual Offences Act 2003 Sec 55).*

2) have risen slightly from 23 in 2004 to 39 in 2006. Comparable data for The Ukraine is not available after 2002.

**Figure 2.**

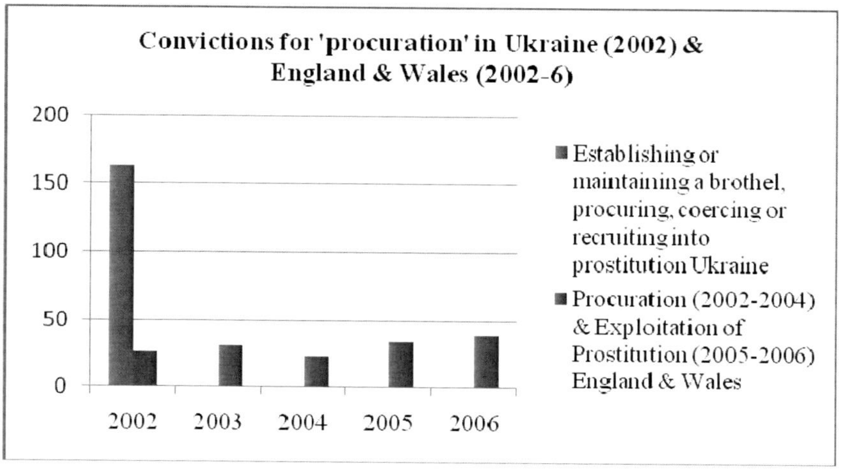


*Source: Home Office, 2007, Ministry of Justice, 2007 & Lucenko, et al, 2004*

Defendants may be more likely to admit to 'procuration' or keeping a brothel than trafficking charges, due to the more lenient sanctions that can be imposed. Even with evidence of coercion as an aggravating factor, the minimum sentence upon conviction of 'causing, inciting or controlling prostitution for gain' is between two years minimum and seven years maximum. In contrast, a conviction under 'Trafficking for sexual exploitation' will receive a sentence of between two to 14 years, depending upon aggravating factors. Clearly, the message here is that trafficking for sexual exploitation is a much more serious offence than sexual exploitation, despite the fact that the 'victims' may be experiencing comparable levels of victimisation. Discussions relating to these incongruities are beginning to emerge in the Appeal Courts in the UK, and will be considered later in the chapter.

## Factors that can determine 'success' at court

The authors have witnessed some of the factors that can lead to the collapse of cases in England and Wales. This is without the judicial and official levels of corruption that are manifest in The Ukraine. In the first place, translation issues can pose enormous problems for all parties involved. If a witness is interviewed during police questioning in her mother-tongue, her translated words will be closely scrutinised by the prosecution and the defence. Any flaws in translation can potentially render her testimony invalid, which can hinder a fair trial. Furthermore, the length of time that cases take to get to trial can have serious implications for the witnesses, especially those who choose to return home or are deported. Travelling back to the UK months later, facing their trafficker and rapist, re-living their ordeal under rigorous cross-examination, whilst trying to recover, can all be debilitating and contribute to illness, post traumatic stress and worse. If the victim has a history of drug use or prostitution, previous convictions or any other 'bad character' background, there is anecdotal evidence that her testimony may be discredited and even discarded. Financial difficulties can be compounded by further risks, especially when witnesses are denied access to services in the UK. The Poppy Project has evidence of cases where women still at risk from their traffickers have sought legal advice and been told they will not receive legal aid. In one case, the Project was made aware of a woman who was forced to continue being exploited in the sex industry in order to pay for her asylum claim, further jeopardising her claim as she was still in contact with her pimps / traffickers (Poppy Project, 2006). Victims' identities are not always sufficiently protected through the use of protective measures in court[40] because these are *ad-hoc* and not used systematically. The decision to employ them is a judicial one and the Judge is not *required* to consider a victims' particular vulnerability as a victim of trafficking. In addition, unlike in The Ukraine, there is currently no link between a victim's willingness and ability to testify in court and their on-going protection in the UK – witnesses may therefore testify without any protective measures yet still face being removed from the UK to their country of origin, potentially facing reprisals (Poppy Project, 2006). Such a situation is far from desirable, especially considering the weight that the government in England & Wales is currently attaching to TfSE.

Although the UK government's action plan says the Crown Prosecution Service regards human trafficking cases as a priority, there have been only 67 convictions[41] so far for trafficking under the Sexual Offences Act 2003, and these

---

40 Such as testifying with an alias, using protective screens or video-links, not releasing victim's names to the media.

41 Vernon Coaker, UK Parliament, November 26th 2007. This figure does not tally with data released from the Ministry of Justice that specifically relates to TfSE. Even if the

are difficult to pinpoint in official statistics, possibly due to publication dates42. The Joint Parliamentary Committee on Human Rights (2006) has stated that there have been too few prosecutions under existing laws, and even the Under-Secretary of State has highlighted the fact that there have been no convictions to date for forced labour under the Asylum and Immigration Act 2004 (Coaker, 2007). Furthermore, it was announced that under Operation Radium [see footnote 7], which was launched in August 2007, that 20 arrests had already been made in connection with TFSE. None of those arrests have resulted in a trial to date (June 2008), four people have since been charged with trafficking offences, and are awaiting trial. If there really are 25.000 'sex slaves' working in massage parlours and brothels[43] in the UK, those conviction figures are derisory.

**Figure 3.**

**Successful prosecutions: trafficking for sexual exploitation cases**

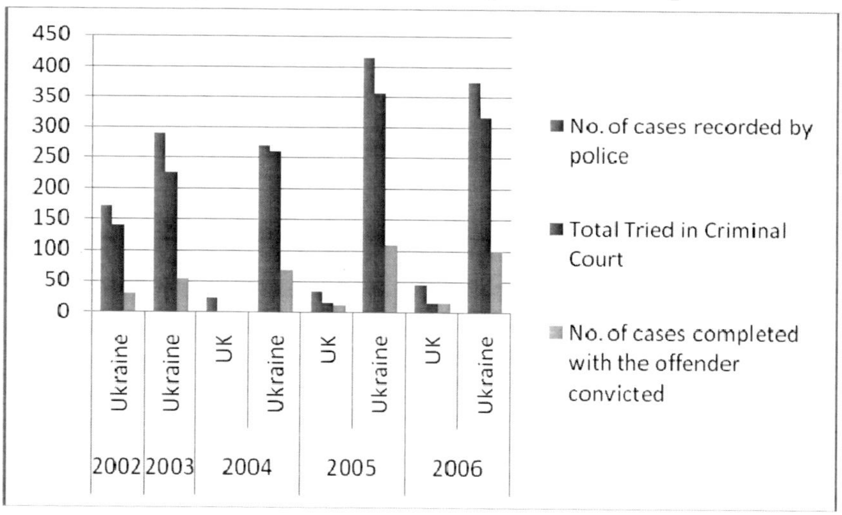


*Source: Levchenko, (2007); Svab (2007) (The Ukraine) & Home Office & Ministry of Justice (2007) UK.*

Figure 3 compare cases brought, trials and convictions in England and Wales with broadly comparable data from The Ukraine. The graph shows that, despite the growing number of criminal case opened and reaching the court, the number

11 noted but unofficial convictions for 2007 are included (MacShane, 2007) official statistics in UK only show 38 convictions for TfSE.

42 Parliamentary discussion took place prior to publication of statistics.

43 As suggested by MacShane, in UK Parliamentary discussion, November 26th 2007.

of cases completed and the offenders convicted is still comparatively low in both countries. Only of 13% of recorded criminal cases in 2006 in The Ukraine resulted in successful conviction, compared with 35% in England and Wales in the same year. In The Ukraine, 26% of cases that reached the courts resulted in a conviction, compared with 94% in England and Wales. As a source country, The Ukraine is likely to have a comparatively high incidence of human trafficking, as the recruitment stage of the trafficking process is undertaken within the country. This does not explain the relatively low conviction rate, however. Furthermore, there are difficulties, as mentioned previously in how such crimes are defined in the two countries.

In The Ukraine, it has not been possible to discover the sanctions imposed following all of the convictions. Did the judges follow the letter of the law and impose recommended terms of sentencing, or did an appeal process successfully convert it to a suspended sentence, as described earlier in this chapter? The authors cannot address this question at present. In England and Wales, sentencing guidelines recommend a maximum imprisonment length of 14 years and it appears that the full sentencing range is being administered upon conviction, depending upon aggravating factors included in the case. Furthermore, appeals seeking for sentence reduction have been denied (see R. v Maka [2005],)[44] where the Appeal Judges noted the increasing and degrading nature of human trafficking, which had echoes of slavery).[45] Some appeals have resulted in an increase in sentence (see R. v Plakici [2004]). In the case of Plakici, it should be noted that the appeal took place after the implementation of the Sexual Offences Act (2003), which gave judges more specific direction. However, recently sentences have also been reduced on appeal, as in the case of R v Roci, R v Ismailaj [2005] and R. v Makai [2007]. In Makai [2007], the Appeal Judges conceded that one of the effects of activities associated with prostitution is that women are forced "to work alone and make their own arrangements to work, a position at odds with any other sector of lawful employment". This solitary work can itself evoke many negative repercussions, which can be addressed somewhat by working with an 'agent' or facilitator (trafficker). The judges went on to suggest that "women's vulnerability is likely to be compounded by legislation which compels a prostitute to work alone rather than in a regularised sector". The judges considered that the traffickers in this case had been helping women

44 See Gilbert's (2007) useful discussion of Maka and Plakici for more information regarding these cases.

45 Or see R. v Kizlaite, R. v Axhami [2007]

find work that was dangerous for foreign women alone to undertake. Further, they observed that the appellant's level of criminality was low in other areas, and that the offence was a "reflection of the economic realities of intra-community migration and an inconsistent legal approach to prostitution". These mitigating factors contributed to a sentence reduction from 40 to 30 months for the appellant. The message from this appeal decision is somewhat at odds with the image of the trafficker as an evil exploiter. Although the judges' decision may have been appropriate in this case, the potential of the trafficker as a 'facilitator / helper' may benefit from a more detailed examination, if it is to be considered as a mitigating factor in some cases.

In March 2007, the Home Office in England and Wales, and the Scottish Executive published the UK Action Plan on human trafficking. The plan recommended a number of proposals, such as closer scrutiny of internal trafficking, including British women and girls who "may have been lured into prostitution, but from which they cannot escape due to the use of violence or coercion" (Home Office, 2007). To date, the authors have found no evidence to suggest that this has become a priority for any police target or has resulted in prosecutions. Instead, offences involving illegal immigration receive the greatest attention. This has precipitated problems when it comes to identifying trafficked persons and protecting their human rights. Practitioners (such as social workers, NGOs, or police) often do not imagine that people legally entitled to be in the UK could possibly have been trafficked (Skrivankova, GAATW, 2007), leading to too strong a focus on the immigration status of trafficked persons. In addition, the plan announced the establishment of a new UK Human Trafficking Centre (UKHTC) which aimed to become a central point for the development of expertise and operational co-ordination in relation to the trafficking of human beings. It was stated that the UK would not sign the Council of Europe Convention[46] until they were clear that they were in a position to ratify. There are some recent documented plans that the UK government intends to ratify by the end of 2008 (Avenall, 2008), but the convention entered into force in February 2008, without the UK as a party.

A sticking point for the UK in the Council of Europe Convention has been Article 13, which obliges states to provide *a recovery and reflection period of at least*

[46] The first European treaty in this field, which sets out measures not only to prevent trafficking in human beings and to prosecute the traffickers but also to give real protection to victims of trafficking and safeguard their human rights.

*30 days* where there are reasonable grounds to believe that a person is a victim of trafficking. Such a period shall be sufficient for the person concerned to recover and escape the influence of traffickers and/or to take an informed decision on cooperating with the competent authorities. During this period it shall not be possible to enforce any expulsion order against him or her. This provision is without prejudice to the activities carried out by the competent authorities in all phases of the relevant national proceedings, and in particular when investigating and prosecuting the offences concerned (Chapter III, Article 13.1). During this (30 day period), the victim should be offered opportunity to recover from the violations they have experienced and decide whether or not to co-operate with the authorities. The 'reflection period' should be unconditional – bearing no relationship with the victim's decision or refusal to co-operate with the authorities. Article 13 stipulates that the competent authorities are not permitted to implement enforcement measures such as deportation during this period. 30 days is arguably not long enough to recover sufficiently, and some have recommended that the Government should grant a longer period, such as 3 months (Home Office, 2007). Not much mention is made of the victim's wishes in this decision – whether she would prefer to return, stay or wait a while to reflect, which again suggests that the victim's position is not a priority. Even less information is available in the UK regarding the status of the victims following their identification by the authorities. Further, Article 14 of the Council of Europe Convention recommends issuing renewable residence permits[47] to victims of trafficking. Currently victims who give evidence have no guarantee that they will receive the right to remain in the UK even though as a result of co-operating they may have placed themselves and their family at increased risk of retaliation and harm from traffickers (Amnesty International UK, 2007).

## Conclusions

We have analysed the experiences of two different countries, one operating as a source for the traffickers, and another as a sink for the women trafficked; one with a tradition of justice through fair trials, and the other with a demonstrable

47 The 'victims' personal circumstances to be taken into consideration include, but are not limited to, their safety, health and family situation. States must set a length compatible with Article's purpose and that permits must be 'renewable'.

tradition of a corrupt judiciary. Shelley (2007) suggested that in some countries, "massive corruption undermines the capacity of the legal system to combat trafficking because police, border and customs officials have been bought off by the traffickers and smugglers". In The Ukraine, low conviction rates and lenient sentencing may partly be explained by endemic corruption at various levels of law enforcement, combined with prejudice against prostitutes, often the victims of trafficking. The number of cases reaching the courts in both countries raises questions about the level of protection afforded to such victims, the lack of 'unconditional' secure accommodation for witnesses and victims, lack of trust in the authorities (law enforcement officers in particular), and finally inadequate training of law enforcement officers in this area.[48] Official statistics seem to suggest that successful prosecutions are difficult to achieve, due, in part to the prosecution criteria used, and a very complicated trial process, which often relies on co-operation from individuals and bodies overseas.

These difficulties are compounded by disagreements *between* human rights campaigners: from those who would make the sex industry more illegal and prosecute and punish men involved as clients and otherwise[49], to the Human Rights Caucus, which seeks to separate sex work and trafficking, and to define trafficking based on working conditions.[50] In England and Wales and in The Ukraine, the public's understandable concern for victims of trafficking may be being exploited to promote a moralistic and dangerous crusade against prostitution. "*. . . anti-trafficking measures are still being used to justify a raft of measures which are aimed at suppressing sex work in general*" (International Collective of Prostitutes, 2008).

Questions also arise relating to crossing borders. Kapur (2005) suggests that an unhelpful division has been presented, which separates the worlds, where the problem exists 'over there', where the occupants themselves are in need of rehabilitation, recovery and civilisation (cited from Mohanty, 1991). She continues "both governmental and non-governmental initiatives reinforce the images presented in the media that promote stereotyped construction of the trafficked victim as foreign, innocent and ignorant" (cited from Doezema, 2001).

48 This point has been highlighted in the UK, and plans to provide comprehensive training for police officers have been prioritised (Avenall, 2008).

49 Some even sought to include prostitution and other sex work in the definition of trafficking in human beings (Ditmore, 2005).

50 Also joined by sex workers and those advocating sex workers rights, who recognise sex work as a form of work, and who seek to improve conditions, and affording legal recognition to the sex industry.

If so much of the responsibility lies with the economic devastation in some countries and opportunities that have arisen through the opening of borders, then what use can backward-looking legislation do in the overall picture? A much more fundamental and holistic approach is necessary, if we are to cull the market that *demands* such a business as trafficking in humans. This highlights further issues, relating to the role of men, per se, which has largely been "ignored, both as agents of positive change and as buyers of sexual services . . . and seldom discussed in trafficking contexts" (Abraham, 2001).

Further challenges exist in eroding the prejudices and polarities that exist between (smuggled) women who 'choose' prostitution, and are 'guilty' (and undeserving of human rights protection), and the (trafficked) woman who is 'innocent' (Anderson, 2007). Clearly, workers, migrant or not, cannot be divided into two entirely separate and distinct groups. Violence, confinement, coercion, deception and exploitation can and do occur within both legally regulated and irregular systems of work, and within legal and illegal systems of migration (*ibid*). Trafficking does not have to take place across international borders: one does not need to be 'illegal' in order to be trafficked, as one does not need to be a 'prostitute'. Traffickers as men (and women) are represented as 'other', as 'agents of evil' and simultaneously, conjure up images that vilify corrupt governments, single out alien criminal gangs and highlight the helplessness of the victims. Such images, and the dichotomous understanding on which it has been constructed, fails to comprehend the complexities within the nature of trafficking and its weaknesses. "The focus of anti-trafficking initiatives at the domestic, regional and international level is rarely on providing women-who-move with human rights – the tools that are critical to fighting abuse, violence and harm [that] they may experience in the course of movement" (Kapur, 2005). Instead, the focus remains firmly on detection, identification of suitable victims and fitting culprits.

The migrant (sex) worker is thus cast as a transgressor, incomprehensible, and existing completely outside the framework of liberal democracy, defined as a threat to the nation-state and as backward, uncivilised and dangerous (*ibid*). Simultaneously, the trafficker is cast as evil, opportunistic and exploitative. A more explicit distinction must be made between the sexual exploiter and the facilitator/travel arranger. Not all women who are moved around the world are exploited in prostitution and not all sexually exploited women are moved around.

Although the issues discussed in this chapter relate to two very different countries, many of the problems experienced therein are shared. Definitional and legal terminology can be difficult to interpret for law enforcement agents, victims and even judges. Laws relating to TfSE are still relatively new in many countries, which can result in tentative or inappropriate uses of them initially. Appeals provide jurists with a clearer understanding of the application of the law. Though the disparity in sentences that are available for these offences are marked and recent appeals in the UK have demonstrated that the situation is far from satisfactory in terms of clarification of gravity of actions. It is hoped that the next few years will provide a much more supportive framework for understanding the complicated nature of the application of legislation relating to trafficking in humans for sexual exploitation.

## References

Abraham, S., Going nowhere: Trafficking of women & children in international sex trade, Dominant Publishers, 2001

Adams, N., The Criminal Justice & Immigration Bill: Implications for Safety, Seminar, Friday February 29th, 2008, *The Cambridge Socio-Legal Group*, 2008, Occasional Seminar Series

Anderson, B., *Motherhood, apple pie and slavery: Reflections on trafficking debates*, Centre on Migration, Policy and Society, Working Paper No. 48, University of Oxford, 2007

Anderson, B. and J. O'Connell Davidson, *Is trafficking in human beings demand driven? A multi-country pilot study*, for IOM (December 2003). Accessed online at: http://www.iom.int/iomwebsite/Publication/ServletSearchPublication?event=detail&id=2932: (last visited April, 2008).

Avenall, J. *Trafficking for sexual exploitation: a process review of Operation Pentameter*, Home Office Research Report 7, 2008

Branigan, T, "Tories attack government for lack of action against trafficking". In *The Guardian*, Friday January 4 2008

Coaker, V., *Hansard*, Parliamentary Discussion, November 26th, 2007

Di Nicola, A., Research into human trafficking: Issues and problems. In: M. Lee, (ed.) *Human Trafficking*, Willan, 2007

Ditmore, M., Trafficking in lives. In: K. Kempadoo, (ed.), Trafficking and prostitution reconsidered: New perspectives on migration, sex work, and human rights, Paradigm Publishers, 2005

Doward, J., Trafficked children 'sent back to gangs'. *The Observer*, Sunday February 17 2008

Farley, M. *et al.*, Prostitution and trafficking in nine countries: An update on violence and posttraumatic stress disorder. *Journal of Trauma Practice*, 2003, Vol. 2, *no. 3/4*: 33-74

Gilbert, A., Sentencing in human trafficking Cases. *Criminal Law*, 2007, *177*, 3-5

Global Alliance Against Traffic in Women, Collateral Damage: The Impact of Anti-Trafficking Measures on Human Rights around the World, (GAATW), 2007

Hibbert, J., From prison to safe haven, March 19th, 2007, in *BBC News*, accessed on line at:
http://news.bbc.co.uk/1/hi/england/london/6429145.stm

Home Office, UK Action Plan on Tackling Human Trafficking, 2007

House of Lords, House of Commons, Joint Committee on Human Rights: Fifth Report, 2008
www.publications.parliament.uk/pa/jt200708/jtselect/jtrights/37/3702.htm

House of Lords, House of Commons, Joint Committee on Human Rights, Human Trafficking: Update, Twenty-first Report of Session 2006-07, HL Paper, 2007, 179, accessed online at:
www.publications.parliament.uk/pa/jt200607/jtselect/jtrights/179/179.pdf

International Collective of Prostitutes (ICP), *Packed meeting in Parliament backs New Zealand's decriminalisation*, 16 January 2008, accessed online at:
www.allwomencount.net/EWC%20Sex%20Workers/PackedMeeting16Jan08.htm

International Organisation for Migration, *Regional and country figures*. [On-line] available at:
http://www.iom.int/jahia/Jahia/lang/en/pid/1

Joint Committee on Human Rights, *Fourth Report*, 2008

Jordan, A., A. Miller and J. O'Connell Davidson, Open letter to ambassador John Miller Director, Office to Monitor and Combat Trafficking in Persons, 2005, accessed online at:
http://www.genderhealth.org/pubs/LtrMillerTrafficking.pdf

Kapur, R., Cross-border movements and the law: Renegotiating the boundaries of difference. In: K. Kempadoo, (ed.), *Trafficking and prostitution reconsidered: New perspectives on migration, sex work, and human rights*, Paradigm Publishers, 2005

Kelly, L. and L. Regan, *Stopping traffic: Exploring the extent of, and responses to, trafficking in women for sexual exploitation in the UK*, Police Research Series: Paper 125, Home Office, Policing and Reducing Crime Unit, Research, Development and Statistics Directorate, 2000

Kempadoo, K. (ed.), Trafficking and prostitution reconsidered: New perspectives on migration, sex work, and human rights. Paradigm Publishers, 2005

KIIS (2007) *Stan korupcii v Ukraini* [Corruption in The Ukraine]. Kiev: USAID

King, E., "Woman raped in people trafficking racket, court told". In: *Wisbech Standard*, 1st April, 2008

Levchenko, K., "Osnovnue problemu porushennya prav ljudunu v torgivli ludmi". [The problems of human rights violation in cases of human trafficking]. In *Prava cheloveka v The Ukraine* - 2006. Doklad pravozashitnih organizacij. [Human rights in The Ukraine – 2006]. Edited by E. Zakharova, I. Rapp, V. Javorski. Kharkov: Prava cheloveka, 2007

Lewis, P, Woman smuggled baby into UK 'to qualify for housing priority'. In: *The Guardian*, Saturday April 12th, 2008

Lucenko, E., L. Matiyashek, I. Shvab, and S. Shivon, S., *Torgovlya ludmi v Ukraini*. [Human trafficking in The Ukraine]. Kiev: British Council, 2004

Lucenko, E., L. Matiyashek, S. Scanlan, and I. Shvab, I., *Trafficking in The Ukraine*. Kiev: British Council, 2005

Maljevic, B., F. Miko, International human trafficking. In: K.L. Thachuk, (ed.), *Transnational Threats*, Praeger Security International, 2007

Pakes, F., *Comparative Criminal Justice*, Willan, 2003

Poppy Project, Home Office and Scottish Executive: Tackling Human Trafficking – Consultation on Proposals for a UK Action Plan, Response from the POPPY Project, April 2006

Pyshchulina, O., An evaluation of Ukrainian legislation to counter and criminalise human trafficking. In: S. Stoecker and L. Shelley, (ed.) *Human traffic and transnational crime: Eurasian and American perspectives*. Oxford: Rowman &Littlefield Publishers, Inc., 2005

Roberts, Y., Raped, beaten and helpless: UK's sex slaves. In: *The Observer*, Sunday 2 April 2006

Safety First Coalition, Briefing from the Safety First Coalition: *Criminal Justice & Immigration Bill 2008*, Aspects relating to prostitution, accessed online at:

www.allwomencount.net/EWC%20Sex%20Workers/CJ&IBLordsBriefing.htm

Sanghera, J., "Unpacking the Trafficking Discourse" in Kempadoo, K. (ed), *Trafficking and prostitution reconsidered: New perspectives on migration, sex work, and human rights*, Paradigm Publishers, 2005

Scott, J. G., How modern governments made prostitution a social problem: Creating a responsible prostitute population. The Edwin Mellen Press, 2005

Shelley, L., Human trafficking as a form of transnational crime. In: M. Lee, (ed.), *Human Trafficking*, Willan, 2007

Spencer, J., The illicit movement of people across borders: The UK as a destination country and the disorganisation of criminal activity. In: P.C. van Duyne, A. Maljevic, M. van Dijck, M., K. von Lampe and J. Harvey (eds.), *Crime business and crime money in Europe: The dirty linen of illicit entrepreneurship*. Nijmegen, Wolf Legal Publishers, 2007

Summers, D., "UK must ratify human trafficking treaty", say Tories. In: *The Guardian*, Thursday January 3 2008

Surtees, R., Traffickers and trafficking in Southern and Eastern Europe: Considering the other side of human trafficking". *European Journal of Criminology*, 2008, vol. 5, *no. 1*, January

Svab, I., *Putannya rozsliduvannya ta rozgljadu v sudah sprav s torgivli ljudmu*. [Questions of investigation and hearing of the human trafficking cases in courts]. Kiev: KLGZ, 2007

Swedish Ministry of Industry, Employment and Communications, *Fact Sheet: Prostitution and trafficking in women*, 2004, accessed online at http://www.sweden.gov .se/content /1/c6/1/87/74/6bc6c972.pdf

United Nations Population Fund, Trafficking in human misery, 2008, accessed at: http://www.unfpa.org/gender/violence1.htm

US Department of State, Bureau of Justice Affairs, *The Link between prostitution and sex trafficking*, 2004, accessed online at: http://www.state.gov/documents/organization/38901.pdf

# Hot sands or the 'romantics' of the desert Women smuggling from Egypt to Israel

*Dina Siegel*[1]

## Human trafficking: the general picture

Since the collapse of the Soviet Union, hundreds of thousands[2] of women arrive in the West searching for better economic opportunities. Many choose to work in the sex industry. These women consider themselves as independent businesswomen and look upon sex-work as a profession and a matter of free choice. It appears, however, that often they come with particular expectations (and experiences), but with little or no idea about their future employment status. (Aronowitz, 2003: 87; Korvinus *et.al*, 2006: 289). Many of them become confronted with a dark side of the business, with an 'evil empire' (Spencer, 2008:54), which is generally presented in the media and previes in criminological literature, namely women trafficking for sexual exploitation (see Goodey, 2003; Lee, 2007; and Stoecker and Shelley, 2005).

In this 'evil empire', trafficked women are recruited and controlled by violence and intimidation. *'Trafficking victims are deprived of their identities, moved vast distances away from their families, language and culture in inhumane conditions and are tortured to induce compliance'* (ibid:131). The business of human trafficking is also very lucrative. For traffickers, trafficked individuals are 'commodities', a renewable resource (Shelley, 2005: 72).

In spite of these and similar heart-breaking media reports, numerous campaigns of human rights activists and the growing concern of policy-makers trying to combat human trafficking, different statistical reports show

---

1 The author is professor of criminology at the Willem Pompe Instituut, University of Utrecht.
This chapter was first published in: P.C. van Duyne, S. Donati, J. Harvey, A. Maljevic and K. von Lampe (eds.), *Crime, money and criminal mobility in Europe*. Nijmegen, Wolf Legal Publishers, 2009

2 The statistics are controversial and vary from one source to another (see The United National Population Fund, 2005; U.S. Department, 2007, 2008; Belser, 2005; etc.)

that the phenomenon is far from disappearing. On the contrary new routes, methods of recruiting and transportation emerge and new actors enter the scene. Traditionally much attention is devoted to the flow of human traffic from the previous socialist countries to Western Europe or the Balkan countries where international peace keeping forces have been (or are being) served (Maljević, 2005). This attention is understandable, but too narrow. Eastern European women demonstrated a broader geographical mobility and entrepreneurial conduct. In this chapter I will focus on the (old-new), and until recently less known traffickers, namely the Bedouin in the Negev and Sinai deserts and on their role in the business of women trafficking and smuggling.

## Sandy attractions

In his fascinating analysis of the hashish smuggling by Bedouin in South Sinai, Emanuel Marx (2008: 39) predicted "*hashish smugglers will sooner or later deal in even more profitable outlawed and heavily-taxed commodities, such as weapons, diamonds, and addictive drugs like heroin and tobacco*". What Marx did not mention as another lucrative illegal activity of the Bedouin, is women smuggling. Smuggling of women in the Middle East, however, became widely discussed in the Israeli and Egyptian media and has been a part of the international public debate since the beginning of the 1990s. It is usually presented as a result of socio-economic reforms and the rise of organised crime, especially in the former socialist countries. About 1000 women are being smuggled through the Egyptian-Israeli border annually (Goldshmid, 2006). Since 2003, about 72% of trafficked women in Israel arrived through this border. In interviews with 340 women working as prostitutes, which took place in 2005, 85% of them appeared to reach Israel from Egypt, mainly accompanied by Bedouin (ibid).

Until 2000, women who came to work in the sex industry in Israel, primarily from countries of the former Soviet Union, were looked upon as criminals, "*who entered the country clandestinely in order to engage in shady business*" (Levinkron and Dahan, 2003: 5). Following an Amnesty International report, which criticised Israel for closing her eyes on inhuman 'women trafficking' (2000), the Israeli Knesset passed a law, prohibiting trafficking in women for prostitution (Amendment no.56 to the Penal Code).

Prostitution itself, however, remains legal[3], providing a convenient environment for the many voluntary sex workers in Israel.

This chapter will answer two questions. The first one is: why do women from the former Soviet Union and other East European countries arrive to work in prostitution in Israel? Israel is much less prosperous than many West European countries, and the conditions of work in the sex industry are very poor – if one believes the numerous governmental and human rights reports, which appeared at the end of the 1990s and the beginning of the 2000s. In addition, there are plenty of restrictions and border controls, which make the entry into the country very difficult. In spite of all these factors, Israel is considered one of the most popular countries for the so-called voluntary prostitution (US Department, 2001). This contrasts with the general picture of a flow of (trafficked) women from Eastern Europe to the west: the cross-border crime image of Western and Eastern Europe (Arromaa and Lehti, 2007), being the main topic of this volume.

The second question has to do with the 'romantics' of the journey and the guide (*provodnik*). The 'exotic' Bedouin who transport young women on camels and jeeps through the desert from Egypt to Israel can be rather associated with some adventurous Hollywood film than with organised crime activities. What is then the real role of these 'romantic' traffickers, how and why have they become involved in these illegal activities?

## Earlier studies and methods

In an earlier study, we tried to combine economic and cultural explanations of women trafficking, taking Russian women in Turkey as a case study (Siegel and Yesilgoz, 2003). Cultural perceptions are rarely taken seriously in criminological studies as a valid explanation of crime. Their value, however, can add an important complementary dimension for a better understanding of criminological questions. What did women on their way to work as prostitutes in Israel expect before they took the risk of crossing the desert? How do they view their work in the sex industry? How do Bedouin refer to the illegal activities they conduct? And how do they perceive their work and the women they smuggle across the border to Israel?

---

3 Though being a client of a prostitute is illegal, it is rarely persecuted de facto.

Though making links to history, this study is based on data gathered in 2007. During my short fieldwork in the summer of 2007 I conducted in-depth interviews with eight women from the former Soviet Union. All of them arrived to Israel from Egypt accompanied by Bedouins. I also obtained first-hand information from a Bedouin smuggler, who was himself involved in human smuggling. In addition, I visited a small Israeli town near Be'er Sheva, known for the frequent conflicts between the Bedouin and the local Jewish population and another town in the South of Israel known for the large presence of Bedouin traders and observed their activities. I also interviewed representatives of the local authorities about the smuggling and other illegal activities by Bedouin in Negev. I studied most of the available written sources, reports and press articles on this subject in Israeli, Russian-Israeli and international newspapers and journals. Remarkably, except for some journalistic publications (see Malarek, 2004), no anthropological or criminological research has yet been conducted on what, from the Israeli and Egyptian press, appears to be a well-known social phenomenon. This study will perhaps be the first attempt to discuss and analyse it within a sociological framework.

## Smuggling and trade in women in historical context

In the Ottoman period, kidnapping and smuggling of women was connected to prostitution. Trade in female slaves was a daily activity, publicly accepted in all parts of the empire. There were markets, where women from Sudan, Persia, the Caucasus and from Slavic countries were sold and later used as 'instruments of pleasure' for men, who did not fulfil their sexual fantasies with their own wives (Siegel and Yesilgoz, 2003: 77, 78). Sex was inevitably connected with a man's reputation: the more women one had, the better for his reputation and the clearer his manifestation of power, wealth and masculinity. Therefore, bringing in new young women from all over the world and selling them to men was a logical and even inevitable process, profitable both for traders and for their clients. In the Ottoman empire many slaves ". . . *were white females, principally of Slavic origin captured during Ottoman campaigns, or by their Tatar collaborators in Eastern Europe, with only a few of other provenance – Circassian, Caucasian, Hungarian, and Austrian*" (Ben-Naeh, 2006: 317).[4]

This 'white slavery' became associated with deceiving or forcing young white women into prostitution (Doezema, 2000: 24)."*The view of 'white slavery' as myth can account for its persistence and power despite the fact that very few actual cases of 'white slavery' existed*" (ibid). I will agree and follow here the argument of Doezema that the 'trafficked women' can be compared with this myth of 'white slaves', which "*bears as little resemblance to women migrating for work in the sex industry as did her historical counterpart*" (2000: 23).

Here perhaps is an appropriate place to mention the on-going discussion about the difference in definition between human smuggling and human trafficking. Human smuggling is considered a transnational criminal activity, based on a consensus between smuggler and smuggled person, in which both parties agree on conditions of a transfer across the national borders. Trafficking on the other hand, could be considered as an equivalent to illegal trade, and usually involves aspects of coercion, if not violence (see Aronowitz, 2003). Trafficking of humans is mainly associated with forced prostitution, in contrast to voluntary prostitution. The victims of human trafficking are usually described as passive and naïve girls, who want to escape from the tentacles of evil traffickers, mainly members of criminal organisations. Voluntary sex-workers, on the other hand are independent businesswomen, who have opted for prostitution as a profession (Spencer, 2008; Markovska and Moore, 2008). This distinction is important especially for social workers, NGOs, and other assistant groups: innocent girls, forced into prostitution, allegedly need their protection and help, in contrast to sex workers, 'fallen women', who deserve all evils (Doezema, 2000; Markovska and Moore, 2008). The process of the construction of the victim and the remedies the social workers offer them in the form of anti-trafficking campaigns and support facilities, such as shelters and protection programmes is a result of these definitions, though these also reflect the traumas of real victimisation. There is a broad literature on human trafficking, in addition to a huge number of governmental and non-governmental reports, to that effect (Aromaa and Lethi, 2007).

In this chapter I will focus only on one specific aspect of the abovementioned discussion, namely on women from the former Soviet

---

4 The slaveholding, including for sexual purposes was also common among Jews (also in Muslim countries) (Ben-Nahe, 2006: 316; Bristow, 1983).

Union looking for work in the sex industry in countries other than Europe and who are smuggled into Israel by Bedouin. The conditions of their stay in Israel and their future either as successful businesswomen or victims of trafficking will not be discussed any further, perhaps because much more in-depth research would be needed to draw any valid conclusions on this issue.

## Organisation of smuggling

### Arrival and transit

The 230 km long border between Israel and Egypt – from Kerem Shalom to Eilat – is the least secured border of Israel. It was established after Israel returned the Sinai Peninsula to Egypt in 1982. In many sectors it does not even have a security fence, which is justified by the notion that the strong shifting desert winds would inadvertently bury such a fence in sand. And for better fortifications Israel will need to invest much more resources and time, something Israel has only chosen to do in other areas, such as, for example, the Gaza strip (Gleis, 2007). Unlike the border between Israel and Jordan, which is characterised by cooperation between the authorities, along the border with Egypt cooperation is very limited (Goldshmid, 2006). The same is true for the borders with Lebanon and Syria. However, here the borders are heavily fortified; and there is also a visible presence of United Nations peacekeepers.

Since the beginning of the 1980s Egyptian authorities have invested in the development of tourism, building hotels and entertainment facilities, and advertising tourist attractions all around the world. Since the mid 1990s, Egypt has become one of the most popular holiday destinations for Russians. Almost one million Russian tourists visited Egypt in 2006[5], attracted by low prices and warm weather. In tourist places, such as Hurghada on the Red Sea, there are so many Russians that shops have Russian signs and shop owners learn Russian. Egypt is especially popular among young Russian women. Many women find jobs as waitresses or dancers in nightclubs, often combining vacation with business. According to Heba Aziz (2000), one of the main attractions for tourists is a so-called Bedouin way of life, which is

5 'Russian tourists give massive boost to Egypt', *Middle East Times*, March 22, 2007

highly emphasised in these places. "*Female travellers get attracted to the Bedouin way of life, the traditional Bedouin dress and the stories about the desert and the Interior (most of the accounts are staged and fabricated by the locals, both Egyptian and Bedouin, to meet the fantasy of the tourists)*" (Aziz, 2000: 44). The vacation relationships sometimes end in marriages between Bedouin and tourists. For Bedouins ". . . *marrying foreign women means sources they never reached before*" (Gardner, 2000: 62).

Other Russian women choose to work in prostitution in big hotels, charging about $30 per hour. There are several reports of police operations among the tourists, who sometimes dismantle international prostitution rings, including women from the former Soviet Union (see Benninger-Budel, 2001: 28). Such prostitution rings are supposed to be engaged in women trafficking and forced prostitution. In many cases, however, the distinction between forced or voluntary prostitution remains unclear.

Among the female tourists in Egypt there are many women who look for an opportunity to find work in Israel. At the beginning of the 2000s Israel implemented a number of regulations against human trafficking, including stricter control at Ben Gurion International Airport and the seaport of Haifa (Gleis, 2007). This has been the main reason of the displacement of the phenomenon to Egypt and the increasing role of Bedouin smugglers along unconventional routes through the desert. Egypt, in fact, has become a transit country. Lina, my Ukrainian informant explained: "*If a Russian woman comes alone to Egypt, she is viewed as a tourist, but if she comes alone to Israel – she is a whore*".

The reports about Russian women crossing the Egypt-Israeli border, with assistance of Bedouin, appear regularly in the international press.[6] Israeli sources reported on Russian women who were disappearing from Egyptian hotels at night, even before they unpacked their suitcases.[7] Also the involvement of criminal networks, mainly combinations of Russian, Georgian, Egyptian and Bedouin men and women, is often mentioned in this context.[8] From these reports it looks like Egypt has become two things. Firstly, a country of destination for Russian female tourists, who try to make

---

6 'Bedouin trying to smuggle Russian women into Israel was killed by Egyptian police', *Pravda*, December 23, 2002; 'Israel a human trafficking haven', August 18, 2004, *Fox News*

7 Hotline for Migrant Workers, 'Trafficking in women via Egypt during 2003', *Report for the U.S. Embassy*, Tel Aviv, 12 January, 2004

8 *Narod moi*, no.24, December 28, 2004, *Nekuda*, no.12 (65), December 2004, *Spektr*, no.10 (76), October 2004.

quick money during their holidays, or to have fun with the romantic Bedouin men. Secondly, as remarked before, it is also one of the most important transit countries for human smuggling to other countries of the Middle East or to Israel.[9]

There are two possibilities for women to travel to Egypt and further on to Israel. The first one is a 'spontaneous' decision, which they make upon their arrival in Egypt, mainly as tourists. They either learn about this possibility upon their arrival, or they have contact addresses of other women, who are already prepared to go to Israel, or men –'agents' in their own description– who provide the logistics for the further journey. The second possibility is an organised trip, an 'all-in', from the beginning arranged at home in their own country. In this case, women land in airports of Cairo, Sharm-el-Sheikh or Hurghada, where they are usually met by agents, who take them to Sinai by car. From there they cross the border accompanied by Bedouin. They are transported through the Egypt-Israel border together with other illegal commodities, such as drugs. Mainly these are groups of 3-20 women, but there were also cases of individual transportation.

There are a number of methods used to transfer women from Egypt to Israel: on foot, by jeep or by camel. For much of the route the road is modern, which makes it quite convenient to take cars, but modern roads also imply more police control, and this is precisely what the Bedouins are trying to avoid. Travelling by camel is much slower. The caravan can be on the way for a few days. Police controls can also happen on caravan routes, but less frequently than on main roads. Sometimes Bedouin inform each other on GSM about approaching controls. There have been reports of women who had to hide from such controls in caves for hours, without food and water.[10] The duration of the journey can even take up to two weeks (Levikron and Dahan, 2003).

---

9 During my visit to Abu Dhabi and Dubai in March 2007, I had conversations with Russian women, who told me that many women were flying to Arab Emirates through Egypt to work in prostitution.

10 Machon Todaá (Awareness Centre), Second Annual Report, Tel Aviv, 31 March, 2002, on: http://www.macom.org.il/todaa-un-20001-ch3.asp

## The role of Bedouin

The women are transferred from Egypt by Sinai Bedouin and then passed on to Israeli Bedouin, usually from the same tribe, mainly the Tarabin, Sawarka, Rumaylat, Tayaha, Hanajra, Ahaywat and to lesser extend Azazma tribes. My Bedouin informant told me:

> "*Smuggling of women demands much more preparations than smuggling of drugs, but the profits are bigger. On the other hand drugs are illegal, but women are not. If police asks questions you can always say that these are tourists, who wanted to have a camel ride, or something like this. If they have correct documents there will be no problems.*"

In other cases the smugglers get the women to wear Bedouin garments[11], pretending to be members of a local tribe.

In the region, Bedouin conduct the majority of illegal smuggling between Egypt, Israel and the Palestinian Territories. Emanuel Marx argues that

> "*the requirements of the smuggling trade fitted easily into the Bedouin's existing social realities and practices, such as their familiarity with cities, the wide dispersal and increasing mobility of the Bedouin labour migrants, the free access of all tribesmen to pastures anywhere in South Sinai, the Bedouin's reliance on dispersed networks of kinsmen and friends . . .*" (Marx, 2007: 34).

According to Marx smuggling, especially of hashish, became an important factor of the Sinai Bedouin's economy since the 1980s, though smuggling of hashish, tobacco, salt and other 'illegal products' existed for generations (Dumreicher, 1931; Marx, 2007: 34-35). Smugglers were looked upon as businessmen, who contributed to the local economy and therefore were praised for it. Illicit trade in drugs has proved to be a lucrative activity among nomadic people in different places and in different periods (Dumreicher, 1931; Claudot-Hawad, 2006; Marx 2007). Smuggling varies from region to region. In some places Bedouin are busy with smuggling of electronics, in other with drugs (Gardner and Marx, 2000: 23), or cigarettes.[12] There are reports of smuggling illicit labourers from China[13], and refugees from the Darfur province in Sudan.[14] Since the first Palestinian *intifada* there are also

---

11 *International Herald Tribune*, June 18, 2007

12 *Ibid*

13 *Associated Press*, June 13, 2006.

14 *Middle East Times*, August 8, 2007

reports on the smuggling of weapons, basically into the Gaza Strip through tunnels.[15]

In contrast to Western traffickers, who invest illicit proceeds in real estate or transfer money to bank accounts in Switzerland or Luxembourg, Bedouin have other ideas about the right investment. The most important form of investment is a marriage, not with a smuggled Russian woman, but with a Bedouin one, or maybe more than one. According to Lila Abu-Lughod: "*Polygamy among Awlad 'Ali is on the increase thanks to the influx of wealth from smuggling . . .*" (1986: 228). Emrys Peters, an anthropologist who spent many years among Bedouin, found that women were mainly viewed by males as commodities. Bedouin women have a value because of their ability to bear children. "*Like other commodities, it is owned by males, and its transfer from one set of males to another is a contractual arrangement*" (1990: 248). Many Bedouin strive to have large families and many children. "*They treat children as workers in the household economy, as allies in local politics, and as the most reliable helpers in sickness and old age*" (Gardner and Marx, 2000: 24). All other commodities, which can contribute to the enlargement of their families, are considered useful. The profits from the smuggled women from the former Soviet Union allow them to purchase a Bedouin wife. In this case the smuggled Russian women may be viewed as an appropriate means by which to make money in order to be able to buy another commodity, namely a Bedouin wife.
Masha, my Russian informant told me:

> "*The Bedouins were counting us before putting us on the jeep. But they were not counting per person, but: 'one thousand, two thousand, etc.' in Israeli shekels. They made money on us, like on sheep or on camels.*"

Both the smuggling of drugs and the smuggling of Russian women brings to Bedouin large profits, which can add to the enlargement of their families and the improvement of living standards, thereby increasing personal reputation and power within the tribe. In this sense, smuggling of Russian women, similar to drugs and other illicit commodities, can be viewed as a contribution to polygamy: the Bedouin becomes wealthier; which allows him to marry more women, which in turn means more children. Thus, one commodity, namely the smuggled women, creates another commodity – Bedouin wives. The latter contributes not only to the economic situation and reproduction of

15 *International Herald Tribune,* June 18, 2007

a Bedouin, but also to his position in terms of power and wealth. Therefore, there is a correlation between smuggling and reputation.

Looking at women smuggling from this point of view it can be considered as an important economic activity in Bedouin society, in which the legality of the act is unimportant compared but its socio-economic outcome. Similar to smuggling of drugs, Bedouin consider smuggling of women as a normal business. The smuggled women are brought to Israel, where they become employed in the sex industry, while the Bedouin are gaining capital on their smuggling activities in order to invest it later in marriage with one or more Bedouin wives.

## Social networks

Since the beginning of the Great Immigration[16] in 1987 more than a million former Soviet citizens have arrived in Israel, forming the largest wave of immigration in the short history of Israel (Siegel, 1998). Israel has been one of the most important countries for Russian organised crime to find new markets and clients. Criminal groups found the conditions favourable to widen their activities, which included, for example, the extortion of compatriots, smuggling of illegal migrants, and drugs smuggling (Siegel, 2005). One interesting development following the immigration of post-Soviet criminals to Israel was the establishment of cooperative relationships with local gangs, irrespective of ethnicity. In the case of smuggling, these were mainly Bedouin and local Arab groups, though there was also evidence of cooperation between Russian criminal groups and Israelis. For example, Russian couriers were recruited to smuggle synthetic drugs from Israel, or from Israeli-subsidised European clandestine laboratories, to the former Soviet Union and to the United States (Blickman *et. al*, 2003).

In the case of the East European women (the Soviet Union having broken up) who choose to work in prostitution in Israel, the assistance of Bedouin in bringing them across the borders is only one part of a much more complex cross-border network of interrelationships. These are based upon individuals who provide valuable information, establish contacts with the owners of illegal brothels, or with other sex workers who are already working in the sex

16 This is the denotation of the massive outflow of Russian Jews (or of those declared themselves as such) due to the relaxation of the migration regulation in the Soviet Union (see Siegel, 1998).

industry in Israel. These networks are at odds with the prevailing image depicted in criminological sources of criminal networks made up of violent and manipulative individuals who force women into submission by organising their trip; taking away their documents and exploiting them later in prostitution (see also Spencer, 2007).

Rita, a 20-year old teacher from Moldova told me:

> "*Two friends of mine worked in Israel last summer; they came back with packs of dollars. One of them told me exactly what I needed to do: first contact Sasha, her cousin, who arranged the whole trip. I paid him 1.000 US dollars. He gave me exact information where to stay in Egypt; he gave me a telephone number of I., a Bedouin, who took me to the border with Israel. On the other side there was a jeep, with another Bedouin, who took me to Eilat. In Eilat I called Sasha's friend, Josef, also Russian. He arranged for me a place in a massage parlour.*"

In other sources there are reports of criminal networks which divide their tasks in transferring women and illegal labourers to Israel. According to Levinkron and Dahan, 66% of women came to Israel in response to information of acquaintances (2003: 21), a phenomenon described also in other countries (see e.g. Hughes, 2001: 11). There are always 'agents' who provide women with addresses and contacts (Siegel and Yesilgoz, 2003: 80). In some cases there are men, who also accompany them on their trip. In addition there are different pimps and smugglers.

There is also rivalry among different smuggling groups, which is sometimes manifested in threats and physical violence. Rival smugglers, for example, 'steal' women from each other. In case of Suleiman S. the arrangement was made between the smuggler and a man from Moldova, to transfer a few people, men and women from Sharm el-Sheikh to Israel. S. found out that a group of other smugglers had stolen 'his' clients by taxi. He ordered one of his men to follow the taxi and transfer them to his jeep, by threat of gun.[17]

---

17 Criminal file Suleiman S. vs. State of Israel, Supreme Court Reports 2002, quoted in Levenkron and Dahan, 2003: 22.

One representative of the local authorities in the South of Israel told me:
"*Bedouin smugglers possess weapons, mainly rifles, AK-47s. They use them either to conduct robberies, especially of cattle in moshavim (farms), or they sell them for good price in the Gaza Strip to terrorists.*"[18]

## Good life?

Bedouin profit from smuggling women from Egypt to Israel not only in economic terms, but also in terms of strengthening their social position and reputation. But what about the women, these 'victims of women trafficking', these 'white slaves', or with whatever other synonyms women may be presented in the media or reports of governmental and non-governmental organisations?

The authors of a report on women trafficking to Israel based on interviews with trafficked women who were expecting deportation from Israel (Levenkron and Dahan, 2003) were surprised that not all the interviewed women considered themselves as victims, and some of them even claimed that they were well-treated. The authors immediately excused these women by both arguing that those were actually comparing the conditions with an even worse situation at home, and showing that their claims could not be real, because they were complaining that they were not allowed to laugh and to talk to each other, when sitting in a 'too cooled' air-conditioned brothel. In the authors' vision prostitution and trafficking could never have any positive effect on a woman's life.

Australian TV aired an interview with a Russian girl, Marusya, who stated that she knew exactly what kind of job she expected in Israel and how much money she would earn. "*For the first month I worked to repay the travel costs. All girls had to. But the people I worked for were nice people. I am not sorry*".[19]

Another informant in Israel, Asya, who arrived from Moldova to Egypt, and then was transported by Bedouins to Israel, told me:

"*We had to spend a night by the Bedouin tent. There was a woman there, I don't know exactly what was her role, a wife, or a sister of our provodnik, but she was very friendly, she gave us food and blankets, because it was quite cold in the desert.*

---

[18] Israeli press reported that in Ramat HaNegev almost all streetlight cables have been stolen. Bedouin also steal fuel, generators, antennas, etc. (*The Jewish Voice*, May 2007), on: http://jewishvoiceandopinion.com/a/jvo200705c.html

[19] *Australian Broadcast Corporation* (ABC), TV Programme, 21 June 2004.

*Also our Bedouin was nice; he stopped every time we asked him. He gave us cigarettes and sweets."*

Luba, another 19-year-old Russian woman told me:

"*The only inconvenience I remember from this journey through the desert is the lack of communication with I., who took us with his jeep. He could not talk Russian, and we could not speak English or Arabic. We did not know how long we would have to ride."*

Part of the money earned by the women in Israel is send back to their villages, where their parents, and sometimes, small children are left behind. 100-200 dollars per month, which these families receive from abroad, can make enormous differences in their standard of living.

Masha, my informant, told me:

"*I have a very sick child back home. In order to give him a proper treatment all our incomes together: my salary (as a hairdresser – $70), my husband's salary (truck driver, $140), pension of both my parents, and my mother-in-law (together $130) - will not be enough even to hospitalise him. One month working in prostitution in Israel will be more than enough to save my child. What choice do I have?"*

Prostitution is a business, and many women from the former socialist countries see an opportunity to make money from sex work. The exchange of information with other women, who already work in prostitution in Israel and stories and rumours in their immediate environment at home encourage them to take this step. The continuous campaigns of different NGO's to warn girls about all kind of threats in a dangerous *zagranitza* (abroad) and numerous dramatic reports on violent criminal organisations, poor conditions, lack of security and hostile environment obviously do not stop thousands of women to make the decision.

The idea to go to Israel is, however, less clear. There are much more prosperous and safe countries than Israel with much more liberal and glamorous life styles, such as countries of Western Europe. The continuous ethnic and military conflicts and suicide terrorist attacks do not contribute to the attractiveness of Israel either. In spite of all this, Israel remains one of the most popular destination countries for sex workers.

There are several reasons for this choice. Firstly, there are strong ties between post-Soviet Israelis and their families and friends in their native countries. In the Soviet period, when the Soviet Jews were immigrating to Israel or to the United States, the contacts were usually broken because of fear of repressions. Under the Soviets any contact with foreigners was considered suspicious. Since the fall of communism, however, and as a result of the *perestroika* and *glasnost* reforms, freedom of movement and exchange of information with abroad became a fact. Indeed, many immigrants from the former Soviet Union visit their countries and have intensive contacts there. When the non-Jewish women decide to go to work in Israel in the sex industry, they are usually well informed about the Israeli laws and potential problems. Having acquaintances in Israel, even though not even too close ones such as ex-classmates or ex-neighbours, gave my informants a feeling of security that they would have a place to hide if necessary.

In addition, there is a reputation of tolerance of prostitution on the side of the police and if women will be caught and deported from the country, they will not have to pay a cent on travel costs, because the Israeli government provides the funds for deportation. It is thus a win-win situation: if they are not caught the women will be going back with money, and if caught, they are going back for free.

Another reason to choose Israel has to do with the many facilities, such as peep-show clubs, massage parlours and night clubs, which mushroomed in Israel with the post-Soviet immigration. These are easily accessible and always have a demand for new sex workers.

According to Jewish tradition "*prostitution is acceptable as long as the prostitutes are not Jewish*" (Lemish, 2000: 340). Dafna Lemish found that most of the women entering Israel for work in the prostitution were not Jewish, and they also had no intention of staying in Israel for too long. However, the media tended to blur the distinction between the Jewish women, who emigrated from the former Soviet Union during the mass immigration in the beginning of the 1990s and the non-Jewish sex workers who arrived to Israel approximately at the same time. In the press a general picture of the 'Russian whores' emerged, which contributed a lot to the creation of a negative attitude and criminalisation of the new immigrants in the mid 1990s. Even ten years later this image still exists. An example is a debate in 2007 on a proposal for the exemption of the visa requirements for Russian tourists, during which the Public Security Minister warned that 'tens of thousands of prostitutes' could enter the country should visa requirements be eliminated.[20] These new regulations for visa exemption have indeed become another reason for Russian sex workers to choose Israel.

[20] *Haáretz*, August, 8, 2007.

## Conclusion

While it cannot be ignored that the flow of women to the EU continues unabated, many women from the previous Soviet Union and socialist satellites countries opt for another window of opportunity. Using their network relationships, thousands of young women take the risk of crossing the border between Egypt and Israel and of being secretly transported through the desert in order to become prostitutes in Israel. For many of them this option is perhaps much better than living in poverty in the villages of the Russian countryside, Moldova or Romania. Some earn money and go back to their families. Others find themselves in shabby brothels exploited by greedy pimps. The fate of all these women in Israel was not the focus of the present study. This chapter presents some empirical data on one fragment of a long journey: whom did the women contact, how did they travel, what were their experiences? In addition to the smuggled women, I focused on the smugglers, the Bedouin: how and why do they smuggle these women, where do they invest their profits, what is their position and reputation in their community?

Sex work and sex trafficking is a very hot issue, widely discussed in public debate, in governmental and human rights reports and sociological literature, but there is still very scarce empirical data, evidence 'from the field' both on victims and on traffickers. This case study from the 'hot sands' of the Middle East will contribute to our knowledge and understanding of the phenomenon. It demonstrates that looking at the traditional traffic channels neglects on-going movement of women making the best of their network information at home and abroad to make an income out of the sex industry. Many of them ignore the usual routes to red light districts in the western cities and pass the hot sands to their preferred working stations in Israel.

## References

Abu-Lughod, L., *Veiled sentiments. Honour and poetry in a Bedouin society*. Berkeley & Los Angeles: University of California Press, 1986

*Amnesty International Report*, 2000, London

Aromaa, K. and M. Lethi, Trafficking in human beings: policy problems and recommendations. In: P.C. van Duyne, A. Maljević, M. van Dijck, K. von Lampe and J. Harvey (eds.), *Crime business and crime money in Europe. The dirty linen of illegal enterprise.* Nijmegen, Wolf Legal Publishers, 2007

Aronowitz, A.A., Trafficking in human beings: an international perspective. In: D. Siegel, H.G. van de Bunt and D. Zaitch (eds.), *Global Organized Crime. Trends and developments*, Dordrecht: Kluwer Academic Publisher, 2003

Aziz, H., Employment in a Bedouin community: The case of the town of Dahab in South Sinai. *Nomadic Peoples*, 2000, vol. 4, *issue 2*, pp. 28-48

Belser, P., *Forced labour and human trafficking: Estimating the profits*, Geneva: International Labour Office, 2005

Benninger-Budel, C., Violence against Women in Egypt, in: *Report prepared for the Committee on the Elimination of Discrimination against Women.* OMCT, 2001

Ben-Naeh, Y., Blond, tall, with honey-coloured eyes: Jewish ownership of slaves in the Ottoman Empire, in: *Jewish History*, 2006, *no. 20*, pp. 315-332

Blickman, T., D. Korf, D. Siegel and D. Zaitch, D., *Synthetic drugs trafficking in Amsterdam.* Amsterda/Turin:TNI/Gruppo Abele, 2003

Bristow, E., *Prostitution and prejudice: the Jewish fight against white slavery, 1870-1939.* New York: Schocken Books, 1983

Doezema, J., Loose women or lost women? The re-emergence of the myth of 'white slavery' in contemporary discourses of 'trafficking in women', in: *Gender Issues*, 2000, vol. 18, *no.1*, pp. 23-50

Dumreicher, A., *Traders and smugglers in the desert of Egypt.* London: Methuen, 1931

Gardner, A., At home in South Sinai, in: *Nomadic Peoples*, 2000, vol. 4, issue 2, pp. 48-68

Gardner, A. and E. Marx, Employment and unemployment among Bedouin. *Nomadic Peoples*, 2000, vol. 4, *issue 2*, pp. 21-28

Geil, J., Trafficking and the Role of the Sinai Bedouin, In: *Terrorism Monitor*, 2007, vol. 5, Issue 12 (June 21) on: http://www.jamestown.org/terrorism/news/article.php?articleid=2373485&printhis=1

Goldshmid, R., *Havrachot derech gvul israel-mitzraim* (Trafficking through the Israeli-Egyptian border). Merkaz hamichkar u-hameida, 16 November 2006. (In Hebrew)

Goodey, J., Migration, crime and victimhood. *Punishment and Society*, 2003, 5 (4): 415-431

Hughes, The 'Natasha' trade: The transnational shadow market of trafficking in women. *Journal of International Affairs*, 2000, 53 (2): 625-651

Janssen, M.L., *Reizende sekswerkers: Latijns- Amerikaanse vrouwen in de Europese prostitutie.* Apeldoorn: Het Spinhuis, 2007

Korvinus, D., D. Koster en H. de Jonge van Ellemeet, Mensenhandel: het begrip uitbuiting in art. 273a Sr, *TREMA*, 2006, 7: 286-290

Lee, M., (ed.), *Human trafficking*, Devon, Portland: Willam Publishing, 2007

Lemish, D., The whore and the other. Israeli images of female immigrants from the former USSR. *Gender & Society*, 2000, vol.14, *no.2*, April, pp. 338-349

Levenkron, N. and I. Dahan, Women as commodities: trafficking in women in Israel, 2003). Hotline for migrant workers; Isha L' Isha – Feminist Center, Haifa, 'Adva' Center. (In English and in Russian), on: http://www.owl.ru/win/books/israel/index.htm

Maljević, A., Trafficking in women in Bosnia and Herzegovina. In: P.C. van Duyne, K. von Lampe, M. van Dijck and J.L. Newell (eds.), *The organised crime economy. Managing crime markets in Europe.* Nijmegen, Wolf Legal Publishers, 2005

Malarek, V., *The Natashas. Inside the new global sex trade.* New York: Arcade Publishers, 2004

Markovska, A. and C. Moore, Stilettos and steel toe-caps: legislation of human trafficking and sexual exploitation, and its enforcement in the UK and The Ukraine. In: P.C. van Duyne, J. Harvey, M. Maljevic, M. Scheinost and K. von Lampe (eds.), *European crime-markets at cross-roads: Extended and extending criminal Europe.* Nijmegen: Wolf Legal Publishers, 2007

Marx, E., Hashish smuggling by Bedouin in South Sinai. In: D. Siegel and H. Nelen (eds.), *Organised Crime.* Dordrecht: Springer, 2008

Peters, E., *The Bedouin of Cyrenaica.* Cambridge: Cambridge University Press, 1990

Shelley, L., Russian and Chinese trafficking: A comparative perspective. In: S. Stoecker and L. Shelley (eds.), *Human trafficking and transnational crime. Eurasian and American perspective.* London, Boulder, new York, Toronto, Oxford: Rowman & Littlefield Publishers, INC, 2005

Siegel, D., Recent trends in women trafficking and voluntary prostitution: Russian-speaking sex-workers in the Netherlands, *Transnational Crime*, 2005, 4 (1): 4-23.

Siegel, D., Russische bizniz. Amsterdam: Meulenhoff, 2005

Siegel, D. and Y. Yesilgoz, Natashas and Turkish men: new trends in women trafficking and prostitution. In: D. Siegel, H. van de Bunt and D. Zaitch (eds.), *Global Organised Crime. Trends and Developments.* Dordrecht: Kluwer Academic Publishers, 2003

Spencer, J., Media constructing organized crime concepts in an extended criminal Europe: Trafficking women for sexual exploitation. In: P.C. van Duyne, J. Harvey, A. Maljevic, M. Scheinost and K. von Lampe (eds.), *European crime-markets at cross-roads: Extended and extending criminal Europe.* Nijmegen: Wolf Legal Publishers, 2007

Stoecker, S. and L. Shelley, *Human traffic and transnational crime. Eurasian and American perspective.* Lanham, Boulder, New York, Toronto, Oxford: Rowman & Littlefield Publishers, INC, 2005

United Nations Population Fund, 2005, *State of world population 2005: The Promise of Equality – Gender Equity, Reproduction Health and the Millennium Development Goals*, on:
http://www.unfpa.org/upload/lib_pub_file/493_filename_en_swp05.pdf

U.S. Department, 2001, *Trafficking in Persons Report Washington, D.C.*

U.S. Department, 2007, *Trafficking in Persons Report. Washington, D.C.*

*U.S. Department, 2008, Trafficking in Persons Report. Washington, D.C.*

# The illicit movement of people across borders.
## The UK as a destination country and the disorganisation of criminal activity[1]

*Jon Spencer*[2]

## Introduction

The movement of people across borders is not a new phenomenon: human beings have traversed land and sea over time and for a variety of reasons. For some people migration met the need of discovery, to find out what lay beyond the horizon, for others it was to find a place more hospitable and productive, for others it was to escape persecution and exploitation and for many it was to seek a new beginning in more stable and predictable economic circumstances. Those who cross borders in the twenty-first century, other than for reasons of tourism, do so for very similar reasons as those who have gone before them; essentially in an attempt to improve their life and the lives of those for whom they feel responsible. Depending on national economic and political situations such cross-border movements have been welcomed, rejected or strictly regulated. One of the consequences of this rejection or regulation of mobility has been the criminalisation of the migrant (Melossi, 2003).

There are a number of key ideas that inform the day to day practice of law enforcement professionals in their work in the area of illegal immigration. In many respects the practice of law enforcement in this area is built on a shared operational experience and the application of intelligence that has been gathered by law enforcement personnel across EU member states. This

---

1 The research reported on here was an EU commissioned project funded by the AGIS Programme, The Directorate General Justice, Freedom and Security. (*Illegal Movement of People Across Borders* (JAI/2004/AGIS/085 (48)).
This chapter was first published in: P.C. van Duyne, A. Maljevic, M. van Dijck, K. von Lampe and J. Harvey (eds.), *Crime business and crime money in Europe. The dirty linen of illicit enterprise*. Nijmegen, Wolf Legal Publishers, 2007

2 The author is Director of the Criminal Justice Research Unit, School of Law, University of Manchester, UK.

relationship between the practice of law enforcement in this area and the use of intelligence is further complicated by a series of professional and cultural perspectives that contribute to the construction of how professional practice is undertaken. Law enforcement professionals have perceptions of law enforcement officers in other member states and of their own professional practice. One particular member state's law enforcement practice may be viewed either positively or negatively and these views, many based either on anecdotal evidence, personal experience, stereotyping and the implementation of organisational policy based on co-operative working shape how law enforcement personnel interact with each other and to what extent they are prepared to share information, intelligence and operational strategy.

Finally, the political and media environment within which law enforcement professionals operate is also a critical determinant of the manner in which the problem of illegal immigration is constructed. There is an interplay between the political and the news gathering processes and the media reporting of illegal immigration. This makes for a difficult and unpredictable terrain across which law enforcement personnel have to operate. There is a need to maintain credibility with the media (and ultimately 'the public') and politicians in order to ensure that funding is forthcoming. There is also an imperative to ensure that the law enforcement operation is also maintained at a level that reproduces the definitions and construction of the illegal immigrant and the process of illegal immigration.

This chapter is concerned with the movement of people across borders: particularly the illegal movement of people into the European Union (the UK in particular), and the relationship between the illegal movement of people and 'organised crime'. The chapter is based on research carried out between 2004 and 2006 for the EU AGIS Programme. This research was undertaken in three countries: Estonia, Finland and the UK, however, this chapter only draws on that data relevant to the UK experience. The chapter is concluded with a discussion that explores whether the conceptualisation of illegal immigration as an activity of 'organised crime' is one that assists the law enforcement process or whether it actually hinders the understanding of illegal immigration as the relationship between crime and illegal immigration may be disorganised and chaotic.

## Defining the problem

In 2005 the publication by UK Home Office of 'A survey of the illegally resident population in detention in the UK' (Black *et al.*, 2005) was an attempt to "increase understanding of the illegally resident population by describing in depth the characteristics of that part of it that is in detention" (Black *et al.* 2005: 2). However, the report only interviewed those people deemed to be in the UK illegally at five UK immigration centres and so excluded a significant number of people being in the UK illegally who were either in the community or in prison. Consequently, the research is lacking data. This deficit is acknowledged by the authors, as are the problems of classification and definition between 'illegal immigrant' and 'asylum seeker'. This highlights at least two problems in this area; first the difficulty in accessing and obtaining reliable representative data and, second, the definitional lack of clarity. The definitional problems are further exacerbated when refugees and the victims of trafficking are included as potential 'illegal immigrants'. All of the definitional groups – asylum seeker, refugee, trafficked person, illegal immigrant, migrant labourer – come with either stark differences in their legal status or nuanced shifts in emphasis that make them more or less deserving. So, for example, an asylum seeker is considered to have a genuine reason for crossing a border illegally as does a 'trafficked person' as they are constructed as a victim of crime. A woman working in the sex industry who crossed the border illegally does not have any other genuine reason for crossing the border but pursuing her profession elsewhere and is therefore not constructed as a victim of crime but rather as the 'criminal' unless she can invoke the status of victim by being perceived as having been 'trafficked' into the sex industry. However, the differences in the two life histories of the trafficked woman and the woman who crossed the border illegally may not be so very different. In understanding how these processes of definition operate it is important to identify those who have the power to define:

> ". . . service providers and state agents define trafficking, and especially the extent to which they introduce additional requirements which do not appear in the protocol in order to construct a category of deserving victims or ration scarce resources . . ." (Kelly 2005: 238)

So, the definers are generally those who are providing victim services or enforcing the law. The process of definition is also political. The trafficked person, for example, acquires a status of victim, although this status is highly conditional on them accepting the concept of victim, or in playing the part (Kelly 2005). Chapkis (2003) argues that the process of defining victims is a complex interaction between social anxieties and the use of the law to manage these anxieties and the control of immigration, so the ". . . law mobilizes anxieties surrounding sexuality and gender in the service of immigration control" (Chapkis 2003: 924).

The definitional process is further complicated by the introduction of 'organised crime' as a driving force behind illegal immigration and trafficking. For example Kelly notes that organised crime is a:

> ". . . major issue for Europe, both in terms of the countries where crime groups are based, where the illicit economy acts as a brake on both the movement out of economic transition and democratization processes, and on the Western countries where organised crime has taken advantage of diasporas to put down roots. The Netherlands, for example, has identified 100 different ethnically organised crime groups operating within its borders." Kelly 2005: 252)

A problem with a perspective such as this is that the myths concerning 'organised crime' are reproduced (Van Duyne, 2004) and so the complexity of the relationship between criminalisation, criminal networks and structures and victimisation are subsumed under the heading of 'organised crime'. This term is rarely helpful and in relation to illegal immigration it only serves to further definitional confusion by reifying the concept of 'organised crime'. Van Duyne (2006) has compared the attempts by law enforcement officials to measure 'organised crime' as being similar to counting clouds. This comparison is drawn because as Van Duyne argues clouds change, split and reform, disappear and reappear in a new form in another place. These constantly changing formations of clouds are similar to the constantly changing formations of organised crime (Van Duyne 2006: 1). Furthermore as von Lampe *et al.* (2006) point out there is no one standard definition of organised crime. The approach seems to be that law enforcement professionals know organised crime when they see it but what they see may not be the same thing:

> "there may be many people who are convinced that they know organised crime when they see it. But they obviously see different things."
> (von Lampe *et al.* 2006: 17-18)

They further argue that the professionals tend to describe what they see as fitting into one of three models: the hierarchical model, the local or ethnic model and the enterprise model (Albanese 1989 cited in von Lampe *et al.* 2006: 18). The process of describing organised crime as fitting into one of these models only serves to reduce the concept of organised crime to one that loses any sense of complexity and ambiguity (von Lampe *et al.* 2006). However, it is not surprising that law enforcement professionals experience this sense of confusion in relation to organised crime because as von Lampe *et al.* (2006) argue there is no 'common theoretical understanding' (von Lampe *et al.*, 2006: 41) in the literature on organised crime and this 'allows a confusing picture to emerge'(von Lampe *et al.* 2006: 41). Van Duyne (2006) takes this argument one stage further by noting that if the research is not based on a theoretically unified definition then research findings are problematic in terms of comparison (Van Duyne 2006: 2). This is of particular importance as Van Duyne (2006) claims that threat assessments derived from such problematic research have no firm basis: their statements lack validity.

So, all of this only adds to the confusion and lack of intellectual rigour that is applied to the idea of 'organised crime'. The research on illegal immigration reported on here suggests that policy implementers especially find solace in locating criminal behaviours within the structure of 'organised crime' as it allows for the panoply of threat assessments and strategic responses to be generated and reproduced. In this world of confusion, law enforcement professionals need to know that they are practicing in a world of certainties and an ever changing nature of criminal activity means that their world of practice is anything but certain. So, the standard and accepted definitions of 'organised crime' are invoked to provide a sense of knowing the unknowable. This suggests that a myth of understanding the problem is created because with the social acceptance of the words 'organised crime' law enforcement professionals act as if they know the underlying meaning. However, in many cases it is apparent that they do not understand the complexity of the term 'organised crime'.

The problem of definition also contributes to the political dialogue in relation to illegal immigration because not only is the definition of organised crime problematic, so is that of the status of the migrant, as Kelly (2005) notes:

> "Assessing what data we do have is made more complex by the fact that governments, the media, and even researchers continue to conflate

migration, asylum, refugees, trafficking, and smuggling. Indeed it may prove impossible to resolve this conceptual confusion, since in some instances it serves political and ideological ends." (Kelly 2005: 239)

The ideological and political ends served by the confusion over the status of migrants combined with the ambiguity of the definition of organised crime can result in there being a discourse that links a popular conceptualisation of organised crime with the confused and negative stereotypes of migrants. At times such a conflation of different ideas is utilised by politicians to justify repressive and harsh immigration policies, for example in the case of Roma people at-tempting to gain access to the UK from the Czech Republic in 2001 (House of Lords 2004) and other more targeted policing, for example the formation of The Serious and Organised Crime Agency (SOCA) in the UK in 2006.

## Illegal immigration and the UK response

Illegal immigration during the 1990s in the UK was a high profile political issue. The system of dealing with asylum applications was slow and there was a large 'backlog' of pending cases so that in October 1995, there were 66.655 pending applications for asylum (Hansard, 1995: 96). By 2005 this number had been significantly reduced but there had been a peak in applications for asylum between 1999 and 2002. Newspapers frequently reported that immigration would be the cause of significant increases in the population, for example in 2004, the Daily Telegraph reported that "4,4 million immigrants will boost the population" (Daily Telegraph 2004a) and in the same edition it was also claimed that "Immigration has hit record levels" (Daily Telegraph 2004b). The Daily Telegraph was concerned at the influx of 'Eastern European' nationals due to European Union enlargement and noted the flow of UK citizens migrating who are replaced by 'non-British nationals'. In attempting to grapple with the reasons for immigration into the UK the Daily Telegraph sets out what the newspaper considers the reasons for large scale migration to the UK: "It is important to dispense with some additional myths surrounding immigration. First: asylum-seekers are not the major cause of migration into the UK. Refugees and others granted special leave to remain under the asylum rules account for only 10% of immigration to Britain. Most permanent immigration consists of people who are economic migrants together with their dependants." (Daily Telegraph 02.07.2006)

Here we witness the definitional confusion in full flight with asylum seekers and refugees gaining a positive status whilst 'economic migrants' are attached a negative significance. The article goes on to argue that such migrants are a drain on the UK's resources:

> "Unskilled migrants and their families often are net consumers of taxes: their children are educated in state schools, they are looked after when they have medical problems by the NHS, and they are eligible for state benefits if they are unable to find work. The new arrivals place a significant strain on the housing stock and delivery of public services in the neighbourhoods where new immigrants live: schools, hospitals and GP surgeries become more crowded, and state-subsidised housing gets more difficult to obtain." (Daily Telegraph 02.07.2006)

There is a total absence of any reporting of positive effects that migrants may have on the economy or any positive contribution they make to civil society. The Daily Telegraph was not on its own in reporting the effects and costs of migration. In 2003 the Daily Mail newspaper reported that migrants were responsible for the increase in HIV/Aids in the UK and the newspaper takes no time in reporting the costs of this increase to the National Health Service (NHS).

> "Immigration is spreading HIV into new parts of the population; 70 % of all heterosexual HIV infections in Britain in 2000/1 were in people from Africa. This hits the taxpayer. Each case costs on average £15.000 a year to treat, and new drug treatments mean longer lives for patients; ten years on that level of treatment would be common." (Daily Mail 05.08.2003)

The paper also uses the label of immigration to highlight what it intimates is preferential treatment for migrants at the expense of justice, so the headline "Migrant drunk-driver free in days after killing boy" sums up those anxieties and concerns related to migration and the lack of authority of the criminal justice system. These examples illustrate that within the UK during the late 1990s and up to the present time immigration is seen as a volatile and sensitive topic for politicians and can interrupt and end political careers. In 2004 the Minister of State for Immigration, Beverly Hughes, resigned because of her perceived lack of action in relation to a 'visa scam' that was alleged to be taking place in Bucharest (The Guardian 2004). In 2006 the then Home Secretary, Charles Clarke, admitted that the Home Office did not know where over one thousand 'foreign' prisoners were after their release from prison. Whilst Charles Clarke rode out the political storm that followed the revelations in relation to 'foreign' prisoners, he was axed in the subsequent cabinet re-shuffle. One of the key issues that resulted in Clarke's sacking was the perceived failure to 'remove' these 'foreign' prisoners from the UK after their release (BBC 2006). These examples demonstrate that governments walk a particularly fine line in the UK when dealing with immigration. Opinion polls taken during 2004 and 2005 in the UK indicate that respondents generally disapproved of the government's policy towards migration with the Conservative Party, at a time of particularly low popularity, leading the government in the polls on the immigration issue (UK Polling Report 2007).

In the UK over the past decade one strategy of government has been to place illegal immigration within the criminal justice sphere and there have been a number of criminal justice 'initiatives' to reduce illegal immigration. During the latter part of 2006 and the early part of 2007 the government published a number of policy papers in relation to immigration (see for example Home Office 2007a&b). The government's understanding of illegal immigration is that:

> "Organised crime feeds on the migration pressure from those seeking a better life for themselves outside the country where they live and we estimate that as much as three quarters of illegal migration is facilitated by criminal gangs." (Home Office(a) 2007: 9)

Once again we see here the definitional confusion with organised crime and criminal gangs being conflated when they are very different types of criminal 'organisation'. So, the 'facts' begin to form an official narrative of how and how many, people cross the UK border illegally. As with drugs and money - laundering the threatening imagery is inflated by a deliberate numbers game (Reuter and Greenfeld, 2001; Reuter and Truman, 2004; Van Duyne and Levi, 2005; Van Duyne *et al.*, 2006). The estimation of the total amount of illegal immigration facilitated by 'organised crime' or criminal gangs as seventyfive percent is an interesting figure especially when the government has little or no accurate estimate of the number of people illegally in the country. Woodbridge (2005) utilises the *Residual Method* as a means of estimating the number of illegal immigrants in the UK. As can be seen the

*Residual Method* is not a very accurate means of estimating the population without a legal right to stay:

> "The Residual Method takes as its starting point the foreign-born population recorded in the UK census conducted in April 2001 and then deducts an estimate of the foreign-born population here legally. The difference is an estimate of the number of unauthorised migrants in the UK." (Woodbridge 2005)

Woodbridge estimates the illegal population in 2005 to be 430.000 (Woodbridge 2005: 1). According to the Home Office some three-hundred and twenty-two thousand people were brought into the UK illegally by 'organised crime' or criminal gangs. If this is accurate, this is an organisation with very special entrepreneurial skills matched only by those that avoid detection. However, the combination of press reports, political pressure and the constructions of illegal immigration methods and figures that emanate from law enforcement agencies only serves to compound the myths of organised crime and criminal gangs as the perpetrators of people smuggling. The threat imagery conveyed by these narratives justifies the increase in police powers, the re-organisation of policing and its removal from democratic accountability.[3] In addition, it provides a cover of toughness and 'Britishness' for politicians eager to exploit the populist seam of public opinion. The construction of organised crime within this 'official' narrative is one that is 'transnational' and 'structured' to exploit global opportunities. The setting up of SOCA in 2006 indicates that the government views organised crime as a threat and as having transnational ties. This view fails to take account of the work of scholars such as Hobbs who argue against such a pervasive view:

> "The notion of organised crime, particularly in the current vogue form of 'trans-nationality', needs to be reconsidered in the light of empirical research, which indicates that ever mutating interlocking networks of locally based serious criminality typifies the situation." (Hobbs 1998: 419)

So, Hobbs cautions against putting our trust in the usual constructions of organised crime and argues for a local understanding of such form of

---

[3] This is not typically British: the whole organised crime policy development in the US and subsequently in the EU is characterized by fear mongering, sometimes deliberately orchestrated (Van Duyne, 2004) and covered by policy supporting 'research'

criminality (Hobbs 1998). It is with this in mind that we can now turn to the findings of research that informs this chapter.

## Getting into the UK without permission

One of the aims of the research was to investigate how individuals cross borders illegally and the relationship between crossing the border, organised crime and corruption. As noted above, the research was undertaken in three countries, Estonia, Finland and the UK, however, the findings reported here refer solely to the UK.

### Research design and execution of the project

The research investigated the issues of corruption by 'organised crime' in relation to border controls and immigration using as a case study the Finnish – Russian and the Estonian– Russian border, the methods of illegal facilitation of people across borders, the role of crime groups and networks as well as 'organised crime' and the relationship between illegal facilitation and exploitation in the labour market.

The project investigated the flow of people illegally from Russia (3rd Country) into Finland (destination and transit country) and Estonia (transit country) and how facilitated people are moved onward. Particular attention was focused on the possible processes of corruption in relation to existing structures. The research also investigated how illegal immigration results in new forms of organised crime. The four key research questions were:

1. How is corruption used to secure the passage of people across borders?
2. Is there evidence that border controls are weak?
3. How are people moved from one EU member state to another?
4. What is the impact of illegal forms immigration on crime rates and organised crime and criminal groups/networks in destination countries?

The fieldwork was undertaken between July 2005 and July 2006 and included interviews with law enforcement practitioners and policy makers, direct observation with immigration officers at border crossing points and focus groups with key personnel working in the UK immigration service, police and government officials. The qualitative data was analysed using Atlas.ti software package.

## Findings: the official UK narrative and what people do

The UK's relative 'popularity' with migrants has resulted in a number of strategic responses to prevent illegal immigration. SOCA was established in 2006 and one of its areas of activity was to tackle 'organised immigration crime':

> "The UK is an attractive destination for illegal migrants from all over the world. Serious organised criminals see immigration crime as lucrative and relatively low risk."
> (Home Office(c) 2007: 7)

Consequently a significant amount of resources have been committed by the UK government with the establishment of SOCA and the re-organisation of the Immigration and Nationality Directorate into the Border and Immigration Agency. At the same time the EU has also committed resources to securing the external borders with the establishment of FRONTEX[4] in 2005 with the aim of securing co-operation between member states to ensure border security. FRONTEX is in addition to EUROPOL which has a mission to combat serious and organised crime across member states. This plethora of agencies securing external borders and combating internal serious crime demonstrates that the UK's position although specific to the political conditions within the UK is in step with the EU approach to illegal immigration. That is: strengthening borders and using law enforcement as a means of ensuring border security. Both the EU and the UK government share a concern over the activities of organised crime.

The official perspective on the issue of people smuggling and trafficking forms an official narrative that is invoked by policy makers and implementers.

---

4 "Frontex, the EU agency based in Warsaw, was created as a specialised and independent body tasked to coordinate the operational cooperation between Member States in the field of border security. The activities of Frontex are intelligence driven. Frontex complements and provides particular added value to the national border management systems of the Member States" http://www.frontex.europa.eu/

It is understandable that in order to appear to be efficient, and to be effective to their political masters, the official narrative is the means of establishing both effectiveness and legitimacy.

The 'official' narrative is that of the person who has gained entry as victim. This is usually a woman who has been trafficked into the UK. She enters an agreement to go to the UK for work and once she has arrived she finds herself imprisoned and forced into prostitution. A UK case that received a high level of media coverage and was frequently quoted by research respondents was that of the Demarku brothers who ran brothels and forced trafficked women to work in their brothels as prostitutes. The reporting of the case contained a language which suggested an 'organised crime' approach. For example the Demarku brothers were called a 'family firm'. However, whilst there is no doubt of the seriousness of their crime there is little else in the reporting that suggests they were part of organised crime (see BBC(a) 2007) other than the headline *Sex Trafficking Gang Sent to Jail.* Other news reports of similar incidents also fail to discuss or provide any substantial evidence of the involvement of 'organised crime'. However, what many of the accounts suggest is that trafficking and the exploitation of women is usually undertaken by small groups of men, sometimes supported by women[5], who are either closely related or known to each other and live in the same locality (see for example BBC (b&c) 2007). However, the establishment of REFLEX[6] teams in 2000 by the UK government "was set up to deal with organised immigration crime" (Home Office 2006). The provision of an additional sixty million pounds of funding in 2004 was designed specifically to engage in combating trans-national organised crime in a number of 'key' areas including people smuggling and trafficking. The lessons in understanding of the nature of serious crime as described by Hobbs (1998) are not incorporated into this narrative form and this further supports van Duyne's argument that:

> ". . . organised crime is mainly a political construct and otherwise ill defined with no observational value or explanatory power." (Van Duyne 2006: 14)

---

5 Women appear to be not only victims, but perpetrators too. Female victims turned into active supporters, particularly in the stage of recruiting, being better able to instil trust with targeted victims (Maljević, 2005).

6 REFLEX is a joint operation between police, immigration and customs and located across the UK. The aim of REFLEX is to combat 'organised' immigration crime through intelligence and policing operations.

However, the official narrative of organised crime as a 'transnational' threat and as one of the drivers of people smuggling and trafficking appears to be deeply embedded in the ideas of policy makers.

In contrast to this official narrative, amongst some law enforcement practitioners there is a realisation of the local nature of serious crime; and they frame both their understanding and action within this context. Firstly, they understand the nature of illegal migration as means of people attempting to improve their economic situation as one law enforcement practitioner commented on 'rescuing' women working in a local brothel:

> "In general people want to stay here and they come of their own free will . . . There were 3 [overseas] girls there and we thought we were rescuing them but at the airport they started demanding the money they had earned and their mobile phones back. It turned out that they were students and came over for 3 months at a time and they knew they could leave at any time and they earned lots of money." (AGIS Research Respondent 12)

This respondent also understood the local nature of serious crime: "The Criminal families and gangs in [this area] are pretty tough, they will hassle you and stand up and fight." (AGIS Research Respondent 12)

They also had a pragmatic view of people smuggling that demonstrated a degree of scepticism towards the idea of 'trafficking': "The snapshot we have is that there is no trafficking but people are smuggled in of their own free will . . . It is doubtful that once people are smuggled into the sex industry they are then forced to do other things that they don't want to as there are that many girls that come you can always get someone who will do whatever out of their own free will." (AGIS Research Respondent 12)

However, on occasions the official narrative makes a guest appearance, as in this statement concerning forged documents:

> "If it is a good counterfeit then it is likely to come from the Russian Mafia as them (sic) have the expertise to make them . . . After the Iron Curtain broke down KGB officers were not getting much money and therefore they diversified into this sort of thing." (AGIS Research Respondent 12)

The view of this respondent, and shared by other law enforcement practitioners interviewed, is that illegal immigration is a result of people moving of their own free will in order to advantage themselves economically. This respondent links illegal immigration to criminal activities but views this is an activity at the local level rather than as part of 'trans-national organised crime'.

The 'international' aspect of illegal immigration is also understood by law enforcement practitioners and it can be seen how this understanding tends to support the 'official' narrative:

> "There is a growing acknowledgement, I think, internationally . . . that the problem of . . . illegal immigration . . . is no longer a national problem. Forged documents are not simply a problem that we have in the UK of people crossing our border, it's a global problem which everybody now appreciates is an issue they have to become actively involved in." (AGIS Respondent 3)

So, the international aspect of forged documents, which can be understood as a 'support industry' to illegal cross-border mobility, and the market in such documents, prompts an international response by law enforcement agencies. This to some extent provides an explanation for the way in which law enforcement practitioners are seen to accept the official narrative. However they appear to be more cautious in their adherence to the narrative structure as in the quote below; so that adherence to the 'official' narrative is measured:

> "So we have met individuals who have travelled through Europe to a number of European countries and arrived in the UK at some point or other. And have been in contact with lots of different organised criminal gangs who have charged different rates for different things." (AGIS Respondent 29)

This respondent recognises implicitly the localised nature of the criminal enterprise but uses the word 'organised' as a form of deference to the 'official' narrative. This is not uncommon as law enforcement personnel describe their experiences in their own words and at times translate this into the 'official' language of their profession. This respondent is less deferential:

> "So what we did find is groups that facilitate certain bits of the journey, but not all of it. They also provide contacts for the next leg of the journey." (AGIS Respondent 16)

These views of practitioners on illegal immigration are much more in step with Hobbs (1998) and the argument that the criminal enterprise should be understood at the local level.

## Criminal disorganisation

There is a problem in attempting to understand the activity of illegal immigration through the concept of organised crime. "'organized crime' is a notoriously difficult concept to define and to measure, and relative to the confident claims that are made about it, little is known about 'its' operation in practice in many European (and for that matter, non-European) countries." (Levi and Maguire 2004)

However, the 'official' narrative persists as the website for the UK Human Trafficking Centre (UKHTC) says: "Organised criminals see human trafficking as a lucrative and relatively low risk crime, viewing the individual victims merely as another profitable commodity" (UKHTC 2007). For all of this 'official' narrative what is apparent from the qualitative data is that law enforcement practitioners understand the process of the illegal crossing of borders as being the consequence of localised criminal enterprises. The participant observation data also confirms this view. On one occasion at a cross channel crossing point the author observed the apprehension of a man and a woman. They were claiming to be a married couple whereas the male had driven from the UK to the Russian Federation and collected the woman who was travelling on false papers. The immigration officers' responses to this situation were that it was not possible to know how this situation had come about because neither of the two people apprehended would provide any information. They could speculate from a simple scenario, that the woman had been refused a visa to join her male partner and so they had resorted to illegal entry, to a scenario that placed the male as a courier bringing women into the UK illegally as a commercial operation for 'organised crime'. The immigration officers tended towards a view that if there was any gain through criminal activity it would be at a local level and that the male was probably either doing a 'favour' for a friend rather than being a full-time courier facilitating women into the UK from the Russian Federation.

The interview data, the participant observation data, and an analysis of press reports indicate that organised crime is neither a significant feature of the experiences of those who enter the UK illegally nor of law enforcement personnel. The localised nature of the criminal activity is accepted and also its ephemeral nature. What the data suggests is that while illegal migration presents criminal opportunities –the provision of forged documents, the taking of people across border or the corruption of officials– all this can happen at a number of different levels and for different reasons. So, it might be that the person providing the service does so at a market rate, or because they have the wherewithal to provide the service, mode of transport regularly crossing borders, and they take the advantage to make illicit gains from their opportunity. It may be that the person providing the service does so because they have the opportunity to do so only occasionally and they exploit that opportunity when it arises. It may be that the person providing the service does so because of kinship, family or local loyalty and the economic benefits are a by-product of their activities. All of this suggests not an organised criminal network but rather a series of criminal opportunities, exploited at a local level, that are not established and concretized but rather criminal associations that 'change, split and reform, disappear and re-appear in a new form in another place' (Van Duyne 2006: 1). Illegally crossing borders provides for criminal networks and groups, entrepreneurial opportunities that are similar to the opportunities of other 'contraband' goods. So we can expect to see similarities between tobacco smuggling, illegal labour subcontracting and moving people, illegally, across borders. There is evidence in the data to suggest that the organising models as detailed by Bruinsma and Bernasco (2004) has a degree of validity. They argue that there are essentially three organising models. First of a defined network where there are linkages between each person who is critical to the enterprise. This is the form of network that is involved in the movement of drugs because the drugs need to be protected from the time they are acquired by the crime network to the point of sale and this requires there to be a closer network where there are connections between those involved with their illegal importation and distribution. This form of network would also apply to trafficking enterprises as it does to cigarettes. However, as Hornsby and Hobbs (2006) describe, the network may not look like an 'organised crime gang' as in one of their case studies it was older people and benefit claimants (Hornsby and Hobbs 2006):

> "Within such networks, familiarity generates sponsorship, followed by acceptance. This is based upon the knowledge of network participants who are familiar by sight, referral or association, and convene via a network of acquaintances" (Hornsby and Hobbs 2006: 4)

Van Duyne and Houtzager (2005) have described the processes of criminal subcontracting in the Netherlands and the Dutch 'koppelbaas' as *crime entrepreneurs*. This appears to be a much more professionally organised form of entrepreneurship than that described by Hornsby and Hobbs (2006), yet it is clear that the organisation described by van Duyne and Houtzager (2005) bear little relationship to the fictional accounts of organised crime that rely on Mario Puzo and Hollywood as the describers of 'organised crime'. This description of the 'koppelbaas' highlights a different form of organisation to that of a highly structured network but more one that is comprised of small groups interacting with an upperworld constructor having a common interest.

The 'illegal migration service providers' on the other hand, are not so much engaged on a large scale enterprise but more on smaller 'bits of businesses' where they are undertaking an illegal task for some reward. So, for example it might be a driver of a truck and two or three 'friends'. The friends are the contacts for those people wanting to try their luck in crossing the border in the back of a truck. They put the person making the illegal journey in touch with the driver. There is an exchange of cash which is divided between the 'partners'. This organisation is much looser in terms of criminal enterprise but it is an important feature in organising the illegal movement of people across the border. Furthermore the truck driver may have contacts with 'partners' in the new country who will provide further services, here the truck driver acts as an introduction agent and he may or may not receive cash benefits for his 'recommendation'. To the external gaze this form of interaction between the parties appears much more disorganised and random than the highly structured hierarchical organisation of the fictional organised crime groups. The activities of these criminal entrepreneurs are market based and as Van Duyne comments: "Such illegal markets are not the realm of sinister, evil forces, but dynamic, interactive places in which criminal entrepreneurs meet the demands of many ordinary, usually law-abiding citizens." (Van Duyne 2003: 1)

This description highlights the entrepreneurial nature of the criminal enterprise and this is also evident, as noted by some respondents, in the illegal movement of people across borders. There is one final model as described by Bruinsma and Bernasco (2004) in which there is no connection between one small group of entrepreneurs and another group. In this instance the person would be driven over the border and once in the 'new' country they would be left to their own devices and make their own contacts. Such contacts are usually established through word of mouth within the illegal immigrant community.

These three strategies for organising the illegal movement of people across borders suggests that there is a level of organisation, but that which is only necessary and beneficial to the enterprise. However, people are slightly different contraband to drugs and cigarettes: usually the smuggler has had to invest in the contraband goods or has a significant investment in their disposal. In relation to people they pay to be moved prior to departure. If apprehended the driver will in many cases say that he had no knowledge of them in the back of the truck and they must have got into the truck when he stopped for food. He declares himself innocent of any intention to facilitate a person across the border. There are few prosecutions for facilitation and so the driver is warned to be more vigilant next time and the person attempting to cross the border is refused entry. The driver has still been paid for his troubles and the immigrant is less likely to be able to afford another ride in the future and so will have to resort to trying to conceal themselves under trucks which is exceptionally dangerous and can have tragic consequences.

What these research data suggests is not a form of 'organised crime' but rather a form of criminal disorganisation, where opportunities are exploited, economic advantage taken but also where there is no 'firm', no organised 'gang' or hierarchical structure to people smuggling. The acceptance of a different and more complex narrative, one that accommodates the local and the ephemeral, would provide those who are attempting to enforce border controls with a more dynamic view of what is taking place and for governments to take a more humanitarian approach to the problems of illegal immigration rather that the pursuit of policies that are oppressive and punitive.

## References

BBC, *Clarke is fired in cabinet purge*
http://news.bbc.co.uk/1/hi/uk_politics/4975938.stm (Accessed May 29th 2007)

BBC(a), *Sex Trafficking Gang Sent to Jail*
http://news.bbc.co.uk/1/hi/uk/4487712.stm (Accessed June 1st 2007)

BBC(b), *Sex slave regrets 'ruined' life*

http://news.bbc.co.uk/1/hi/england/leicestershire/6366085.stm (accessed 1st June 2007)

BBC(c), '*They raped me again and again*' http://news.bbc.co.uk/1/hi/england/6224171.stm (Accessed 1st June 2007)

Black, R., M. Collyer, R. Skeldon and C. Waddington, *A survey of the illegally resident population in detention in the UK*. Home Office Report 20/05, 2005

Bruinsma, G. and W. Bernasco, Criminal groups and Transnational Illegal Markets: A More Detailed Examination on the Basis of Social Network Theory. *Crime, Law and Social Change*, 2004, *vol.* 41: 79-94

Chapkis, W., Trafficking, migration and the law. Protecting innocents, punishing immigrants. *Gender and Society*, 2003, vol. 17, *no. 6*

Daily Mail, Migrants blamed for diseases. London, Daily Mail 05.08.2003

Daily Mail, Migrant drunk-driver free in days after killing boy. London, *Daily Mail* 02.03.2005

Daily Telegraph(a), 4.4 million migrants will boost the population. London, *Daily Telegraph* 30.04.2004

Daily Telegraph(b), Immigration hits record level. London. *Daily Telegraph* 30.04.2004

Daily Telegraph, Never have we seen immigration on such a scale; we just can't cope. London, *Daily Telegraph* 02.07.2006

Duyne, P.C. van, Counting Clouds and Measuring Organised Crime. In: P.C. van Duyne, M. Maljevic, M. van Dijck, K. von Lampe and J.L. Newell, (eds.), *The organisation of crime for profit*. Nijmegen, Wolf Legal Publishers, 2006

Duyne, P.C. van, The creation of a threat image. Media, policy making and organised crime. In: P.C. van Duyne, M. Jager, K. von Lampe and J.L. Newell (eds.) Threats and phantoms of organised crime, corruption and terrorism. Nijmegen, Wolf Legal Publishers, 2004

Duyne P.C, van, Greasing the organisation of crime-markets in Europe. In: P.C. van Duyne, K. von Lampe and J.L. Newell (eds.), Criminal Finances and Organising Crime in Europe. Nijmegen, Wolf Legal Publishers, 2003

Duyne P.C. van and M. Houtzager, Criminal Subcontracting in the Netherlands; the Dutch koppelbaas as crime entrepreneurship. In: P.C. van Duyne, K. von Lampe, Maarten van Dijck and J.L. Newell (eds.), *The organised crime economy. Managing crime markets in Europe*. Nijmegen, Wolf Legal Publishers, 2005

Duyne, P.C. van and M. Levi, *Drugs and money. Managing the drug trade and crimemoney in Europe*. London, Routledge, 2005

Hansard 1995-96, 4th *December, Vol 95, Column 20*

Hobbs, D., Going down the glocal; the local context of organised crime. *The Howard Journal of Criminal Justice*, vol. 37, *no. 4*: 407-422

Home Office(a), *Enforcing the Rules: A strategy to ensure and enforce compliance with our immigration laws*. London, Home Office, 2007

Home Office(b), *Simplifying Immigration law; An initial consultation*. London, Home Office, 2007

Home Office (c), *Serious organised crime agency annual plan 2007-8*. London, Home Office, 2007.

Home Office, *People trafficking from Lithuania*. London, Home Office, 2006 http://www.homeoffice.gov.uk/about-us/freedom-of-information/releasedinformation/foi-archive-immigration/1965-trafficking-lithuania?view=Html (Accessed June 5th 2007)

House of Lords, *Regina v. Immigration Officer at Prague Airport and another (Respondents) ex parte European Roma Rights Centre and others (Appellants)* Session 200405 [2004] UKHL 55 on appeal from: [2003]EWCA Civ 666

Hornsby R. and D. Hobbs, A zone of ambiguity. The political economy of cigarette bootlegging. *British Journal of Criminology*, 2007, vol. 47: 551-571

Kelly, Liz, 'You can find anything you want'. A critical reflection on research on trafficking of persons into and with Europe. *International Migration*, 2005, *vol. 43*

von Lampe, K., Maarten van Dijck and J.L. Newell (eds.), *The organised crime economy. Managing crime markets in Europe*. Nijmegen, Wolf Legal Publishers, 2005

von Lampe, K., M. van Dijck, R. Hornsby, A. Markina and K. Verpoest, Organised crime is . . . Findings from a cross-national review of literature. In: P.C. van Duyne, M. Maljevic, M. van Dijck, K. von Lampe and J.L. Newell (eds), *The organisation of crime for profit*. Nijmegen, Wolf Legal Publishers, 2006

Levi, M. and M. Maguire, Reducing and preventing organised crime: An evidence-based critique. *Crime, Law & Social Change*, 2004, *vol.* 41: 397–469

Maljevic, A., Trafficking women in Bosnia and Herzegovina. In: P.C. van Duyne, K. von Lampe, M. van Dijck and J.L. Newell (eds.), *The organised crime economy. Managing crime markets in Europe.* Nijmegen, Wolf Legal Publishers, 2005

Melossi, D., 'In a peaceful life'. Migration and the crime of modernity in Europe/Italy. *Punishment and Society*, 2003, vol. 5, *no. 4*: 371-397

Reuter, P. and V. Greenfeld, Measuring global drug markets: how good are the numbers and why should we care about them? *World Economics*, 2001, *no. 4*, 159-173

Reuter, P. and E.M. Truman, *Chasing dirty money. The fight against money laundering.* Washington, DC, Institute for International Economics, 2004

The Guardian, *Final straw for Hughes.* London, The Guardian 01.04.2004

UKHTC *Human Trafficking in the UK.* http://www.ukhtc.org/uk.htm (Accessed 29th May 2007)

UK Polling Report, *Immigration* http://www.ukpollingreport.co.uk/blog/issues/immigration/(Accessed May 23rd 2007)

Woodbridge, J., *Sizing the (illegal) immigrant Population in the United Kingdom, 2001.* On-line Report 29/05 London, Home Office, 2005